MABEL COLLINS COLLECTION SEVEN BOOKS

LIGHT ON THE PATH

THE ILLUMINED WAY

THROUGH THE GATES OF GOLD

A CRY FROM AFAR

ILLUSSIONS

THE IDYLL OF THE WHITE LOTUS

SENSA

(A MYSTERY PLAY ADAPTED FROM
THE IDYLL OF THE WHITE LOTUS)

®2019 THE SUCCESS AND PROSPERITY LIBRARY

This book is a product of its time, and it does not necessarily reflect the same views on race, gender, sexuality, ethnicity, and interpersonal relations as it would if it was written today.

THE ESOTERIC COLLECTION # 170

For available titles please search AMAZON for "THE ESOTERIC COLLECTION" or join our newsletter at: THESUCCESSANDPROSPERITYLIBRARY@GMAIL.COM.

CONTENTS

- BOOK ONE. LIGHT ON THE PATH 1
  - Introduction 1
  - I. 2
  - II 6
  - Karma 9
- BOOK TWO. THE ILUMINED WAY 13
  - Publishers' Announcement. 13
  - Comments on Light on the Path 14
  - The Demand of the Neophyte. 27
  - The Seclusion of the Adept. 30
- BOOK THREE. THROUGH THE GATES OF GOLD 36
  - PROLOGUE 36
  - CHAPTER I. THE SEARCH FOR PLEASURE 36
    - I 36
    - II 39
    - III 40
    - IV 41
    - V 42
    - VI 44
    - VII 45
  - CHAPTER II. THE MYSTERY OF THRESHOLD 46
    - I 46
    - II 48
    - III 49
  - CHAPTER III. THE INITIAL EFFORT 49
  - CHAPTER IV. THE MEANING OF PAIN 56
  - CHAPTER V. THE SECRET OF STRENGTH 64
  - EPILOGUE 72
  - THROUGH THE GATES OF GOLD 72
- BOOK FOUR. A CRY FROM AFAR 79
  - CHAPTER I 79
  - CHAPTER II. 84
  - CHAPTER III. 86
  - CHAPTER IV. 90
- BOOK FIVE. THE IDYLL OF THE WHITE LOTUS 92
  - PREFACE 92
  - PROLOGUE 92

- PART I. 92
  - CHAPTER I. 92
  - CHAPTER II. 96
  - CHAPTER III. 101
  - CHAPTER IV. 105
  - CHAPTER V. 111
  - CHAPTER VI. 117
  - CHAPTER VII. 121
  - CHAPTER VIII. 124
  - CHAPTER IX. 125
  - CHAPTER X. 130
  - CHAPTER XI. 132
- PART II. 136
  - CHAPTER I. 136
  - CHAPTER II. 138
  - CHAPTER III. 141
  - CHAPTER IV. 142
  - CHAPTER V. 145
  - CHAPTER VI. 146
  - CHAPTER VII. 151
  - CHAPTER VIII. 152
  - CHAPTER IX. 156
  - CHAPTER X. 158

BOOK SIX. ILLUSIONS **161**
- PREFACE. 161
- ILLUSION I. That Man is Imprisoned in the Body. 163
- ILLUSION II. That the Unborn are Unknown. 171
- ILLUSION III. That there is any Secret in the Mind or Memory of Man. 176
- ILLUSION IV. That the Earth exists apart from Man. 183
- ILLUSION V. That Nature is indifferent to Man. 187

BOOK SEVEN. THE STORY OF SENSA **189**
- ACT I. 190
- ACT II 202
- ACT III 214

BOOK ONE.
LIGHT ON THE PATH

INTRODUCTION

The following treatise, "*Light on the Path*," is a classic among occultists, and is the best guide known for those who have taken the first step on the Path of Attainment. Its writer has veiled the meaning of the rules in the way always customary to mystics, so that to the one who has no grasp on the Truth these pages will probably appear to be a mass of contradictions and practically devoid of sense. But to the one to whom a glimpse of the inner life has been given, these pages will be a treasury of the rarest jewels, and each time he opens it he will see new gems. To many this little book will be the first revelation of that which they have been all their lives blindly seeking. To many it will be the first bit of spiritual bread given to satisfy the hunger of the soul. To many it will be the first cup of water from the spring of life, given to quench the thirst which has consumed them. Those for whom this book is intended will recognize its message, and after reading it they will never be the same as before it came to them. As the poet has said: "Where I pass all my children know me," and so will the Children of the Light recognize this book as for them. As for the others, we can only say that they will in time be ready for this great message.

The book is intended to symbolize the successive steps of the neophyte in occultism as he progresses in the lodge work. The rules are practically those which were given to the neophytes in the great lodge of the Brotherhood in ancient Egypt, and which for generations have been taught by guru to chela in India. The peculiarity of the rules herein laid down, is that their inner meaning unfolds as the student progresses on the Path. Some will be able to understand a number of these rules, while the others will see but dimly even the first steps. The student, however, will find that when he has firmly planted his foot on one of these steps, he will find the one just ahead becoming dimly illuminated, so as to give him confidence to take the next step. Let none be discouraged; the fact that this book attracts you is the message to you that it is intended for you, and will in time unfold its meaning. Read it over and over often, and you will find veil after veil lifted, though veil upon veil still remains between you and the Absolute. It will be noticed by you that the words of the book will remain in your mind, and will become a part of you. You will learn to love this book, and will want it always with you. It will be as music to your soul. To those who know not this book, we would say that it is not our work, but was written down by "M. C.," a student of occultism, presumably at the dictation of someone high in authority. Its words and teachings bear witness to the nobility and grandeur of the soul who aspired it. To us, it is as a guiding star. May it be the same to you. Peace be unto you. Yogi Ramacharaka

I

These rules are written for all disciples: Attend you to them.

Before the eyes can see, they must be incapable of tears. Before the ear can hear, it must have lost its sensitiveness. Before the voice can speak in the presence of the Masters, it must have lost the power to wound. Before the soul can stand in the presence of the Masters, its feet must be washed in the blood of the heart.

Kill out ambition.[1]

2. Kill out desire of life.

3. Kill out desire of comfort.

4. Work as those work who are ambitious. Respect life as those do who desire it. Be happy as those are who live for happiness.

Seek in the heart the source of evil and expunge it. It lives fruitfully in the heart of the devoted disciple as well as in the heart of the man of desire. Only the strong can kill it out. The weak must wait for its growth, its fruition, its death. And it is a plant that lives and increases throughout the ages. It flowers when the man has accumulated unto himself innumerable existences. He who will enter upon the path of power must tear this thing out of his heart. And then the heart will bleed, and the whole life of the man seem to be utterly dissolved. This ordeal must be endured: it may come at the first step of the perilous ladder which leads to the path of life: it may

---

[1] *Ambition is the first curse: the great tempter of the man who is rising above his fellows. It is the simplest form of looking for reward. Men of intelligence and power are led away from their higher possibilities by it continually. Yet it is a necessary teacher. Its results turn to dust and ashes in the mouth; like death and estrangement it shows the man at last that to work for self is to work for disappointment. But though this first rule seems so simple and easy, do not quickly pass it by. For these vices of the ordinary man pass through a subtle transformation and reappear with changed aspect in the heart of the disciple. It is easy to say: I will not be ambitious; it is not so easy to say: When the Master reads my heart, he will find it clean utterly. The pure artist who works for the love of his work is sometimes more firmly planted on the right road than the occultist, who fancies he has removed his interest from self, but who has in reality only enlarged the limits of experience and desire, and transferred his interest to the things which concern his larger span of life. The same principle applies to the other two seemingly simple rules. Linger over them and do not let yourself be easily deceived by your own heart. For now, at the threshold, a mistake can be corrected. But carry it on with you and it will grow and come to fruition, or else you must suffer bitterly in its destruction.*

not come until the last. But, O disciple, remember that it has to be endured, and fasten the energies of your soul upon the task. Live neither in the present nor the future, but in the eternal. This giant weed cannot flower there: this blot upon existence is wiped out by the very atmosphere of eternal thought.

5. Kill out all sense of separateness. [2]

6. Kill out desire for sensation.

7. Kill out the hunger for growth.

8. Yet stand alone and isolated, because nothing that is embodied, nothing that is conscious of separation, nothing that is out of the eternal, can aid you. Learn from sensation and observe it, because only so can you commence the science of self-knowledge, and plant your foot on the first step of the ladder. Grow as the flower grows, unconsciously, but eagerly anxious to open its soul to the air. So must you press forward to open your soul to the eternal. But it must be the eternal that draws forth your strength and beauty, not desire of growth. For in the one case you develop in the luxuriance of purity; in the other you harden by the forcible passion for personal stature.

9. Desire only that which is within you.

10. Desire only that which is beyond you.

11. Desire only that which is unattainable.

12. For within you is the light of the world—the only light that can be shed upon the Path. If you are unable to perceive it within you, it is useless to look for it elsewhere. It is beyond you, because when you reach it you have lost yourself. It is unattainable, because it forever recedes. You will enter the light, but you will never touch the flame.

13. Desire power ardently.

14. Desire peace fervently.

15. Desire possessions above all.

---

[2] Do not fancy you can stand aside from the bad man or the foolish man. They are yourself, though in a less degree than your friend or your master. But if you allow the idea of separateness from any evil thing or person to grow up within you, by so doing you create Karma, which will bind you to that thing or person till your soul recognises that it cannot be isolated. Remember that the sin and shame of the world are your sin and shame; for you are a part of it; your Karma is inextricably interwoven with the great Karma. And before you can attain knowledge you must have passed through all places, foul and clean alike. Therefore, remember that the soiled garment you shrink from touching may have been yours yesterday, may be yours to-morrow. And if you turn with horror from it, when it is flung upon your shoulders, it will cling the more closely to you. The self-righteous man makes for himself a bed of mire. Abstain because it is right to abstain—not that yourself shall be kept clean.

16. But those possessions must belong to the pure soul only, and be possessed therefore by all pure souls equally, and thus be the especial property of the whole only when united. Hunger for such possessions as can be held by the pure soul, that you may accumulate wealth for that united spirit of life which is your only true self. The peace you shall desire is that sacred peace which nothing can disturb, and in which the soul grows as does the holy flower upon the still lagoons. And that power which the disciple shall covet is that which shall make him appear as nothing in the eyes of men.

17. Seek out the way.[3]

18. Seek the way by retreating within.

19. Seek the way by advancing boldly without.

20. Seek it not by any one road. To each temperament there is one road which seems the most desirable. But the way is not found by devotion alone, by religious contemplation alone, by ardent progress, by self-sacrificing labor, by studious observation of life. None alone can take the disciple more than one step onward. All steps are necessary to make up the ladder. The vices of men become steps in the ladder, one by one, as they are surmounted. The virtues of man are steps indeed, necessary—not by any means to be dispensed with. Yet, though they create a fair atmosphere and a happy future, they are useless if they stand alone. The whole nature of man must be used wisely by the one who desires to enter the way. Each man is to himself absolutely the way, the truth, and the life. But he is only so when he grasps his whole individuality firmly, and, by the force of his awakened spiritual will recognises this individuality as not himself, but that thing which he has with pain created for his own use, and by means of which he purposes, as his growth slowly develops his intelligence, to reach to the life beyond individuality. When he knows that for this his wonderful, complex, separated life exists, then, indeed, and then only, he is upon the way. Seek it by plunging into the mysterious and glorious depths of your

---

[3] These four words seem, perhaps, too slight to stand alone. The disciple may say: Should I study these thoughts at all; did I not seek out the way? Yet do not pass on hastily. Pause and consider awhile. Is it the way you desire, or is it that there is a dim perspective in your visions of great heights to be scaled by yourself, of a great future for you to compass? Be warned. The way is to be sought for its own sake, not with regard to your feet that shall tread it. There is a correspondence between this rule and the seventeenth of the second series. When after ages of struggle and many victories the final battle is won, the final secret demanded, then you are prepared for a further path. When the final secret of this great lesson is told, in it is opened the mystery of the new way—a path which leads out of all human experience, and which is utterly beyond human perception or imagination. At each of these points it is needful to pause long and consider well. At each of these points it is necessary to be sure that the way is chosen for its own sake. The way and the truth come first, then follows the life.

own inmost being. Seek it by testing all experience, by utilizing the senses in order to understand the growth and meaning of individuality, and the beauty and obscurity of those other divine fragments which are struggling side by side with you, and form the race to which you belong. Seek it by study of the laws of being, the laws of nature, the laws of the supernatural; and seek it by making the profound obeisance of the soul to the dim star that burns within. Steadily, as you watch and worship, its light will grow stronger. Then you may know you have found the beginning of the way. And when you have found the end, its light will suddenly become the infinite light.[4]

21. Look for the flower to bloom in the silence that follows the storm: not till then.

It shall grow, it will shoot up, it will make branches and leaves and form buds, while the storm continues, while the battle lasts. But not till the whole personality of the man is dissolved and melted—not until it is held by the divine fragment which has created it, as a mere subject for grave experiment and experience—not until the whole nature has yielded and become subject unto its higher self, can the bloom open. Then will come a calm such as comes in a tropical country after the heavy rain, when Nature works so swiftly that one may see her action. Such a calm will come to the harassed spirit. And in the deep silence the mysterious event will occur which will prove that the way has been found. Call it by what name you will, it is a voice that speaks where there is none to speak—it is a messenger that comes, a messenger without form or substance; or it is the flower of the soul that has opened. It cannot be described by any metaphor. But it can be

---

[4] Seek it by testing all experience, and remember that when I say this I do not say: Yield to the seductions of sense in order to know it. Before you have become an occultist you may do this; but not afterwards. When you have chosen and entered the path you cannot yield to these seductions without shame. Yet you can experience them without horror: can weigh, observe, and test them; and wait with the patience of confidence for the hour when they shall affect you no longer. But do not condemn the man that yields; stretch out your hand to him as a brother pilgrim whose feet have become heavy with mire. Remember, O disciple, that great though the gulf may be between the good man and the sinner, it is greater between the good man and the man who has attained knowledge; it is immeasurable between the good man and the one on the threshold of divinity. Therefore be wary lest too soon you fancy yourself a thing apart from the mass. When you have found the beginning of the way the star of your soul will show its light; and by that light you will perceive how great is the darkness in which it burns. Mind, heart, brain, all are obscure and dark until the first great battle has been won. Be not appalled and terrified by this sight; keep your eyes fixed on the small light and it will grow. But let the darkness within help you to understand the helplessness of those who have seen no light, whose souls are in profound gloom. Blame them not, shrink not from them, but try to lift a little of the heavy Karma of the world; give your aid to the few strong hands that hold back the powers of darkness from obtaining complete victory. Then do you enter into a partnership of joy, which brings indeed terrible toil and profound sadness, but also a great and ever-increasing delight.

felt after, looked for, and desired, even amid the raging of the storm. The silence may last a moment of time or it may last a thousand years. But it will end. Yet you will carry its strength with you. Again and again the battle must be fought and won. It is only for an interval that Nature can be still. [5]

These written above are the first of the rules which are written on the walls of the Hall of Learning. Those that ask shall have. Those that desire to read shall read. Those who desire to learn shall learn.

Peace be with you. Δ

II

Out of the silence that is peace a resonant voice shall arise. And this voice will say: It is not well; thou hast reaped, now thou must sow. And knowing this voice to be the silence itself thou wilt obey.

Thou who art now a disciple, able to stand, able to hear, able to see, able to speak; who hast conquered desire and attained to self-knowledge; who hast seen thy soul in its bloom and recognised it; and heard the voice of the silence, go thou to the Hall of Learning and read what is written there for thee.[6]

---

[5] The opening of the bloom is the glorious moment when perception awakes: with it comes confidence, knowledge, certainty. The pause of the soul is the moment of wonder, and the next moment of satisfaction, that is the silence.

Know, O disciple, that those who have passed through the silence: and felt its peace, and retained its strength; they long that you shall pass through it also. Therefore, in the Hall of Learning, when he is capable of entering there, the disciple will always find his master.

Those that ask shall have. But though the ordinary man asks perpetually, his voice is not heard. For he asks with his mind only; and the voice of the mind is only heard on that plane on which the mind acts. Therefore, not until the first twenty-one rules are past do I say those that ask shall have.

To read, in the occult sense, is to read with the eyes of the spirit. To ask is to feel the hunger within—the yearning of spiritual aspiration. To be able to read means having obtained the power in a small degree of gratifying that hunger. When the disciple is ready to learn, then he is accepted, acknowledged, recognised. It must be so, for he has lit his lamp, and it cannot be hidden. But to learn is impossible until the first great battle has been won. The mind may recognise truth, but the spirit cannot receive it. Once having passed through the storm and attained the peace, it is then always possible to learn, even though the disciple waver, hesitate, and turn aside. The voice of the silence remains within him, and though he leave the path utterly, yet one day it will resound and rend him asunder and separate his passions from his divine possibilities. Then, with pain and desperate cries from the deserted lower self, he will return.

Therefore I say: Peace be with you. My peace I give unto you can only be said by the Master to the beloved disciples who are as himself. There are some even among those who are ignorant of the Eastern wisdom to whom this can be said, and to whom it can daily be said with more completeness.

Δ Regard the three truths. They are equal.

[6] To be able to stand is to have confidence; to be able to hear is to have opened the doors of the soul; to be able to see is to have attained perception; to be able to speak is to have

1. Stand aside in the coming battle, and though thou fightest be not thou the warrior.

2. Look for the warrior and let him fight in thee.

3. Take his orders for battle and obey them.

4. Obey him, not as though he were a general, but as though he were thyself, and his spoken words were the utterance of thy secret desires; for he is thyself, yet infinitely wiser and stronger than thyself. Look for him, else in the fever and hurry of the fight thou mayest pass him; and he will not know thee unless thou knowest him. If thy cry meet his listening ear, then will he fight in thee, and fill the dull void within. And if this is so, then canst thou go through the fight cool and unwearied, standing aside and letting him battle for thee. Then it will be impossible for thee to strike one blow amiss. But if thou look not for him, if thou pass him by, then there is no safeguard for thee. Thy brain will reel, thy heart grow uncertain, and in the dust of the battle-field thy sight and senses will fail, and thou wilt not know thy friends from thy enemies.

He is thyself, yet thou art but finite and liable to error. He is eternal and is sure. He is eternal truth. When once he has entered thee and become thy warrior, he will never utterly desert thee, and at the day of the great peace he will become one with thee.

5. Listen to the song of life.[7]

---

attained the power of helping others; to have conquered desire is to have learned how to use and control the self; to have attained to self-knowledge is to have retreated to the inner fortress from whence the personal man can be viewed with impartiality; to have seen thy soul in its bloom is to have obtained a momentary glimpse in thyself of the transfiguration which shall eventually make thee more than man; to recognise is to achieve the great task of gazing upon the blazing light without dropping the eyes, and not falling back in terror, as though before some ghastly phantom. This happens to some, and so when the victory is all but won it is lost; to hear the voice of the silence is to understand that from within comes the only true guidance; to go to the Hall of Learning is to enter the state in which learning becomes possible. Then will many words be written there for thee, and written in fiery letters for thee easily to read. For when the disciple is ready the Master is ready also.

[7] Look for it, and listen to it first in your own heart. At first you may say it is not there; when I search I find only discord. Look deeper. If again you are disappointed, pause and look deeper again. There is a natural melody, an obscure fount in every human heart. It may be hidden over and utterly concealed and silenced—but it is there. At the very base of your nature you will find faith, hope, and love. He that chooses evil refuses to look within himself, shuts his ears to the melody of his heart, as he blinds his eyes to the light of his soul. He does this because he finds it easier to live in desires. But underneath all life is the strong current that cannot be checked; the great waters are there in reality. Find them, and you will perceive that none, not the most wretched of creatures, but is a part of it, however he blind himself to the fact and build up for himself a phantasmal outer form of horror. In that sense it is that I say to you—All those beings among whom you struggle on are fragments of the Divine. And so deceptive is the illusion in which you live, that it is hard to guess where you will first detect the sweet voice in the hearts of others. But know that it is certainly within

6. Store in your memory the melody you hear.

7. Learn from it the lesson of harmony.

8. You can stand upright now, firm as a rock amid the turmoil, obeying the warrior who is thyself and thy king. Unconcerned in the battle save to do his bidding, having no longer any care as to the result of the battle, for one thing only is important, that the warrior shall win, and you know he is incapable of defeat—standing thus, cool and awakened, use the hearing you have acquired by pain and by the destruction of pain. Only fragments of the great song come to your ears while yet you are but man. But if you listen to it, remember it faithfully, so that none which has reached you is lost, and endeavour to learn from it the meaning of the mystery which surrounds you. In time you will need no teacher. For as the individual has voice, so has that in which the individual exists. Life itself has speech and is never silent. And its utterance is not, as you that are deaf may suppose, a cry: it is a song. Learn from it that you are part of the harmony; learn from it to obey the laws of the harmony.

9. Regard earnestly all the life that surrounds you.

10. Learn to look intelligently into the hearts of men.[8]

11. Regard most earnestly your own heart.

12. For through your own heart comes the one light which can illuminate life and make it clear to your eyes.

Study the hearts of men; that you may know what is that world in which you live and of which you will to be a part. Regard the constantly changing and moving life which surrounds you, for it is formed by the hearts of men; and as you learn to understand their constitution and meaning, you will by degrees be able to read the larger word of life.

13. Speech comes only with knowledge. Attain to knowledge and you will attain to speech.[9]

---

yourself. Look for it there, and once having heard it, you will more readily recognise it around you.

[8] From an absolutely impersonal point of view, otherwise your sight is coloured. Therefore impersonality must first be understood. Intelligence is impartial: no man is your enemy: no man is your friend. All alike are your teachers. Your enemy becomes a mystery that must be solved, even though it take ages: for man must be understood. Your friend becomes a part of yourself, an extension of yourself, a riddle hard to read. Only one thing is more difficult to know—your own heart. Not until the bonds of personality are loosed can that profound mystery of self begin to be seen. Not till you stand aside from it will it in any way reveal itself to your understanding. Then, and not till then, can you grasp and guide it. Then, and not till then, can you use all its powers, and devote them to a worthy service.

[9] It is impossible to help others till you have obtained some certainty of your own. When you have learned the first twenty-one rules and have entered the Hall of Learning with your powers developed and sense unchained, then you will find there is a fount within you from

14. Having obtained the use of the inner senses, having conquered the desires of the outer senses, having conquered the desires of the individual soul, and having obtained knowledge, prepare now, O disciple, to enter upon the way in reality. The path is found: make yourself ready to tread it.

15. Inquire of the earth, the air, and the water, of the secrets they hold for you. The development of your inner senses will enable you to do this.

16. Inquire of the holy ones of the earth of the secrets they hold for you. The conquering of the desires of the outer senses will give you the right to do this.

17. Inquire of the inmost, the one, of its final secret which it holds for you through the ages.

The great and difficult victory, the conquering of the desires of the individual soul, is a work of ages; therefore expect not to obtain its reward until ages of experience have been accumulated. When the time of learning this seventeenth rule is reached, man is on the threshold of becoming more than man.

18. The knowledge which is now yours is only yours because your soul has become one with all pure souls and with the inmost. It is a trust vested in you by the Most High. Betray it, misuse your knowledge, or neglect it, and it is possible even now for you to fall from the high estate you have attained. Great ones fall back, even from the threshold, unable to sustain the weight of their responsibility, unable to pass on. Therefore look forward always with awe and trembling to this moment, and be prepared for the battle.

19. It is written that for him who is on the threshold of divinity no law can be framed, no guide can exist. Yet to enlighten the disciple, the final struggle may be thus expressed:

Hold fast to that which has neither substance nor existence.

20. Listen only to the voice which is soundless.

21. Look only on that which is invisible alike to the inner and the outer sense.

Peace be with you.

KARMA

Consider with me that the individual existence is a rope which stretches from the infinite to the infinite, and has no end and no commencement, neither is it capable of being broken. This rope is formed of innumerable

---

which speech will arise. After the thirteenth rule I can add no words to what is already written. My peace I give unto you. ∆

fine threads, which, lying closely together, form its thickness. These threads are colourless, are perfect in their qualities of straightness, strength, and levelness. This rope, passing as it does through all places, suffers strange accidents. Very often a thread is caught and becomes attached, or perhaps is only violently pulled away from its even way. Then for a great time it is disordered, and it disorders the whole. Sometimes one is stained with dirt or with colour; and not only does the stain run on further than the spot of contact, but it discolours other of the threads. And remember that the threads are living—are like electric wires, more, are like quivering nerves. How far, then, must the stain, the drag awry, be communicated! But eventually the long strands, the living threads which in their unbroken continuity form the individual, pass out of the shadow into the shine. Then the threads are no longer colourless, but golden; once more they lie together, level. Once more harmony is established between them; and from that harmony within the greater harmony is perceived.

This illustration presents but a small portion—a single side of the truth: it is less than a fragment. Yet, dwell on it; by its aid you may be led to perceive more. What it is necessary first to understand is, not that the future is arbitrarily formed by any separate acts of the present, but that the whole of the future is in unbroken continuity with the present as the present is with the past. On one plane, from one point of view, the illustration of the rope is correct.

It is said that a little attention to occultism produces great Karmic results. That is because it is impossible to give any attention to occultism without making a definite choice between what are familiarly called good and evil. The first step in occultism brings the student to the tree of knowledge. He must pluck and eat; he must choose. No longer is he capable of the indecision of ignorance. He goes on, either on the good or on the evil path. And to step definitely and knowingly even but one step on either path produces great Karmic results. The mass of men walk waveringly, uncertain as to the goal they aim at; their standard of life is indefinite; consequently their Karma operates in a confused manner. But when once the threshold of knowledge is reached, the confusion begins to lessen, and consequently the Karmic results increase enormously, because all are acting in the same direction on all the different planes: for the occultist cannot be half-hearted, nor can he return when he has passed the threshold. These things are as impossible as that the man should become the child again. The individuality has approached the state of responsibility by reason of growth; it cannot recede from it.

He who would escape from the bondage of Karma must raise his individuality out of the shadow into the shine; must so elevate his existence that these threads do not come in contact with soiling substances, do not become so attached as to be pulled awry. He simply lifts himself out of the region in which Karma operates. He does not leave the existence which he is experiencing because of that. The ground may be rough and dirty, or full of rich flowers whose pollen stains and of sweet substances that cling and become attachments—but overhead there is always the free sky. He who desires to be Karmaless must look to the air for a home; and after that to the ether. He who desires to form good Karma will meet with many confusions, and in the effort to sow rich seed for his own harvesting may plant a thousand weeds, and among them the giant. Desire to sow no seed for your own harvesting; desire only to sow that seed the fruit of which shall feed the world. You are a part of the world; in giving it food you feed yourself. Yet in even this thought there lurks a great danger which starts forward and faces the disciple who has for long thought himself working for good, while in his inmost soul he has perceived only evil; that is, he has thought himself to be intending great benefit to the world while all the time he has unconsciously embraced the thought of Karma, and the great benefit he works for is for himself. A man may refuse to allow himself to think of reward. But in that very refusal is seen the fact that reward is desired. And it is useless for the disciple to strive to learn by means of checking himself. The soul must be unfettered, the desires free. But until they are fixed only on that state wherein there is neither reward nor punishment, good nor evil, it is in vain that he endeavours. He may seem to make great progress, but some day he will come face to face with his own soul, and will recognise that when he came to the tree of knowledge he chose the bitter fruit and not the sweet; and then the veil will fall utterly, and he will give up his freedom and become a slave of desire. Therefore be warned, you who are but turning toward the life of occultism. Learn now that there is no cure for desire, no cure for the love of reward, no cure for the misery of longing, save in the fixing of the sight and hearing upon that which is invisible and soundless. Begin even now to practise it, and so a thousand serpents will be kept from your path. Live in the eternal.

The operations of the actual laws of Karma are not to be studied until the disciple has reached the point at which they no longer affect himself. The initiate has a right to demand the secrets of nature and to know the rules which govern human life. He obtains this right by having escaped from the limits of nature and by having freed himself from the rules which govern human life. He has become a recognised portion of the divine element, and is no longer affected by that which is temporary. He then obtains a knowledge of the laws which govern temporary conditions. Therefore you who desire to understand the laws of Karma, attempt first to free yourself from these laws; and this can only be done by fixing your attention on that which is unaffected by those laws.

BOOK TWO.
THE ILUMINED WAY

Publishers' Announcement.

The subject matter of this little book first appeared in a leading English occult magazine, a number of years ago, under the title of "*Comments on Light on the Path,*" running in the shape of a series of essays extending over a period of several months. The extreme modesty of the author caused her to adopt the above mentioned unpretentious title, and to assume that her series of essays were merely "comments" on her previous work, *Light on the Path,* the authorship of which, by-the-way, she had conscientiously disclaimed, contenting her with using the words "written down by," instead of "written by" herself, it being generally understood among occultists that *Light on the Path* had been received by her, and written down, under what might be called "inspiration" from some higher minds. These "comments" were afterward reprinted in various forms, in England and America, often forming part of larger works, and always (so far as known) bearing the original title used in the magazine publication. Wishing to issue a popular edition of this valuable treatise, which would reach many new readers, as well as many with whom it had always been a favorite, we have felt that the original title was not worthy of the treatise, which, so far from being merely "comments," is, in fact, one of the most instructive and valuable pieces of occult teaching which has been handed down to the student for a number of years. So, accordingly, we sought for a title more in keeping with the real merit, purpose, and scope of the work in question. At the suggestion of some, well qualified to offer advice upon the subject, we have decided to publish the book under the title of *The Illumined Way,* believing that such title is far more appropriate, and that it has been justly earned. We feel sure that the old lovers of this treatise, as well as its new students, will agree with us in the matter, and will welcome this beautiful and instructive work under the new name. The author's modesty prevented her from bestowing upon the offspring of her mind an appropriate and worthy title, but we, her friends and students, lovers of both herself and her work, have endeavored to remedy her oversight.

Yours fraternally,

The Yogi Publication Society.

Palmyra, New Jersey,

December 28, 1903.

COMMENTS ON LIGHT ON THE PATH

"Before the eyes can see they must be incapable of tears."

It should be very clearly remembered by all readers of *Light on the Path* that it is a book which may appear to have some little philosophy in it, but very little sense, to those who believe it to be written in ordinary English. To the many, who read in this manner it will be—not caviare so much as olives strong of their salt. Be warned and read but a little in this way.

There is another way of reading, which is, indeed, the only one of any use with many authors. It is reading, not between the lines but within the words. In fact, it is deciphering a profound cipher. All alchemical works are written in the cipher of which I speak; it has been used by the great philosophers and poets of all time. It is used systematically by the adepts in life and knowledge, who, seemingly giving out their deepest wisdom, hide, in the very words which frame it, its actual mystery. They cannot do more. There is a law of nature which insists that a man shall read these mysteries for himself. By no other method can he obtain them. A man who desires to live must eat his food himself: this is the simple law of nature—which applies also to the higher life. A man who would live and act in it cannot be fed like a babe with a spoon; he must eat for himself.

I propose to put into new and sometimes plainer language parts of *Light on the Path*; but whether this effort of mine will really be any interpretation I cannot say. To a deaf and dumb man, a truth is made no more intelligible if, in order to make it so, some misguided linguist translates the words in which it is couched into every living or dead language, and shouts these different phrases in his ear. But for those who are not deaf and dumb one language is generally easier than the rest; and it is to such as these I address myself.

The very first aphorisms of *Light on the Path,* included under
Number I, have, I know well, remained sealed as to their inner meaning to many who have otherwise followed the purpose of the book.

There are four proven and certain truths with regard to the entrance to occultism. The Gates of Gold bar that threshold; yet there are some who pass those gates and discover the sublime and illimitable beyond. In the far spaces of Time all will pass those gates. But I am one who wish that Time, the great deluder, were not so over-masterful. To those who know and love him I have no word to say; but to the others—and there are not so very few as some may fancy—to whom the passage of Time is as the stroke of a sledge-hammer, and the sense of Space like the bars of an iron cage, I will translate and re-translate until they understand fully.

The four truths written on the first page of *Light on the Path,* refer to the trial initiation of the would-be occultist. Until he has passed it, he cannot even reach to the latch of the gate which admits to knowledge. Knowledge is man's greatest inheritance; why, then, should he not attempt to reach it by every possible road? The laboratory is not the only ground for experiment, *science,* we must remember, is derived from *sciens,* present participle of *scire,* "to know,"—its origin is similar to that of the word "discern," "to ken." Science does not therefore deal only with matter, no, not even its subtlest and obscurest forms. Such an idea is born merely of the idle spirit of the age. Science is a word which covers all forms of knowledge. It is exceedingly interesting to hear what chemists discover, and to see them finding their way through the densities of matter to its finer forms; but there are other kinds of knowledge than this, and it is not every one who restricts his (strictly scientific) desire for knowledge to experiments which are capable of being tested by the physical senses.

Everyone who is not a dullard, or a man stupefied by some predominant vice, has guessed, or even perhaps discovered with some certainty, that there are subtle senses lying within the physical senses. There is nothing at all extraordinary in this; if we took the trouble to call Nature into the witness box we should find that everything which is perceptible to the ordinary sight, has something even more important than itself hidden within it; the microscope has opened a world to us, but within those encasements which the microscope reveals, lies the mystery which no machinery can probe.

The whole world is animated and lit, down to its most material shapes, by a world within it. This inner world is called Astral by some people, and it is as good a word as any other, though it merely means starry; but the stars, as Locke pointed out, are luminous bodies which give light of themselves. This quality is characteristic of the life which lies within matter; for those who see it, need no lamp to see it by. The word star, moreover, is derived from the Anglo-Saxon "stir-an," to steer, to stir, to move, and undeniably it is the inner life which is master of the outer, just as a man's brain guides the movements of his lips. So that although Astral is no very excellent word in itself, I am content to use it for my present purpose.

The whole of *Light on the Path* is written in an astral cipher and can therefore only be deciphered by one who reads astrally. And its teaching is chiefly directed towards the cultivation and development of the astral life.

Until the first step has been taken in this development, the swift knowledge, which is called intuition with certainty, is impossible to man. And this positive and certain intuition is the only form of knowledge which enables a man to work rapidly or reach his true and high estate, within the limit of his conscious effort. To obtain knowledge by experiment is too tedious a method for those who aspire to accomplish real work; he who gets it by certain intuition, lays hands on its various forms with supreme rapidity, by fierce effort of will; as a determined workman grasps his tools, indifferent to their weight or any other difficulty which may stand in his way. He does not stay for each to be tested—he uses such as he sees are fittest.

All the rules contained in *Light on the Path,* are written for all disciples, but only for disciples—those who "take knowledge." To none else but the student in this school are its laws of any use or interest.

To all who are interested seriously in Occultism, I say first— take knowledge. To him who hath shall be given. It is useless to wait for it. The womb of Time will close before you, and in later days you will remain unborn, without power. I therefore say to those who have any hunger or thirst for knowledge, attend to these rules.

They are none of my handicraft or invention. They are merely the phrasing of laws in super-nature, the putting into words truths as absolute in their own sphere, as those laws which govern the conduct of the earth and its atmosphere.

The senses spoken of in these four statements are the astral, or inner senses.

No man desires to see that light which illumines the spaceless soul until pain and sorrow and despair have driven him away from the life of ordinary humanity. First he wears out pleasure; then he wears out pain—till, at last, his eyes become incapable of tears.

This is a truism, although I know perfectly well that it will meet with a vehement denial from many who are in sympathy with thoughts which spring from the inner life. *To see* with the astral sense of sight is a form of activity which it is difficult for us to understand immediately. The scientist knows very well what a miracle is achieved by each child that is born into the world, when it first conquers its eye-sight and compels it to obey its brain. An equal miracle is performed with each sense certainly, but this ordering of sight is perhaps the most stupendous effort. Yet the child does it almost unconsciously, by force of the powerful heredity of habit. No one now is aware that he has ever done it at all; just as we cannot recollect the individual movements which enabled us to walk up a hill a year ago. This arises from the fact that we move and live and have our being in matter. Our knowledge of it has become intuitive.

With our astral light it is very much otherwise. For long ages past, man has paid very little attention to it—so little, that he has practically lost the use of his senses. It is true, that in every civilization the star arises, and man confesses, with more or less of folly and confusion, that he knows himself to be. But most often he denies it, and in being a materialist becomes that strange thing, a being which cannot see its own light, a thing of life which will not live, an astral animal which has eyes, and ears, and speech, and power, yet will use none of these gifts. This is the case, and the habit of ignorance has become so confirmed, that now none will see with the inner vision till agony has made the physical eyes not only unseeing, but without tears—the moisture of life. To be incapable of tears is to have faced and conquered the simple human nature, and to have attained an equilibrium which cannot be shaken by personal emotions. It does not imply any hardness of heart, or any indifference. It does not imply the exhaustion of sorrow, when the suffering soul seems powerless to suffer acutely any longer; it does not mean the deadness of old age, when emotion is becoming dull because the strings which vibrate to it are wearing out. None of these conditions are fit for a disciple, and if any one of them exist in him, it must be overcome before the path can be entered upon. Hardness of heart belongs to the selfish man, the egotist, to whom the gate is for ever closed. Indifference belongs to the fool and the false philosopher; those whose lukewarmness makes them mere puppets, not strong enough to face the realities of existence. When pain or sorrow has worn out the keenness of suffering, the result is a lethargy not unlike that which accompanies old age, as it is usually experienced by men and women. Such a condition makes the entrance to the path impossible, because the first step is one of difficulty and needs a strong man, full of psychic and physical vigor, to attempt it.

It is a truth that, as Edgar Allan Poe said, the eyes are the windows for the soul, the windows of that haunted palace in which it dwells. This is the very nearest interpretation into ordinary language of the meaning of the text. If grief, dismay, disappointment or pleasure, can shake the soul so that it loses its fixed hold on the calm spirit which inspires it, and the moisture of life breaks forth, drowning knowledge in sensation, then all is blurred, the windows are darkened, the light is useless. This is as literal a fact as that if a man, at the edge of a precipice, loses his nerve through some sudden emotion he will certainly fall. The poise of the body, the balance, must be preserved, not only in dangerous places, but even on the level ground, and with all the assistance Nature gives us by law of gravitation. So it is with the soul, it is the link between the outer body and the starry spirit beyond; the divine spark dwells in the still place where no convulsion of Nature can shake the air; this is so always. But the soul may lose its hold on that, its knowledge of it, even though these two are part of one whole; and it is by emotion, by sensation, that this hold is loosed. To suffer either pleasure or pain, causes a vivid vibration which is, to the consciousness of man, life. Now this sensibility does not lessen when the disciple enters upon his training; it increases. It is the first test of his strength; he must suffer, must enjoy or endure, more keenly than other men, while yet he has taken on him a duty which does not exist for other men, that of not allowing his suffering to shake him from his fixed purpose. He has, in fact, at the first step to take himself steadily in hand and put the bit into his own mouth; no one else can do it for him.

The first four aphorisms of *Light on the Path,* refer entirely to astral development. This development must be accomplished to a certain extent— that is to say it must be fully entered upon— before the remainder of the book is really intelligible except to the intellect; in fact, before it can be read as a practical, not a metaphysical treatise.

In one of our great mystic Brotherhoods, there are four ceremonies, that take place early in the year, which practically illustrate and elucidate these aphorisms. They are ceremonies in which only novices take part, for they are simply services of the threshold. But it will show how serious a thing it is to become a disciple, when it is understood that these are all ceremonies of sacrifice. The first one is this of which I have been speaking.

The keenest enjoyment, the bitterest pain, the anguish of loss and despair, are brought to bear on the trembling soul, which has not yet found light in the darkness, which is helpless as a blind man is, and until these shocks can be endured without loss of equilibrium the astral senses must remain sealed. This is the merciful law. The "medium," or "spiritualist," who rushes into the psychic world without preparation, is a law-breaker, a breaker of the laws of super-nature. Those who break Nature's laws lose their physical health; those who break the laws of the inner life, lose their psychic health. "Mediums" become mad, suicides, miserable creatures devoid of moral sense; and often end as unbelievers, doubters even of that which their own eyes have seen. The disciple is compelled to become his own master before he adventures on this perilous path, and attempts to face those beings who live and work in the astral world, and whom we call masters, because of their great knowledge and their ability to control not only themselves but the forces around them.

The condition of the soul when it lives for the life of sensation as distinguished from that of knowledge, is vibratory or oscillating, as distinguished from fixed. That is the nearest literal representation of the fact; but it is only literal to the intellect, not to the intuition. For this part of man's consciousness a different vocabulary is needed. The idea of "fixed" might perhaps be transposed into that of "at home." In sensation no permanent home can be found, because change is the law of this vibratory existence, that fact is the first one which must be learned by the disciple. It is useless to pause and weep for a scene in a kaleidoscope which has passed.

It is a very well-known fact, one with which Bulwer Lytton dealt with great power, that an intolerable sadness is the very first experience of the neophyte in Occultism. A sense of blankness falls upon him which makes the world a waste, and life a vain exertion. This follows his first serious contemplation of the abstract. In gazing, or even in attempting to gaze, on the ineffable mystery of his own higher nature, he himself causes the initial trial to fall on him. The oscillation between pleasure and pain ceases for— perhaps an instant of time; but that is enough to have cut him loose from his fast moorings in the world of sensation. He has experienced, however briefly, the greater life; and he goes on with ordinary existence weighted by a sense of unreality, of blank, of horrid negation. This was the nightmare which visited Bulwer Lytton's neophyte in "*Zanoni*"; and even Zanoni himself, who had learned great truths, and been entrusted with great powers, had not actually passed the threshold where fear and hope, despair and joy seem at one moment absolute realities, at the next mere forms of fancy.

This initial trial is often brought on us by life itself. For life is after all, the great teacher. We return to study it, after we have acquired power over it, just as the master in chemistry learns more in the laboratory than his pupil does. There are persons so near the door of knowledge that life itself prepares them for it, and no individual hand has to invoke the hideous guardian of the entrance. These must naturally be keen and powerful organizations, capable of the most vivid pleasure; then pain comes and fills its great duty. The most intense forms of suffering fall on such a nature, till at last it arouses from its stupor of consciousness, and by the force of its internal vitality steps over the threshold into a place of peace. Then the vibration of life loses its power of tyranny. The sensitive nature must suffer still; but the soul has freed itself and stands aloof, guiding the life towards its greatness. Those who are the subjects of Time, and go slowly through all his spaces, live on through a long-drawn series of sensations, and suffer a constant mingling of pleasure and of pain. They do not dare to take the snake of self in a steady grasp and conquer it, so becoming divine; but prefer to go on fretting through divers experiences, suffering blows from the opposing forces.

When one of these subjects of Time decides to enter on the path of Occultism, it is this which is his first task. If life has not taught it to him, if he is not strong enough to teach himself, and if he has power enough to demand the help of a master, then this fearful trial, depicted in *Zanoni*, is put upon him. The oscillation in which he lives, is for an instant stilled; and he has to survive the shock of facing what seems to him at first sight as the abyss of nothingness. Not till he has learned to dwell in this abyss, and has found its peace, is it possible for his eyes to have become incapable of tears.

The difficulty of writing intelligibly on these subjects is so great that I beg of those who have found any interest in this article, and are yet left with perplexities and doubts, to address me in the correspondence column of this magazine. I ask this because thoughtful questions are as great an assistance to the general reader as the answers to them.

"Before the ear can hear, it must have lost its sensitiveness."

The first four rules of *Light on the Path* are, undoubtedly, curious though the statement may seem, the most important in the whole book, save one only. Why they are so important is that they contain the vital law, the very creative essence of the astral man. And it is only in the astral (or self-illuminated) consciousness that the rules which follow them have any living meaning. Once attain to the use of the astral senses and it becomes a matter of course that one commences to use them; and the later rules are but guidance in their use. When I speak like this I mean, naturally, that the first four rules are the ones which are of importance and interest to those who read them in print upon a page. When they are engraved on a man's heart and on his life, unmistakably then the other rules become not merely interesting, or extraordinary, metaphysical statements, but actual facts in life which have to be grasped and experienced.

The four rules stand written in the great chamber of every actual lodge of a living Brotherhood. Whether the man is about to sell his soul to the devil, like Faust; whether he is to be worsted in the battle, like Hamlet; or whether he is to pass on within the precincts; in any case these words are for him.

The man can choose between virtue and vice, but not until he is a man; a babe or a wild animal cannot so choose. Thus with the disciple, he must first become a disciple before he can even see the paths to choose between. This effort of creating himself as a disciple, the re-birth, he must do for himself without any teacher. Until the four rules are learned no teacher can be of any use to him; and that is why "the Masters" are referred to in the way they are. No real masters, whether adepts in power, in love, or in blackness, can affect a man till these four rules are passed.

Tears, as I have said, may be called the moisture of life. The soul must have laid aside the emotions of humanity, must have secured a balance which cannot be shaken by misfortune, before its eyes can open upon the super-human world.

The voice of the Masters is always in the world; but only those hear it whose ears are no longer receptive of the sounds which affect the personal life. Laughter no longer lightens the heart, anger may no longer enrage it, tender words bring it no balm. For that within, to which the ears are as an outer gateway, is an unshaken place of peace in itself which no person can disturb.

As the eyes are the windows of the soul, so are the ears its gateways or doors. Through them comes knowledge of the confusion of the world. The great ones who have conquered life, who have become more than disciples, stand at peace and undisturbed amid the vibration and kaleidoscopic movement of humanity. They hold within themselves a certain knowledge, as well as a perfect peace; and thus they are not roused or excited by the partial and erroneous fragments of information which are brought to their ears by the changing voices of those around them. When I speak of knowledge, I mean intuitive knowledge. This certain information can never be obtained by hard work, or by experiment; for these methods are only applicable to matter, and matter is in itself a perfectly uncertain substance, continually effected by change. The most absolute and universal laws of natural and physical life, as understood by the scientist, will pass away when the life of this universe has passed away, and only its soul is left in the silence. What then will be the value of the knowledge of its laws acquired by industry and observation? I pray that no reader or critic will imagine that by what I have said I intend to depreciate or disparage acquired knowledge, or the work of scientists. On the contrary, I hold that scientific men are the pioneers of modern thought. The days of literature and of art, when poets and sculptors saw the divine light, and put it into their own great language—these days lie buried in the long past with the ante-Phidian sculptors and the pre-Homeric poets. The mysteries no longer rule the world of thought and beauty; human life is the governing power, not that which lies beyond it. But the scientific workers are progressing, not so much by their own will as by sheer force of circumstances, towards the far line which divides things interpretable from things uninterpretable. Every fresh discovery drives them a step onward. Therefore do I very highly esteem the knowledge obtained by work and experiment.

But intuitive knowledge is an entirely different thing. It is not acquired in any way, but is, so to speak, a faculty of the soul; not the animal soul, that which becomes a ghost after death, when lust or liking or the memory of ill-deeds holds it to the neighbourhood of human beings, but the divine soul which animates all the external forms of the individualised being.

This is, of course, a faculty which indwells in that soul, which is inherent. The would-be disciple has to arouse himself to the consciousness of it by a fierce and resolute and indomitable effort of will. I use the word indomitable for a special reason. Only he who is untameable, who cannot be dominated, who knows he has to play the lord over men, over facts, over all things save his own divinity, can arouse this faculty. "With faith all things are possible." The sceptical laugh at faith and pride themselves on its absence from their own minds. The truth is that faith is a great engine, an enormous power, which in fact can accomplish all things. For it is the covenant or engagement between man's divine part and his lesser self.

The use of this engine is quite necessary in order to obtain intuitive knowledge; for unless a man believes such knowledge exists within himself how can he claim and use it?

Without he is more helpless than any drift-wood or wreckage on the great tides of the ocean. They are cast hither and thither indeed; so may a man be by the chances of fortune. But such adventures are purely external and of very small account. A slave may be dragged through the streets in chains, and yet retain the quiet soul of a philosopher, as was well seen in the person of Epictetus. A man may have every worldly prize in his possession, and stand absolute master of his personal fate, to all appearance, and yet he knows no peace, no certainty, because he is shaken within himself by every tide of thought that he touches on. And these changing tides do not merely sweep the man bodily hither and thither like drift-wood on the water; that would be nothing. They enter into the gateways of his soul, and wash over that soul and make it blind and blank and void of all permanent intelligence, so that passing impressions affect it.

To make my meaning plainer I will use an illustration. Take an author at his writing, a painter at his canvas, a composer listening to the melodies that dawn upon his glad imagination; let any one of these workers pass his daily hours by a wide window looking on a busy street. The power of the animating life blinds sight and hearing alike, and the great traffic of the city goes by like nothing but a passing pageant. But a man whose mind is empty, whose day is objectless, sitting at the same window, notes the passers-by and remembers the faces that chance to please or interest him. So it is with the mind in its relation to eternal truth. If it no longer transmits its fluctuations, its partial knowledge, its unreliable information to the soul, then in the inner place of peace already found when the first rule has been learned—in that inner place there leaps into flame the light of actual knowledge. Then the ears begin to hear. Very dimly, very faintly at first. And, indeed, so faint and tender are these first indications of the commencement of true actual life, that they are sometimes pushed aside as mere fancies, mere imaginings.

But before these are capable of becoming more than mere imaginings, the abyss of nothingness has to be faced in another form. The utter silence which can only come by closing the ears to all transitory sounds comes as a more appalling horror than even the formless emptiness of space. Our only mental conception of blank space is, I think, when reduced to its barest element of thought, that of black darkness. This is a great physical terror to most persons, and when regarded as an eternal and unchangeable fact, must mean to the mind the idea of annihilation rather than anything else. But it is the obliteration of one sense only; and the sound of a voice may come and bring comfort even in the profoundest darkness. The disciple, having found his way into this blackness, which is the fearful abyss, must then so shut the gates of his soul that no comforter can enter there nor any enemy. And it is in making this second effort that the fact of pain and pleasure being but one sensation becomes recognisable by those who have before been unable to perceive it. For when the solitude of silence is reached the soul hungers so fiercely and passionately for some sensation on which to rest, that a painful one would be as keenly welcomed as a pleasant one. When this consciousness is reached the courageous man by seizing and retaining it, may destroy the "sensitiveness" at once. When the ear no longer discriminates between that which is pleasant or that which is painful, it will no longer be affected by the voices of others. And then it is safe and possible to open the doors of the soul.

"Sight" is the first effort, and the easiest, because it is accomplished partly by an intellectual effort. The intellect can conquer the heart, as is well known in ordinary life. Therefore, this preliminary step still lies within the dominion of matter. But the second step allows of no such assistance, nor of any material aid whatever. Of course, I mean by material aid the action of the brain, or emotions, or human soul. In compelling the ears to listen only to the eternal silence, the being we call man becomes something which is no longer man. A very superficial survey of the thousand and one influences which are brought to bear on us by others will show that this must be so. A disciple will fulfil all the duties of his manhood; but he will fulfil them according to his own sense of right, and not according to that of any person or body of persons. This is a very evident result of following the creed of knowledge instead of any of the blind creeds.

To obtain the pure silence necessary for the disciple, the heart and emotions, the brain and its intellectualisms, have to be put aside. Both are but mechanisms, which will perish with the span of man's life. It is the essence beyond, that which is the motive power, and makes man live, that is now compelled to rouse itself and act. Now is the greatest hour of danger. In the first trial men go mad with fear; of this first trial Bulwer Lytton wrote. No novelist has followed to the second trial, though some of the poets have. Its subtlety and great danger lies in the fact that in the measure of a man's strength is the measure of his chance of passing beyond it or coping with it at all. If he has power enough to awaken that unaccustomed part of himself, the supreme essence, then has he power to lift the gates of gold, then is he the true alchemist, in possession of the elixir of life.

It is at this point of experience that the occultist becomes separated from all other men and enters on to a life which is his own; on to the path of individual accomplishment instead of mere obedience to the genii which rule our earth. This raising of himself into an individual power does in reality identify him with the nobler forces of life and make him one with them. For they stand beyond the powers of this earth and the laws of this universe. Here lies man's only hope of success in the great effort; to leap right away from his present standpoint to his next and at once become an intrinsic part of the divine power as he has been an intrinsic part of the intellectual power, of the great nature to which he belongs. He stands always in advance of himself, if such a contradiction can be understood. It is the men who adhere to this position, who believe in their innate power of progress, and that of the whole race, who are the elder brothers, the pioneers. Each man has to accomplish the great leap for himself and without aid; yet it is something of a staff to lean on to know that others have gone on that road. It is possible that they have been lost in the abyss; no matter, they have had the courage to enter it. Why I say that it is possible they have been lost in the abyss is because of this fact, that one who has passed through is unrecognizable until the other and altogether new condition is attained by both. It is unnecessary to enter upon the subject of what that condition is at present. I only say this, that in the early state in which man is entering upon the silence he loses knowledge of his friends, of his lovers, of all who have been near and dear to him; and also loses sight of his teachers and of those who have preceded him on his way. I explain this because scarce one passes through without bitter complaint. Could but the mind grasp beforehand that the silence must be complete, surely this complaint need not arise as a hindrance on the path. Your teacher, or your predecessor may hold your hand in his, and give you the utmost sympathy the human heart is capable of. But when the silence and the darkness comes, you lose all knowledge of him; you are alone and he cannot help you, not because his power is gone, but because you have invoked your great enemy.

By your great enemy, I mean yourself. If you have the power to face your own soul in the darkness and silence, you will have conquered the physical or animal self which dwells in sensation only.

This statement, I feel, will appear involved; but in reality it is quite simple. Man, when he has reached his fruition, and civilization is at its height, stands between two fires. Could he but claim his great inheritance, the encumbrance of the mere animal life would fall away from him without difficulty. But he does not do this, and so the races of men flower and then droop and die and decay off the face of the earth, however splendid the bloom may have been. And it is left to the individual to make this great effort; to refuse to be terrified by his greater nature, to refuse to be drawn back by his lesser or more material self. Every individual who accomplishes this is a great redeemer of the race. He may not blazon forth his deeds, he may dwell in secret and silence; but it is a fact that he forms a link between man and his divine part; between the known and the unknown; between the stir of the marketplace and the stillness of the snow-capped Himalayas. He has not to go about among men in order to form this link; in the astral he *is* that link, and this fact makes him a being of another order from the rest of mankind. Even so early on the road towards knowledge, when he has but taken the second step, he finds his footing more certain, and becomes conscious that he is a recognised part of a whole.

This is one of the contradictions in life which occur so constantly that they afford fuel to the fiction writer. The occultist finds them become much more marked as he endeavours to live the life he has chosen. As he retreats within himself and becomes self-dependent, he finds himself more definitely becoming part of a great tide of definite thought and feeling. When he has learned the first lesson, conquered the hunger of the heart, and refused to live on the love of others, he finds himself more capable of inspiring love. As he flings life away it comes to him in a new form and with a new meaning. The world has always been a place with many contradictions in it, to the man; when he becomes a disciple he finds life is describable as a series of paradoxes. This is a fact in nature, and the reason for it is intelligible enough. Man's soul "dwells like a star apart," even that of the vilest among us; while his consciousness is under the law of vibratory and sensuous life. This alone is enough to cause those complications of character which are the material for the novelist; every man is a mystery, to friend and enemy alike, and to himself. His motives are often undiscoverable, and he cannot probe to them or know why he does this or that.

The disciple's effort is that of awakening consciousness in this starry part of himself, where his power and divinity lie sleeping. As this consciousness becomes awakened, the contradictions in the man himself become more marked than ever; and so do the paradoxes which he lives through. For, of course man creates his own life; and "adventures are to the adventurous" is one of those wise proverbs which are drawn from actual fact, and cover the whole area of human experience.

Pressure on the divine part of man re-acts upon the animal part. As the silent soul awakes it makes the ordinary life of the man more purposeful, more vital, more real, and responsible. To keep to the two instances already mentioned, the occultist who has withdrawn into his own citadel has found his strength; immediately he becomes aware of the demands of duty upon him. He does not obtain his strength by his own right, but because he is a part of the whole; and as soon as he is safe from the vibration of life and can stand unshaken, the outer world cries out to him to come and labour in it. So with the heart. When it no longer wishes to take, it is called upon to give abundantly.

Light on the Path has been called a book of paradoxes, and very justly; what else could it be, when it deals with the actual personal experience of the disciple?

To have acquired the astral senses of sight and hearing; or in other words to have attained perception and opened the doors of the soul, are gigantic tasks and may take the sacrifice of many successive incarnations. And yet when the will has reached its strength, the whole miracle may be worked in a second of time.

Then is the disciple the servant of Time no longer.

These two first steps are negative; that is to say they imply retreat from a present condition of things rather than advance towards another. The two next are active, implying the advance into another state of being.

THE DEMAND OF THE NEOPHYTE.

"Before the voice can speak in the presence of the Masters."

Speech is the power of communication; the moment of entrance into active life is marked by its attainment.

And now, before I go any further, let me explain a little the way in which the rules written down in *Light on the Path* are arranged. The first seven of those which are numbered are sub-divisions of the two first unnumbered rules those with which I have dealt in the two preceding papers. The numbered rules were simply an effort of mine to make the unnumbered ones more intelligible. "Eight" to "fifteen" of these numbered rules belong to this unnumbered rule which is now my text.

As I have said, these rules are written for all disciples, but for none else; they are not of interest to any other persons.

Therefore I trust no one else will trouble to read these papers any further. The first two rules, which include the whole of that part of the effort which necessitates the use of the surgeon's knife, I will enlarge upon further if I am asked to do so. But the disciple is expected to deal with the snake, his lower self, unaided; to suppress his human passions and emotions by the force of his own will. He can only demand assistance with a master when this is accomplished, or at all events, partially so. Otherwise the gates and windows of his soul are blurred, and blinded, and darkened, and no knowledge can come to him. I am not, in these papers, purposing to tell a man how to deal with his own soul; I am simply giving, to the disciple, the knowledge. That I am not writing, even now, so that all who run may read, is owing to the fact that super-nature prevents this by its own immutable laws.

The four rules which I have written down for those in the

West who wish to study them, are as I have said, written in the ante-chamber of every living Brotherhood; I may add more, in the ante-chamber of every living or dead Brotherhood, or Order yet to be formed. When I speak of a Brotherhood or an Order, I do not mean an arbitrary constitution made by scholiasts and intellectualists; I mean an actual fact in super-nature, a stage of development towards the absolute God or Good. During this development the disciple encounters harmony, pure knowledge, pure truth, in different degrees, and as he enters these degrees, he finds himself becoming part of what might be roughly described as a layer of human consciousness. He encounters his equals, men of his own self-less character, and with them his association becomes permanent and indissoluble, because founded on a vital likeness of nature. To them he becomes pledged by such vows as need no utterance or framework in ordinary words. This is one aspect of what I mean by a Brotherhood.

If the first rules are conquered, the disciple finds himself standing at the threshold. Then if his will is sufficiently resolute his power of speech comes; a two-fold power. For, as he advances now, he finds himself entering into a state of blossoming, where every bud that opens throws out its several rays or petals. If he is to exercise his new gift, he must use it in its two-fold character. He finds in himself the power to speak in the presence of the masters; in other words, he has the right to demand contact with the divinest element of that state of consciousness into which he has entered. But he finds himself compelled, by the nature of his position, to act in two ways at the same time. He cannot send his voice up to the heights where sit the gods till he has penetrated to the deep places where their light shines not at all. He has come within the grip of an iron law. If he demands to become a neophyte, he at once becomes a servant. Yet his service is sublime, if only from the character of those who share it. For the masters are also servants; they serve and claim their reward afterwards. Part of their service is to let their knowledge touch him; his first act of service is to give some of that knowledge to those who are not yet fit to stand where he stands. This is no arbitrary decision, made by any master or teacher or any such person, however divine. It is a law of that life which the disciple has entered upon.

Therefore was it written in the inner doorway of the lodges of the old Egyptian Brotherhood, "the labourer is worthy of his hire."

"Ask and ye shall have," sounds like something too easy and simple to be credible. But the disciple cannot "ask" in the mystic sense in which the word is used in this scripture until he has attained the power of helping others.

Why is this? Has the statement too dogmatic a sound?

Is it too dogmatic to say that a man must have foothold before he can spring? The position is the same. If help is given, if work is done, then there is an actual claim—not what we call a personal claim of payment, but the claim of co-nature. The divine give, they demand that you also shall give before you can be of their kin.

This law is discovered as soon as the disciple endeavours to speak. For speech is a gift which comes only to the disciple of power and knowledge. The spiritualist enters the psychic-astral world, but he does not find there any certain speech, unless he at once claims it and continues to do so. If he is interested in "phenomena," or the mere circumstance and accident of astral life, then he enters no direct ray of thought or purpose, he merely exists and amuses himself in the astral life as he has existed and amused himself in the physical life. Certainly there are one or two simple lessons which the psychic-astral can teach him, just as there are simple lessons which material and intellectual life teach him. And these lessons have to be learned; the man who proposes to enter upon the life of the disciple without having learned the early and simple lessons must always suffer from his ignorance. They are vital, and have to be studied in a vital manner; experienced through and through, over and over again, so that each part of the nature has been penetrated by them.

To return. In claiming the power of speech, as it is called, the Neophyte cries out to the Great One who stands foremost in the ray of knowledge on which he has entered, to give him guidance. When he does this, his voice is hurled back by the power he has approached, and echoes down to the deep recesses of human ignorance. In some confused and blurred manner the news that there is knowledge and a beneficent power which teaches is carried to as many men as will listen to it. No disciple can cross the threshold without communicating this news, and placing it on record in some fashion or other.

He stands horror-struck at the imperfect and unprepared manner in which he has done this; and then comes the desire to do it well, and with the desire to help others comes the power. For it is a pure desire, this which comes upon him; he can gain no credit, no glory, no personal reward by fulfilling it.

And therefore he obtains the power to fulfil it.

The history of the whole past, so far as we can trace it, shows very plainly that there is neither credit, glory, or reward to be gained by this first task which is given to the Neophyte. Mystics have always been sneered at, and seers disbelieved; those who have had the added power of intellect have left for posterity their written record, which to most men appears unmeaning and visionary, even when the authors have the advantage of speaking from a far-off past. The disciple who undertakes the task, secretly hoping for fame or success, to appear as a teacher and apostle before the world, fails even before his task is attempted, and his hidden hypocrisy poisons his own soul, and the souls of those he touches. He is secretly worshiping himself, and this idolatrous practice must bring its own reward.

The disciple who has the power of entrance, and is strong enough to pass each barrier, will when the divine message comes to his spirit, forget himself utterly in the new consciousness which falls on him. If this lofty contact can really rouse him, he becomes as one of the divine in his desire to give rather than to take, in his wish to help rather than be helped, in his resolution to feed the hungry rather than take manna from Heaven himself. His nature is transformed, and the selfishness which prompts men's actions in ordinary life suddenly deserts him.

THE SECLUSION OF THE ADEPT.

"Before the voice can speak in the presence of the Masters, it must have lost the power to wound."

Those who give a merely passing and superficial attention to the subject of occultism—and their name is Legion— constantly inquire why, if adepts in life exist, they do not appear in the world and show their power? That the chief body of these wise ones should be understood to dwell beyond the fastnesses of the Himalayas, appears to be sufficient proof that they are only figures of straw. Otherwise, why place them so far off?

Unfortunately, Nature has done this and not personal choice or arrangement. There are certain spots on the earth where the advance of "civilisation" is unfelt, and the nineteenth century fever is kept at bay. In these favoured places there is always time, always opportunity, for the realities of life; they are not crowded out by the doings of an inchoate, money-loving, pleasure-seeking society. While there are adepts upon the earth, the earth must preserve to them places of seclusion.

This is a fact in nature which is only an external expression of a profound fact in super-nature.

The demand of the neophyte remains unheard until the voice in which it is uttered has lost the power to wound. This is because the divine-astral life is a place in which order reigns, just as it does in natural life. There is, of course, always the centre and the circumference as there is in nature. Close to the central heart of life, on any plane, there is knowledge, there order reigns completely; and chaos makes dim and confused the outer margin of the circle. In fact, life in every form bears a more or less strong resemblance to a philosophic school. There are always the devotees of knowledge who forget their own lives in their pursuit of it; there are always the flippant crowd who come and go—Of such, Epictetus said that it was as easy to teach them philosophy as to eat custard with a fork. The same state exists in the super-astral life; and the adept has an even deeper and more profound seclusion there in which to dwell. This place of retreat is so safe, so sheltered, that no sound which has discord in it can reach his ears. Why should this be, will be asked at once, if he is a being of such great powers as those say who believe in existence? The answer seems very apparent. He serves humanity and identifies himself with the whole world; he is ready to make vicarious sacrifice for it at any moment—*by living not by dying for it*. Why should he not die for it? Because he is part of the great whole, and one of the most valuable parts of it. Because he lives under laws of order which he does not desire to break. His life is not his own, but that of the forces which work behind him. He is the flower of humanity, the bloom which contains the divine seed. He is, in his own person, a treasure of the universal nature, which is guarded and made safe in order that the fruition shall be perfected. It is only at definite periods of the world's history that he is allowed to go among the herd of men as their redeemer. But for those who have the power to separate themselves from this herd he is always at hand. And for those who are strong enough to conquer the vices of the personal human nature, as set forth in these four rules, he is consciously at hand, easily recognised, ready to answer[10]

But this conquering of self implies a destruction of qualities which most men regard as not only indestructible but desirable.

The "power to wound" includes much that men value, not only in themselves, but in others. The instinct of self-defence and of self-preservation is part of it; the idea that one has any right or rights, either as citizen, or man, or individual, the pleasant consciousness of self-respect and of virtue. These are hard sayings to many; yet they are true. For these words that I am writing now, and those which I have written on this subject, are not in any sense my own. They are drawn from the traditions of the lodge of the Great Brotherhood, which was once the secret splendour of Egypt. The rules written in its ante-chamber were the same as those now written in the ante-chamber of existing schools. Through all time the wise men have lived apart from the mass. And even when some temporary purpose or object induces one of them to come into the midst of human life,

---

[10] *Of course every occultist knows by reading Eliphas Levi and other authors that the "astral" plane is a plane of unequalised forces, and that a state of confusion necessarily prevails. But this does not apply to the "divine astral" plane, which is a plane where wisdom, and therefore order, prevails*

his seclusion and safety is preserved as completely as ever. It is part of his inheritance, part of his position, he has an actual title to it, and can no more put it aside than the Duke of Westminster can say he does not choose to be the Duke of Westminster. In the various great cities of the world an adept lives for a while from time to time, or perhaps only passes through; but all are occasionally aided by the actual power and presence of one of these men. Here in London, as in Paris and St. Petersburgh, there are men high in development. But they are only known as mystics by those who have the power to recognise; the power given by the conquering of self. Otherwise how could they exist, even for an hour, in such a mental and psychic atmosphere as is created by the confusion and disorder of a city? Unless protected and made safe their own growth would be interfered with, their work injured. And the neophyte may meet an adept in the flesh, may live in the same house with him, and yet be unable to recognise him, and unable to make his own voice heard by him. For no nearness in space, no closeness of relations, no daily intimacy, can do away with the inexorable laws which give the adept his seclusion. No voice penetrates to his inner hearing till it has become a divine voice, a voice which gives no utterance to the cries of self. Any lesser appeal would be as useless, as much a waste of energy and power, as for mere children who are learning their alphabet to be taught it by a professor of philology. Until a man has become, in heart and spirit, a disciple, he has no existence for those who are teachers of disciples. And he becomes this by one method only—the surrender of his personal humanity.

For the voice to have lost the power to wound, a man must have reached that point where he sees himself only as one of the vast multitude that live; one of the sands washed hither and thither by the sea of vibratory existence. It is said that every grain of sand in the ocean bed does, in its turn, get washed up on to the shore and lie for a moment in the sunshine. So with human beings, they are driven hither and thither by a great force, and each, in his turn, finds the sunrays on him. When a man is able to regard his own life as part of a whole like this he will no longer struggle in order to obtain anything for himself. This is the surrender of personal rights. The ordinary man expects, not to take equal fortunes with the rest of the world, but in some points, about which he cares, to fare better than the others. The disciple does not expect this. Therefore, though he be, like

Epictetus, a chained slave, he has no word to say about it. He knows that the wheel of life turns ceaselessly. Burne Jones has shown it in his marvellous picture—the wheel turns, and on it are bound the rich and the poor, the great and the small— each has its moment of good fortune when the wheel brings him uppermost—the King rises and falls, the poet is *fêted* and forgotten, the slave is happy and afterwards discarded. Each in his turn is crushed as the wheel turns on. The disciple knows that this is so, and though it is his duty to make the utmost of the life that is his, he neither complains of it nor is elated by it, nor does he complain against the better fortune of others. All alike, as he well knows, are but learning a lesson; and he smiles at the socialist and the reformer who endeavour by sheer force to re-arrange circumstances which arise out of the forces of human nature itself. This is but kicking against the pricks; a waste of life and energy.

In realising this a man surrenders his imagined individual rights, of whatever sort. That takes away one keen sting which is common to all ordinary men.

When the disciple has fully recognised that the very thought of individual rights is only the outcome of the venomous quality in himself, that it is the hiss of the snake of self which poisons with its sting his own life and the lives of those about him, then he is ready to take part in a yearly ceremony which is open to all neophytes who are prepared for it. All weapons of defence and offence are given up; all weapons of mind and heart, and brain, and spirit. Never again can another man be regarded as a person who can be criticised or condemned; never again can the neophyte raise his voice in self-defence or excuse. From that ceremony he turns into the world as helpless, as unprotected, as a new-born child. That, indeed is what he is. He has begun to be born again on to the higher plane of life, that breezy and well-lit plateau from whence the eyes see intelligently and regard the world with a new insight.

I have said, a little way back, that after parting with the sense of individual rights, the disciple must part also with the sense of self-respect and of virtue. This may sound a terrible doctrine, yet all occultists know well that it is not a doctrine, but a fact. He who thinks himself holier than another, he who has any pride in his own exemption from vice or folly, he who believes himself wise, or in any way superior to his fellow men, is incapable of discipleship. A man must become as a little child before he can enter into the kingdom of heaven.

Virtue and wisdom are sublime things; but if they create pride and a consciousness of separateness from the rest of humanity in the mind of a man, then they are only the snakes of self reappearing in a finer form. At any moment he may put on his grosser shape and sting as fiercely as when he inspired the actions of a murderer who kills for gain or hatred, or a politician who sacrifices the mass for his own or his party's interests.

In fact, to have lost the power to wound, implies that the snake is not only scotched, but killed. When it is merely stupefied or lulled to sleep it awakes again and the disciple uses his knowledge and his power for his own ends, and is a pupil of the many masters of the black art, for the road to destruction is very broad and easy, and the way can be found blindfold. That it is the way to destruction is evident, for when a man begins to live for self he narrows his horizon steadily till at last the fierce driving inwards leaves him but the space of a pin's-head to dwell in. We have all seen this phenomenon occur in ordinary life. A man who becomes selfish isolates himself, grows less interesting and less agreeable to others. The sight is an awful one, and people shrink from a very selfish person at last, as from a beast of prey. How much more awful is it when it occurs on the more advanced plane of life, with the added powers of knowledge, and through the greater sweep of successive incarnations!

Therefore I say, pause and think well upon the threshold. For if the demand of the neophyte is made without the complete purification, it will not penetrate the seclusion of the divine adept, but will evoke the terrible forces which attend upon the black side of our human nature.

"Before the soul can stand in the presence of the Masters its feet must be washed in the blood of the heart."

The word soul, as used here, means the divine soul, or "starry spirit."

"To be able to stand is to have confidence;" and to have confidence means that the disciple is sure of himself, that he has surrendered his emotions, his very self, even his humanity; that he is incapable of fear and unconscious of pain; that his whole consciousness is centred in the divine life, which is expressed symbolically by the term "the Masters"; that he has neither eyes, nor ears, nor speech, nor power, save in and for the divine ray on which his highest sense has touched. Then is he fearless, free from suffering, free from anxiety or dismay; his soul stands without shrinking or desire of postponement, in the full blaze of the divine light which penetrates through and through his being. Then he has come into his inheritance and can claim his kinship with the teachers of men; he is upright, he has raised his head, he breathes the same air that they do.

But before it is in any way possible for him to do this, the feet of the soul must be washed in the blood of the heart.

The sacrifice, or surrender of the heart of man, and its emotions, is the first of the rules; it involves the "attaining of an equilibrium which cannot be shaken by personal emotion." This is done by the stoic philosopher; he, too, stands aside and looks equally upon his own sufferings, as well as on those of others.

In the same way that "tears" in the language of occultists expresses the soul of emotion, not its material appearance, so blood expresses, not that blood which is an essential of physical life, but the vital creative principle in man's nature, which drives him into human life in order to experience pain and pleasure, joy and sorrow. When he has let the blood flow from the heart he stands before the Masters as a pure spirit which no longer wishes to incarnate for the sake of emotion and experience.

Through great cycles of time successive incarnations in gross matter may yet be his lot; but he no longer desires them, the crude wish to live has departed from him. When he takes upon him man's form in the flesh he does it in the pursuit of a divine object, to accomplish the work of "the Masters," and for no other end. He looks neither for pleasure nor pain, asks for no heaven, and fears no hell; yet he has entered upon a great inheritance which is not so much a compensation for these things surrendered, as a state which simply blots out the memory of them. He lives now not in the world, but with it; his horizon has extended itself to the width of the whole universe. FINIS.

BOOK THREE.
THROUGH THE GATES OF GOLD

A FRAGMENT OF THOUGHT

Once, as I sat alone writing, a mysterious Visitor entered my study, unannounced, and stood beside me. I forgot to ask who he was or why he entered so unceremoniously, for he began to tell me of the Gates of Gold. He spoke from knowledge, and from the fire of his speech I caught faith. I have written down his words; but, alas, I cannot hope that the fire shall burn so brightly in my writing as in his speech. — M. C.

PROLOGUE

EVERY man has a philosophy of life of his own, except the true philosopher. The most ignorant boor has some conception of his object in living, and definite ideas as to the easiest and wisest way of attaining that object. The man of the world is often, unconsciously to himself, a philosopher of the first rank. He deals with his life on principles of the clearest character, and refuses to let his position be shattered by chance disaster. The man of thought and imagination has less certainty, and finds himself continually unable to formulate his ideas on that subject most profoundly interesting to human nature, — human life itself. The true philosopher is the one who would lay no claim to the name whatever, who has discovered that the mystery of life is unapproachable by ordinary thought, just as the true scientist confesses his complete ignorance of the principles which lie behind science.

Whether there is any mode of thought or any effort of the mind which will enable a man to grasp the great principles that evidently exist as causes in human life, is a question no ordinary thinker can determine. Yet the dim consciousness that there is cause behind the effects we see, that there is order ruling the chaos and sublime harmony pervading the discords, haunts the eager souls of the earth, and makes them long for vision of the unseen and knowledge of the unknowable.

Why long and look for that which is beyond all hope until the inner eyes are opened? Why not piece together the fragments that we have at hand, and see whether from them some shape cannot be given to the vast puzzle?

CHAPTER I. THE SEARCH FOR PLEASURE

I

WE are all acquainted with that stern thing called misery, which pursues man, and strangely enough, as it seems at first, pursues him with no vague or uncertain method, but with a positive and unbroken pertinacity. Its presence is not absolutely continuous, else man must cease to live; but its pertinacity is without any break. There is always the shadowy form of despair standing behind man ready to touch him with its terrible finger if for too long he finds himself content. What has given this ghastly shape the right to haunt us from the hour we are born until the hour we die? What has given it the right to stand always at our door, keeping that door ajar with its impalpable yet plainly horrible hand, ready to enter at the moment it sees fit? The greatest philosopher that ever lived succumbs before it at last; and he only is a philosopher, in any sane sense, who recognizes the fact that it is irresistible, and knows that like all other men he must suffer soon or late. It is part of the heritage of men, this pain and distress; and he who determines that nothing shall make him suffer, does but cloak himself in a profound and chilly selfishness. This cloak may protect him from pain; it will also separate him from pleasure. If peace is to be found on earth, or any joy in life, it cannot be by closing up the gates of feeling, which admit us to the loftiest and most vivid part of our existence. Sensation, as we obtain it through the physical body, affords us all that induces us to live in that shape. It is inconceivable that any man would care to take the trouble of breathing, unless the act brought with it a sense of satisfaction. So it is with every deed of every instant of our life. We live because it is pleasant even to have the sensation of pain. It is sensation we desire, else we would with one accord taste of the deep waters of oblivion, and the human race would become extinct. If this is the case in the physical life, it is evidently the case with the life of the emotions, — the imagination, the sensibilities, all those fine and delicate formations which, with the marvelous recording mechanism of the brain, make up the inner or subtile man. Sensation is that which makes their pleasure; an infinite series of sensations is life to them. Destroy the sensation which makes them wish to persevere in the experiment of living, and there is nothing left. Therefore the man who attempts to obliterate the sense of pain, and who proposes to maintain an equal state whether he is pleased or hurt, strikes at the very root of life, and destroys the object of his own existence. And that must apply, so far as our present reasoning or intuitive powers can show us, to every state, even to that of the Oriental's longed-for Nirvana. This condition can only be one of infinitely subtiler and more exquisite sensation, if it is a state at all, and not annihilation; and according to the experience of life from which we are at present able to judge, increased subtility of sensation means increased vividness, — as, for instance, a man of sensibility and imagination feels more in consequence of the unfaithfulness or faithfulness of a friend than can a man of even the grossest physical nature feel through the medium of the senses. Thus it is clear that the philosopher who refuses to feel, leaves himself no place to retreat to, not even the distant and unattainable Nirvanic goal. He can only deny himself his heritage of life, which is in other words the right of sensation. If he chooses to sacrifice that which makes him man, he must be content with mere idleness of consciousness, — a condition compared to which the oyster's is a life of excitement.

But no man is able to accomplish such a feat. The fact of his continued existence proves plainly that he still desires sensation, and desires it in such positive and active form that the desire must be gratified in physical life. It would seem more practical not to deceive one's self by the sham of stoicism, not to attempt renunciation of that with which nothing would induce one to part. Would it not be a bolder policy, a more promising mode of solving the great enigma of existence, to grasp it, to take hold firmly and to demand of it the mystery of itself? If men will but pause and consider what lessons they have learned from pleasure and pain, much might be guessed of that strange thing which causes these effects. But men are prone to turn away hastily from self-study, or from any close analysis of human nature. Yet there must be a science of life as intelligible as any of the methods of the schools. The science is unknown, it is true, and its existence is merely guessed, merely hinted at, by one or two of our more advanced thinkers. The development of a science is only the discovery of what is already in existence; and chemistry is as magical and incredible now to the ploughboy as the science of life is to the man of ordinary perceptions. Yet there may be, and there must be, a seer who perceives the growth of the new knowledge as the earliest dabblers in the experiments of the laboratory saw the system of knowledge now attained evolving itself out of nature for man's use and benefit.

II

Doubtless many more would experiment in suicide, as many now do, in order to escape from the burden of life, if they could be convinced that in that manner oblivion might be found. But he who hesitates before drinking the poison from the fear of only inviting change of mode of existence, and perhaps a more active form of misery, is a man of more knowledge than the rash souls who fling themselves wildly on the unknown, trusting to its kindliness. The waters of oblivion are something very different from the waters of death, and the human race cannot become extinct by means of death while the law of birth still operates. Man returns to physical life as the drunkard returns to the flagon of wine, — he knows not why, except that he desires the sensation produced by life as the drunkard desires the sensation produced by wine. The true waters of oblivion lie far behind our consciousness, and can only be reached by ceasing to exist in that consciousness, — by ceasing to exert the will which makes us full of senses and sensibilities.

Why does not the creature man return into that great womb of silence whence he came, and remain in peace, as the unborn child is at peace before the impetus of life has reached it? He does not do so because he hungers for pleasure and pain, joy and grief, anger and love. The unfortunate man will maintain that he has no desire for life; and yet he proves his words false by living. None can compel him to live; the galley-slave may be chained to his oar, but his life cannot be chained to his body. The superb mechanism of the human body is as useless as an engine whose fires are not lit, if the will to live ceases, — that will which we maintain resolutely and without pause, and which enables us to perform the tasks which otherwise would fill us with dismay, as, for instance, the momently drawing in and giving out of the breath. Such herculean efforts as this we carry on without complaint, and indeed with pleasure, in order that we may exist in the midst of innumerable sensations.

And more; we are content, for the most part, to go on without object or aim, without any idea of a goal or understanding of which way we are going. When the man first becomes aware of this aimlessness, and is dimly conscious that he is working with great and constant efforts, and without any idea towards what end those efforts are directed, then descends on him the misery of nineteenth-century thought. He is lost and bewildered, and without hope. He becomes sceptical, disillusioned, weary, and asks the apparently unanswerable question whether it is indeed worth while to draw his breath for such unknown and seemingly unknowable results. But are these results unknowable? At least, to ask a lesser question, is it impossible to make a guess as to the direction in which our goal lies?

III

This question, born of sadness and weariness, which seems to us essentially part of the spirit of the nineteenth century, is in fact a question which must have been asked all through the ages. Could we go back throughout history intelligently, no doubt we should find that it came always with the hour when the flower of civilization had blown to its full, and when its petals were but slackly held together. The natural part of man has reached then its utmost height; he has rolled the stone up the Hill of Difficulty only to watch it roll back again when the summit is reached, — as in Egypt, in Rome, in Greece. Why this useless labor? Is it not enough to produce a weariness and sickness unutterable, to be forever accomplishing a task only to see it undone again? Yet that is what man has done throughout history, so far as our limited knowledge reaches. There is one summit to which, by immense and united efforts, he attains, where there is a great and brilliant efflorescence of all the intellectual, mental, and material part of his nature. The climax of sensuous perfection is reached, and then his hold weakens, his power grows less, and he falls back, through despondency and satiety, to barbarism. Why does he not stay on this hill-top he has reached, and look away to the mountains beyond, and resolve to scale those greater heights? Because he is ignorant, and seeing a great glittering in the distance, drops his eyes bewildered and dazzled, and goes back for rest to the shadowy side of his familiar hill. Yet there is now and then one brave enough to gaze fixedly on this glittering, and to decipher something of the shape within it. Poets and philosophers, thinkers and teachers, — all those who are the "elder brothers of the race," — have beheld this sight from time to time, and some among them have recognized in the bewildering glitter the outlines of the Gates of Gold.

Those Gates admit us to the sanctuary of man's own nature, to the place whence his life-power comes, and where he is priest of the shrine of life. That it is possible to enter here, to pass through those Gates, some one or two have shown us. Plato, Shakespeare, and a few other strong ones have gone through and spoken to us in veiled language on the near side of the Gates. When the strong man has crossed the threshold he speaks no more to those at the other side. And even the words he utters when he is outside are so full of mystery, so veiled and profound, that only those who follow in his steps can see the light within them.

IV

What men desire is to ascertain how to exchange pain for pleasure; that is, to find out in what way consciousness may be regulated in order that the sensation which is most agreeable is the one that is experienced. Whether this can be discovered by dint of human thought is at least a question worth considering.

If the mind of man is turned upon any given subject with a sufficient concentration, he obtains illumination with regard to it sooner or later. The particular individual in whom the final illumination appears is called a genius, an inventor, one inspired; but he is only the crown of a great mental work created by unknown men about him, and receding back from him through long vistas of distance. Without them he would not have had his material to deal with. Even the poet requires innumerable poetasters to feed upon. He is the essence of the poetic power of his time, and of the times before him. It is impossible to separate an individual of any species from his kin.

If, therefore, instead of accepting the unknown as unknowable, men were *with one accord* to turn their thoughts towards it, those Golden Gates would not remain so inexorably shut. It does but need a strong hand to push them open. The courage to enter them is the courage to search the recesses of one's own nature without fear and without shame. In the fine part, the essence, the flavor of the man, is found the key which unlocks those great Gates. And when they open, what is it that is found?

Voices here and there in the long silence of the ages speak to answer that question. Those who have passed through have left words behind them as legacies to others of their kin. In these words we can find definite indications of what is to be looked for beyond the Gates. But only those who desire to go that way read the meaning hidden within the words. Scholars, or rather scholiasts, read the sacred books of different nations, the poetry and the philosophy left by enlightened minds, and find in it all the merest materiality. Imagination glorifying legends of nature, or exaggerating the psychic possibilities of man, explains to them all that they find in the Bibles of humanity.

What is to be found within the words of those books is to be found in each one of us; and it is impossible to find in literature or through any channel of thought that which does not exist in the man who studies. This is of course an evident fact known to all real students. But it has to be especially remembered in reference to this profound and obscure subject, as men so readily believe that nothing can exist for others where they themselves find emptiness.

One thing is soon perceived by the man who reads: those who have gone before have not found that the Gates of Gold lead to oblivion. On the contrary, sensation becomes real for the first time when that threshold is crossed. But it is of a new order, an order unknown to us now, and by us impossible to appreciate without at least some clew as to its character. This clew can be obtained undoubtedly by any student who cares to go through all the literature accessible to us. That mystic books and manuscripts exist, but remain inaccessible simply because there is no man ready to read the first page of any one of them, becomes the conviction of all who have studied the subject sufficiently. For there must be the continuous line all through: we see it go from dense ignorance up to intelligence and wisdom; it is only natural that it should go on to intuitive knowledge and to inspiration. Some scant fragments we have of these great gifts of man; where, then, is the whole of which they must be a part? Hidden behind the thin yet seemingly impassable veil which hides it from us as it hid all science, all art, all powers of man till he had the courage to tear away the screen. That courage comes only of conviction. When once man believes that the thing exists which he desires, he will obtain it at any cost. The difficulty in this case lies in man's incredulity. It requires a great tide of thought and attention to set in towards the unknown region of man's nature in order that its gates may be unlocked and its glorious vistas explored.

That it is worth while to do this whatever the hazard may be, all must allow who have asked the sad question of the nineteenth century, — Is life worth living? Surely it is sufficient to spur man to new effort, — the suspicion that beyond civilization, beyond mental culture, beyond art and mechanical perfection, there is a new, another gateway, admitting to the realities of life.

V

When it seems as if the end was reached, the goal attained, and that man has no more to do, — just then, when he appears to have no choice but between eating and drinking and living in his comfort as the beasts do in theirs, and scepticism which is death, — then it is that in fact, if he will but look, the Golden Gates are before him. With the culture of the age within him and assimilated perfectly, so that he is himself an incarnation of it, then he is fit to attempt the great step which is absolutely possible, yet is attempted by so few even of those who are fitted for it. It is so seldom attempted, partly because of the profound difficulties which surround it, but much more because man does not realize that this is actually the direction in which pleasure and satisfaction are to be obtained.

There are certain pleasures which appeal to each individual; every man knows that in one layer or another of sensation he finds his chief delight. Naturally he turns to this systematically through life, just as the sunflower turns to the sun and the water-lily leans on the water. But he struggles throughout with an awful fact which oppresses him to the soul, — that no sooner has he obtained his pleasure than he loses it again and has once more to go in search of it. More than that; he never actually reaches it, for it eludes him at the final moment. This is because he endeavors to seize that which is untouchable and satisfy his soul's hunger for sensation by contact with external objects. How can that which is external satisfy or even please the inner man, — the thing which reigns within and has no eyes for matter, no hands for touch of objects, no senses with which to apprehend that which is outside its magic walls? Those charmed barriers which surround it are limitless, for it is everywhere; it is to be discovered in all living things, and no part of the universe can be conceived of without it, if that universe is regarded as a coherent whole. And unless that point is granted at the outset it is useless to consider the subject of life at all. Life is indeed meaningless unless it is universal and coherent, and unless we maintain our existence by reason of the fact that we are part of that which is, not by reason of our own being.

This is one of the most important factors in the development of man, the recognition — profound and complete recognition — of the law of universal unity and coherence. The separation which exists between individuals, between worlds, between the different poles of the universe and of life, the mental and physical fantasy called space, is a nightmare of the human imagination. That nightmares exist, and exist only to torment, every child knows; and what we need is the power of discrimination between the phantasmagoria of the brain, which concern ourselves only, and the phantasmagoria of daily life, in which others also are concerned. This rule applies also to the larger case. It concerns no one but ourselves that we live in a nightmare of unreal horror, and fancy ourselves alone in the universe and capable of independent action, so long as our associates are those only who are a part of the dream; but when we desire to speak with those who have tried the Golden Gates and pushed them open, then it is very necessary — in fact it is essential — to discriminate, and not bring into our life the confusions of our sleep. If we do, we are reckoned as madmen, and fall back into the darkness where there is no friend but chaos. This chaos has followed every effort of man that is written in history; after civilization has flowered, the flower falls and dies, and winter and darkness destroy it. While man refuses to make the effort of discrimination which would enable him to distinguish between the shapes of night and the active figures of day, this must inevitably happen.

But if man has the courage to resist this reactionary tendency, to stand steadily on the height he has reached and put out his foot in search of yet another step, why should he not find it? There is nothing to make one suppose the pathway to end at a certain point, except that tradition which has declared it is so, and which men have accepted and hug to themselves as a justification for their indolence.

VI

Indolence is, in fact, the curse of man. As the Irish peasant and the cosmopolitan gypsy dwell in dirt and poverty out of sheer idleness, so does the man of the world live contented in sensuous pleasures for the same reason. The drinking of fine wines, the tasting of delicate food, the love of bright sights and sounds, of beautiful women and admirable surroundings, — these are no better for the cultivated man, no more satisfactory as a final goal of enjoyment for him, than the coarse amusements and gratifications of the boor are for the man without cultivation. There can be no final point, for life in every form is one vast series of fine gradations; and the man who elects to stand still at the point of culture he has reached, and to avow that he can go no further, is simply making an arbitrary statement for the excuse of his indolence. Of course there is a possibility of declaring that the gypsy is content in his dirt and poverty, and, because he is so, is as great a man as the most highly cultured. But he only is so while he is ignorant; the moment light enters the dim mind the whole man turns towards it. So it is on the higher platform; only the difficulty of penetrating the mind, of admitting the light, is even greater. The Irish peasant loves his whiskey, and while he can have it cares nothing for the great laws of morality and religion which are supposed to govern humanity and induce men to live temperately. The cultivated gourmand cares only for subtle tastes and perfect flavors; but he is as blind as the merest peasant to the fact that there is anything beyond such gratifications. Like the boor he is deluded by a mirage that oppresses his soul; and he fancies, having once obtained a sensuous joy that pleases him, to give himself the utmost satisfaction by endless repetition, till at last he reaches madness. The bouquet of the wine he loves enters his soul and poisons it, leaving him with no thoughts but those of sensuous desire; and he is in the same hopeless state as the man who dies mad with drink. What good has the drunkard obtained by his madness? None; pain has at last swallowed up pleasure utterly, and death steps in to terminate the agony. The man suffers the final penalty for his persistent ignorance of a law of nature as inexorable as that of gravitation, — a law which forbids a man to stand still. Not twice can the same cup of pleasure be tasted; the second time it must contain either a grain of poison or a drop of the elixir of life.

The same argument holds good with regard to intellectual pleasures; the same law operates. We see men who are the flower of their age in intellect, who pass beyond their fellows and tower over them, entering at last upon a fatal treadmill of thought, where they yield to the innate indolence of the soul and begin to delude themselves by the solace of repetition. Then comes the barrenness and lack of vitality, — that unhappy and disappointing state into which great men too often enter when middle life is just passed. The fire of youth, the vigor of the young intellect, conquers the inner inertia and makes the man scale heights of thought and fill his mental lungs with the free air of the mountains. But then at last the physical reaction sets in; the physical machinery of the brain loses its powerful impetus and begins to relax its efforts, simply because the youth of the body is at an end. Now the man is assailed by the great tempter of the race who stands forever on the ladder of life waiting for those who climb so far. He drops the poisoned drop into the ear, and from that moment all consciousness takes on a dullness, and the man becomes terrified lest life is losing its possibilities for him. He rushes back on to a familiar platform of experience, and there finds comfort in touching a well-known chord of passion or emotion. And too many having done this linger on, afraid to attempt the unknown, and satisfied to touch continually that chord which responds most readily. By this means they get the assurance that life is still burning within them. But at last their fate is the same as that of the gourmand and the drunkard. The power of the spell lessens daily as the machinery which feels loses its vitality; and the man endeavors to revive the old excitement and fervor by striking the note more violently, by hugging the thing that makes him feel, by drinking the cup of poison to its fatal dregs. And then he is lost; madness falls on his soul, as it falls on the body of the drunkard. Life has no longer any meaning for him, and he rushes wildly into the abysses of intellectual insanity. A lesser man who commits this great folly wearies the spirits of others by a dull clinging to familiar thought, by a persistent hugging of the treadmill which he asserts to be the final goal. The cloud that surrounds him is as fatal as death itself, and men who once sat at his feet turn away grieved, and have to look back at his early words in order to remember his greatness.

VII

What is the cure for this misery and waste of effort? Is there one? Surely life itself has a logic in it and a law which makes existence possible; otherwise chaos and madness would be the only state which would be attainable. When a man drinks his first cup of pleasure his soul is filled with the unutterable joy that comes with a first, a fresh sensation. The drop of poison that he puts into the second cup, and which, if he persists in that folly, has to become doubled and trebled till at last the whole cup is poison, — that is the ignorant desire for repetition and intensification; this evidently means death, according to all analogy. The child becomes the man; he cannot retain his childhood and repeat and intensify the pleasures of childhood except by paying the inevitable price and becoming an idiot. The plant strikes its roots into the ground and throws up green leaves; then it blossoms and bears fruit. That plant which will only make roots or leaves, pausing persistently in its development, is regarded by the gardener as a thing which is useless and must be cast out.

The man who chooses the way of effort, and refuses to allow the sleep of indolence to dull his soul, finds in his pleasures a new and finer joy each time he tastes them, — a something subtle and remote which removes them more and more from the state in which mere sensuousness is all; this subtle essence is that elixir of life which makes man immortal. He who tastes it and who will not drink unless it is in the cup finds life enlarge and the world grow great before his eager eyes. He recognizes the soul within the woman he loves, and passion becomes peace; he sees within his thought the finer qualities of spiritual truth, which is beyond the action of our mental machinery, and then instead of entering on the treadmill of intellectualisms he rests on the broad back of the eagle of intuition and soars into the fine air where the great poets found their insight; he sees within his own power of sensation, of pleasure in fresh air and sunshine, in food and wine, in motion and rest, the possibilities of the subtle man, the thing which dies not either with the body or the brain. The pleasures of art, of music, of light and loveliness, — within these forms, which men repeat till they find only the forms, he sees the glory of the Gates of Gold, and passes through to find the new life beyond which intoxicates and strengthens, as the keen mountain air intoxicates and strengthens, by its very vigor. But if he has been pouring, drop by drop, more and more of the elixir of life into his cup, he is strong enough to breathe this intense air and to live upon it. Then if he die or if he live in physical form, alike he goes on and finds new and finer joys, more perfect and satisfying experiences, with every breath he draws in and gives out.

CHAPTER II. THE MYSTERY OF THRESHOLD

I

THERE is no doubt that at the entrance on a new phase of life something has to be given up. The child, when it has become the man, puts away childish things. Saint Paul showed in these words, and in many others which he has left us, that he had tasted of the elixir of life, that he was on his way towards the Gates of Gold. With each drop of the divine draught which is put into the cup of pleasure something is purged away from that cup to make room for the magic drop. For Nature deals with her children generously: man's cup is always full to the brim; and if he chooses to taste of the fine and life-giving essence, he must cast away something of the grosser and less sensitive part of himself. This has to be done daily, hourly, momently, in order that the draught of life may steadily increase. And to do this unflinchingly, a man must be his own schoolmaster, must recognize that he is always in need of wisdom, must be ready to practise any austerities, to use the birch-rod unhesitatingly against himself, in order to gain his end. It becomes evident to any one who regards the subject seriously, that only a man who has the potentialities in him both of the voluptuary and the stoic has any chance of entering the Golden Gates. He must be capable of testing and valuing to its most delicate fraction every joy existence has to give; and he must be capable of denying himself all pleasure, and that without suffering from the denial. When he has accomplished the development of this double possibility, then he is able to begin sifting his pleasures and taking away from his consciousness those which belong absolutely to the man of clay. When those are put back, there is the next range of more refined pleasures to be dealt with. The dealing with these which will enable a man to find the essence of life is not the method pursued by the stoic philosopher. The stoic does not allow that there is joy within pleasure, and by denying himself the one loses the other. But the true philosopher, who has studied life itself without being bound by any system of thought, sees that the kernel is within the shell, and that, instead of crunching up the whole nut like a gross and indifferent feeder, the essence of the thing is obtained by cracking the shell and casting it away. All emotion, all sensation, lends itself to this process, else it could not be a part of man's development, an essential of his nature. For that there is before him power, life, perfection, and that every portion of his passage thitherwards is crowded with the means of helping him to his goal, can only be denied by those who refuse to acknowledge life as apart from matter. Their mental position is so absolutely arbitrary that it is useless to encounter or combat it. Through all time the unseen has been pressing on the seen, the immaterial overpowering the material; through all time the signs and tokens of that which is beyond matter have been waiting for the men of matter to test and weigh them. Those who will not do so have chosen the place of pause arbitrarily, and there is nothing to be done but let them remain there undisturbed, working that treadmill which they believe to be the utmost activity of existence.

II

There is no doubt that a man must educate himself to perceive that which is beyond matter, just as he must educate himself to perceive that which is in matter. Every one knows that the early life of a child is one long process of adjustment, of learning to understand the use of the senses with regard to their special provinces, and of practice in the exercise of difficult, complex, yet imperfect organs entirely in reference to the perception of the world of matter. The child is in earnest and works on without hesitation if he means to live. Some infants born into the light of earth shrink from it, and refuse to attack the immense task which is before them, and which must be accomplished in order to make life in matter possible. These go back to the ranks of the unborn; we see them lay down their manifold instrument, the body, and fade into sleep. So it is with the great crowd of humanity when it has triumphed and conquered and enjoyed in the world of matter. The individuals in that crowd, which seems so powerful and confident in its familiar demesne, are infants in the presence of the immaterial universe. And we see them, on all sides, daily and hourly, refusing to enter it, sinking back into the ranks of the dwellers in physical life, clinging to the consciousnesses they have experienced and understand. The intellectual rejection of all purely spiritual knowledge is the most marked indication of this indolence, of which thinkers of every standing are certainly guilty.

That the initial effort is a heavy one is evident, and it is clearly a question of strength, as well as of willing activity. But there is no way of acquiring this strength, or of using it when acquired, except by the exercise of the will. It is vain to expect to be born into great possessions. In the kingdom of life there is no heredity except from the man's own past. He has to accumulate that which is his. This is evident to any observer of life who uses his eyes without blinding them by prejudice; and even when prejudice is present, it is impossible for a man of sense not to perceive the fact. It is from this that we get the doctrine of punishment and salvation, either lasting through great ages after death, or eternal. This doctrine is a narrow and unintelligent mode of stating the fact in Nature that what a man sows that shall he reap. Swedenborg's great mind saw the fact so clearly that he hardened it into a finality in reference to this particular existence, his prejudices making it impossible for him to perceive the possibility of new action when there is no longer the sensuous world to act in. He was too dogmatic for scientific observation, and would not see that, as the spring follows the autumn, and the day the night, so birth must follow death. He went very near the threshold of the Gates of Gold, and passed beyond mere intellectualism, only to pause at a point but one step farther. The glimpse of the life beyond which he had obtained appeared to him to contain the universe; and on his fragment of experience he built up a theory to include all life, and refused progress beyond that state or any possibility outside it. This is only another form of the weary treadmill. But Swedenborg stands foremost in the crowd of witnesses to the fact that the Golden Gates exist and can be seen from the heights of thought, and he has cast us a faint surge of sensation from their threshold.

III

When once one has considered the meaning of those Gates, it is evident that there is no other way out of this form of life except through them. They only can admit man to the place where he becomes the fruit of which manhood is the blossom. Nature is the kindest of mothers to those who need her; she never wearies of her children or desires them to lessen in multitude. Her friendly arms open wide to the vast throng who desire birth and to dwell in forms; and while they continue to desire it, she continues to smile a welcome. Why, then, should she shut her doors on any? When one life in her heart has not worn out a hundredth part of the soul's longing for sensation such as it finds there, what reason can there be for its departure to any other place? Surely the seeds of desire spring up where the sower has sown them. This seems but reasonable; and on this apparently self-evident fact the Indian mind has based its theory of re-incarnation, of birth and rebirth in matter, which has become so familiar a part of Eastern thought as no longer to need demonstration. The Indian knows it as the Western knows that the day he is living through is but one of many days which make up the span of a man's life. This certainty which is possessed by the Eastern with regard to natural laws that control the great sweep of the soul's existence is simply acquired by habits of thought. The mind of many is fixed on subjects which in the West are considered unthinkable. Thus it is that the East has produced the great flowers of the spiritual growth of humanity. On the mental steps of a million men Buddha passed through the Gates of Gold; and because a great crowd pressed about the threshold he was able to leave behind him words which prove that those Gates will open.

CHAPTER III. THE INITIAL EFFORT

I

It is very easily seen that there is no one point in a man's life or experience where he is nearer the soul of things than at any other. That soul, the sublime essence, which fills the air with a burnished glow, is there, behind the Gates it colors with itself. But that there is no one pathway to it is immediately perceived from the fact that this soul must from its very nature be universal. The Gates of Gold do not admit to any special place; what they do is to open for egress from a special place. Man passes through them when he casts off his limitation. He may burst the shell that holds him in darkness, tear the veil that hides him from the eternal, at any point where it is easiest for him to do so, and most often this point will be where he least expects to find it. Men go in search of escape with the help of their minds, and lay down arbitrary and limited laws as to how to attain the, to them, unattainable. Many, indeed, have hoped to pass through by the way of religion, and instead they have formed a place of thought and feeling so marked and fixed that it seems as though long ages would be insufficient to enable them to get out of the rut! Some have believed that by the aid of pure intellect a way was to be found; and to such men we owe the philosophy and metaphysics which have prevented the race from sinking into utter sensuousness. But the end of the man who endeavors to live by thought alone is that he dwells in fantasies, and insists on giving them to other men as substantial food. Great is our debt to the meta-physicians and transcendentalists; but he who follows them to the bitter end, forgetting that the brain is only one organ of use, will find himself dwelling in a place where a dull wheel of argument seems to turn forever on its axis, yet goes nowhither and carries no burden.

Virtue (or what seems to each man to be virtue, his own special standard of morality and purity) is held by those who practise it to be a way to heaven. Perhaps it is, to the heaven of the modern sybarite, the ethical voluptuary. It is as easy to become a gourmand in pure living and high thinking as in the pleasures of taste or sight or sound. Gratification is the aim of the virtuous man as well as of the drunkard; even if his life be a miracle of abstinence and self-sacrifice, a moment's thought shows that in pursuing this apparently heroic path he does but pursue pleasure. With him pleasure takes on a lovely form because his gratifications are those of a sweet savor, and it pleases him to give gladness to others rather than to enjoy himself at their expense. But the pure life and high thoughts are no more finalities in themselves than any other mode of enjoyment; and the man who endeavors to find contentment in them must intensify his effort and continually repeat it,—all in vain. He is a green plant indeed, and the leaves are beautiful; but more is wanted than leaves. If he persists in his endeavor blindly, believing that he has reached his goal when he has not even perceived it, then he finds himself in that dreary place where good is done perforce, and the deed of virtue is without the love that should shine through it. It is well for a man to lead a pure life, as it is well for him to have clean hands,—else he becomes repugnant. But virtue as we understand it now can no more have any special relation to the state beyond that to which we are limited than any other part of our constitution. Spirit is not a gas created by matter, and we cannot create our future by forcibly using one material agent and leaving out the rest. Spirit is the great life on which matter rests, as does the rocky world on the free and fluid ether; whenever we can break our limitations we find ourselves on that marvellous shore where Wordsworth once saw the gleam of the gold. When we enter there all the present must disappear alike,—virtue and vice, thought and sense. That a man reaps what he has sown must of course be true also; he has no power to carry virtue, which is of the material life, with him; yet the aroma of his good deeds is a far sweeter sacrifice than the odor of crime and cruelty. Yet it may be, however, that by the practice of virtue he will fetter himself into one groove, one changeless fashion of life in matter, so firmly that it is impossible for the mind to conceive that death is a sufficient power to free him, and cast him upon the broad and glorious ocean,—a sufficient power to undo for him the inexorable and heavy latch of the Golden Gate. And sometimes the man who has sinned so deeply that his whole nature is scarred and blackened by the fierce fire of selfish gratification is at last so utterly burned out and charred that from the very vigor of the passion light leaps forth. It would seem more possible for such a man at least to reach the threshold of the Gates than for the mere ascetic or philosopher.

But it is little use to reach the threshold of the Gates without the power to pass through. And that is all that the sinner can hope to do by the dissolution of himself which comes from seeing his own soul. At least this appears to be so, inevitably because his condition is negative. The man who lifts the latch of the Golden Gate must do so with his own strong hand, must be absolutely positive. This we can see by analogy. In everything else in life, in every new step or development, it is necessary for a man to exercise his most dominant will in order to obtain it fully. Indeed in many cases, though he has every advantage and though he use his will to some extent, he will fail utterly of obtaining what he desires from lack of the final and unconquerable resolution. No education in the world will make a man an intellectual glory to his age, even if his powers are great; for unless he positively desires to seize the flower of perfection, he will be but a dry scholar, a dealer in words, a proficient in mechanical thought, and a mere wheel of memory. And the man who has this positive quality in him will rise in spite of adverse circumstances, will recognise and seize upon the tide of thought which is his natural food, and will stand as a giant at last in the place he willed to reach. We see this practically every day in all walks of life. Wherefore it does not seem possible that the man who has simply succeeded through the passions in wrecking the dogmatic and narrow part of his nature should pass through those great Gates. But as he is not blinded by prejudice, nor has fastened himself to any treadmill of thought, nor caught the wheel of his soul in any deep rut of life, it would seem that if once the positive will might be born within him, he could at some time not hopelessly far distant lift his hand to the latch.

Undoubtedly it is the hardest task we have yet seen set us in life, that which we are now talking of,—to free a man of all prejudice, of all crystallized thought or feeling, of all limitations, yet develop within him the positive will. It seems too much of a miracle; for in ordinary life positive will is always associated with crystallized ideas. But many things which have appeared to be too much of a miracle for accomplishment have yet been done, even in the narrow experience of life given to our present humanity. All the past shows us that difficulty is no excuse for dejection, much less for despair; else the world would have been without the many wonders of civilization. Let us consider the thing more seriously, therefore, having once used our minds to the idea that it is not impossible.

The great initial difficulty is that of fastening the interest on that which is unseen. Yet, this is done every day, and we have only to observe how it is done in order to guide our own conduct. Every inventor fastens his interest firmly on the unseen; and it entirely depends on the firmness of that attachment whether he is successful or whether he fails. The poet who looks on to his moment of creation as that for which he lives, sees that which is invisible and hears that which is soundless.

Probably in this last analogy there is a clew as to the mode by which success in this voyage to the unknown bourn ("whence," indeed, "no traveller returns") is attained. It applies also to the inventor and to all who reach out beyond the ordinary mental and psychical level of humanity. The clew lies in that word "creation."

II

The words "to create" are often understood by the ordinary mind to convey the idea of evolving something out of nothing. This is clearly not its meaning; we are mentally obliged to provide our Creator with chaos from which to produce the worlds. The tiller of the soil, who is the typical producer of social life, must have his material, his earth, his sky, rain, and sun, and the seeds to place within the earth. Out of nothing he can produce nothing. Out of a void Nature cannot arise; there is that material beyond, behind, or within, from which she is shaped by our desire for a universe. It is an evident fact that the seeds and the earth, air, and water which cause them to germinate exist on every plane of action. If you talk to an inventor, you will find that far ahead of what he is now doing he can always perceive some other thing to be done which he cannot express in words because as yet he has not drawn it into our present world of objects. That knowledge of the unseen is even more definite in the poet, and more inexpressible until he has touched it with some part of that consciousness which he shares with other men. But in strict proportion to his greatness he lives in the consciousness which the ordinary man does not even believe can exist,— the consciousness which dwells in the greater universe, which breathes in the vaster air, which beholds a wider earth and sky, and snatches seeds from plants of giant growth.

It is this place of consciousness that we need to reach out to. That it is not reserved only for men of genius is shown by the fact that martyrs and heroes have found it and dwelt in it. It is not reserved for men of genius only, but it can only be found by men of great soul.

In this fact there is no need for discouragement. Greatness in man is popularly supposed to be a thing inborn. This belief must be a result of want of thought, of blindness to facts of nature. Greatness can only be attained by growth; that is continually demonstrated to us. Even the mountains, even the firm globe itself, these are great by dint of the mode of growth peculiar to that state of materiality,—accumulation of atoms. As the consciousness inherent in all existing forms passes into more advanced forms of life it becomes more active, and in proportion it acquires the power of growth by assimilation instead of accumulation. Looking at existence from this special point of view (which indeed is a difficult one to maintain for long, as we habitually look at life in planes and forget the great lines which connect and run through these), we immediately perceive it to be reasonable to suppose that as we advance beyond our present standpoint the power of growth by assimilation will become greater and probably change into a method yet more rapid, easy, and unconscious. The universe is, in fact, full of magnificent promise for us, if we will but lift our eyes and see. It is that lifting of the eyes which is the first need and the first difficulty; we are so apt readily to be content with what we see within touch of our hands. It is the essential characteristic of the man of genius that he is comparatively indifferent to that fruit which is just within touch, and hungers for that which is afar on the hills. In fact he does not need the sense of contact to arouse longing. He knows that this distant fruit, which he perceives without the aid of the physical senses, is a subtler and a stronger food than any which appeals to them. And how is he rewarded! When he tastes that fruit, how strong and sweet is its flavor, and what a new sense of life rushes upon him! For in recognising that flavor he has recognised the existence of the subtle senses, those which feed the life of the inner man; and it is by the strength of that inner man, and by his strength only, that the latch of the Golden Gates can be lifted.

In fact it is only by the development and growth of the inner man that the existence of these Gates, and of that to which they admit, can be even perceived. While man is content with his gross senses and cares nothing for his subtle ones, the Gates remain literally invisible. As to the boor the gateway of the intellectual life is as a thing uncreate and non-existent, so to the man of the gross senses, even if his intellectual life is active, that which lies beyond is uncreate and non-existent, only because he does not open the book.

To the servant who dusts the scholar's library the closed volumes are meaningless; they do not even appear to contain a promise unless he also is a scholar, not merely a servant. It is possible to gaze throughout eternity upon a shut exterior from sheer indolence,—mental indolence, which is incredulity, and which at last men learn to pride themselves on; they call it scepticism, and talk of the reign of reason. It is no more a state to justify pride than that of the Eastern sybarite who will not even lift his food to his mouth; he is "reasonable" also in that he sees no value in activity, and therefore does not exercise it. So with the sceptic; decay follows the condition of inaction, whether it be mental, psychic, or physical.

III

And now let us consider how the initial difficulty of fastening the interest on that which is unseen is to be overcome. Our gross senses refer only to that which is objective in the ordinary sense of the word; but just beyond this field of life there are finer sensations which appeal to finer senses. Here we find the first clew to the stepping-stones we need. Man looks from this point of view like a point where many rays or lines centre; and if he has the courage or the interest to detach himself from the simplest form of life, the point, and explore but a little way along these lines or rays, his whole being at once inevitably widens and expands, the man begins to grow in greatness. But it is evident, if we accept this illustration as a fairly true one, that the chief point of importance is to explore no more persistently on one line than another: else the result must be a deformity. We all know how powerful is the majesty and personal dignity of a forest tree which has had air enough to breathe, and room for its widening roots, and inner vitality with which to accomplish its unceasing task. It obeys the perfect natural law of growth, and the peculiar awe it inspires arises from this fact.

How is it possible to obtain recognition of the inner man, to observe its growth and foster it?

Let us try to follow a little way the clew we have obtained, though words will probably soon be useless.

We must each travel alone and without aids, as the traveller has to climb alone when he nears the summit of the mountain. No beast of burden can help him there; neither can the gross senses or anything that touches the gross senses help him here. But for a little distance words may go with us.

The tongue recognises the value of sweetness or piquancy in food. To the man whose senses are of the simplest order there is no other idea of sweetness than this. But a finer essence, a more highly placed sensation of the same order, is reached by another perception. The sweetness on the face of a lovely woman, or in the smile of a friend, is recognised by the man whose inner senses have even a little—a mere stirring of—vitality. To the one who has lifted the golden latch the spring of sweet waters, the fountain itself whence all softness arises, is opened and becomes part of his heritage.

But before this fountain can be tasted, or any other spring reached, any source found, a heavy weight has to be lifted from the heart, an iron bar which holds it down and prevents it from arising in its strength.

The man who recognises the flow of sweetness from its source through Nature, through all forms of life, he has lifted this, he has raised himself into that state in which there is no bondage. He knows that he is a part of the great whole, and it is this knowledge which is his heritage. It is through the breaking asunder of the arbitrary bond which holds him to his personal centre that he comes of age and becomes ruler of his kingdom. As he widens out, reaching by manifold experience along those lines which centre at the point where he stands embodied, he discovers that he has touch with all life, that he contains within himself the whole. And then he has but to yield himself to the great force which we call good, to clasp it tightly with the grasp of his soul, and he is carried swiftly on to the great, wide waters of real living. What are those waters? In our present life we have but the shadow of the substance. No man loves without satiety, no man drinks wine without return of thirst. Hunger and longing darken the sky and make the earth unfriendly. What we need is an earth that will bear living fruit, a sky that will be always full of light. Needing this positively, we shall surely find it.

CHAPTER IV. THE MEANING OF PAIN

I

Look into the deep heart of life, whence pain comes to darken men's lives. She is always on the threshold, and behind her stands despair.

What are these two gaunt figures, and why are they permitted to be our constant followers?

It is we who permit them, we who order them, as we permit and order the action of our bodies; and we do so as unconsciously. But by scientific experiment and investigation we have learned much about our physical life, and it would seem as if we can obtain at least as much result with regard to our inner life by adopting similar methods.

Pain arouses, softens, breaks, and destroys. Regarded from a sufficiently removed standpoint, it appears as medicine, as a knife, as a weapon, as a poison, in turn. It is an implement, a thing which is used, evidently. What we desire to discover is, who is the user; what part of ourselves is it that demands the presence of this thing so hateful to the rest?

Medicine is used by the physician, the knife by the surgeon; but the weapon of destruction is used by the enemy, the hater.

Is it, then, that we do not only use means, or desire to use means, for the benefit of our souls, but that also we wage warfare within ourselves, and do battle in the inner sanctuary? It would seem so; for it is certain that if man's will relaxed with regard to it he would no longer retain life in that state in which pain exists. Why does he desire his own hurt?

The answer may at first sight seem to be that he primarily desires pleasure, and so is willing to continue on that battlefield where it wages war with pain for the possession of him, hoping always that pleasure will win the victory and take him home to herself. This is but the external aspect of the man's state. In himself he knows well that pain is co-ruler with pleasure, and that though the war wages always it never will be won. The superficial observer concludes that man submits to the inevitable. But that is a fallacy not worthy of discussion. A little serious thought shows us that man does not exist at all except by exercise of his positive qualities; it is but logical to suppose that he chooses the state he will live in by the exercise of those same qualities.

Granted, then, for the sake of our argument, that he desires pain, why is it that he desires anything so annoying to himself?

II

If we carefully consider the constitution of man and its tendencies, it would seem as if there were two definite directions in which he grows. He is like a tree which strikes its roots into the ground while it throws up young branches towards the heavens. These two lines which go outward from the central personal point are to him clear, definite, and intelligible. He calls one good and the other evil. But man is not, according to any analogy, observation, or experience, a straight line. Would that he were, and that life, or progress, or development, or whatever we choose to call it, meant merely following one straight road or another, as the religionists pretend it does. The whole question, the mighty problem, would be very easily solved then. But it is not so easy to go to hell as preachers declare it to be. It is as hard a task as to find one's way to the Golden Gate! A man may wreck himself utterly in sense-pleasure,—may debase his whole nature, as it seems,—yet he fails of becoming the perfect devil, for there is still the spark of divine light within him. He tries to choose the broad road which leads to destruction, and enters bravely on his headlong career. But very soon he is checked and startled by some unthought-of tendency in himself,—some of the many other radiations which go forth from his centre of self. He suffers as the body suffers when it develops monstrosities which impede its healthy action. He has created pain, and encountered his own creation. It may seem as if this argument is difficult of application with regard to physical pain. Not so, if man is regarded from a loftier standpoint than that we generally occupy. If he is looked upon as a powerful consciousness which forms its external manifestations according to its desires, then it is evident that physical pain results from deformity in those desires. No doubt it will appear to many minds that this conception of man is too gratuitous, and involves too large a mental leap into unknown places where proof is unobtainable. But if the mind is accustomed to look upon life from this standpoint, then very soon none other is acceptable; the threads of existence, which to the purely materialistic observer appear hopelessly entangled, become separated and straightened, so that a new intelligibleness illumines the universe. The arbitrary and cruel Creator who inflicts pain and pleasure at will then disappears from the stage; and it is well, for he is indeed an unnecessary character, and, worse still, is a mere creature of straw, who cannot even strut upon the boards without being upheld on all sides by dogmatists. Man comes into this world, surely, on the same principle that he lives in one city of the earth or another; at all events, if it is too much to say that this is so, one may safely ask, why is it not so? There is neither for nor against which will appeal to the materialist, or which would weigh in a court of justice; but I aver this in favor of the argument,—that no man having once seriously considered it can go back to the formal theories of the sceptics. It is like putting on swaddling-clothes again.

Granting, then, for the sake of this argument, that man is a powerful consciousness who is his own creator, his own judge, and within whom lies all life in potentiality, even the ultimate goal, then let us consider why he causes himself to suffer.

If pain is the result of uneven development, of monstrous growths, of defective advance at different points, why does man not learn the lesson which this should teach him, and take pains to develop equally?

It would seem to me as if the answer to this question is that this is the very lesson which the human race is engaged in learning. Perhaps this may seem too bold a statement to make in the face of ordinary thinking, which either regards man as a creature of chance dwelling in chaos, or as a soul bound to the inexorable wheel of a tyrant's chariot and hurried on either to heaven or to hell. But such a mode of thought is after all but the same as that of the child who regards his parents as the final arbiters of his destinies, and in fact the gods or demons of his universe. As he grows he casts aside this idea, finding that it is simply a question of coming of age, and that he is himself the king of life like any other man.

So it is with the human race. It is king of its world, arbiter of its own destiny, and there is none to say it nay. Who talk of Providence and chance have not paused to think.

Destiny, the inevitable, does indeed exist for the race and for the individual; but who can ordain this save the man himself? There is no clew in heaven or earth to the existence of any ordainer other than the man who suffers or enjoys that which is ordained. We know so little of our own constitution, we are so ignorant of our divine functions, that it is impossible for us yet to know how much or how little we are actually fate itself. But this at all events we know,—that so far as any provable perception goes, no clew to the existence of an ordainer has yet been discovered; whereas if we give but a very little attention to the life about us in order to observe the action of the man upon his own future, we soon perceive this power as an actual force in operation. It is visible, although our range of vision is so very limited.

The man of the world, pure and simple, is by far the best practical observer and philosopher with regard to life, because he is not blinded by any prejudices. He will be found always to believe that as a man sows so shall he reap. And this is so evidently true when it is considered, that if one takes the larger view, including all human life, it makes intelligible the awful Nemesis which seems consciously to pursue the human race,—that inexorable appearance of pain in the midst of pleasure. The great Greek poets saw this apparition so plainly that their recorded observation has given to us younger and blinder observers the idea of it. It is unlikely that so materialistic a race as that which has grown up all over the West would have discovered for itself the existence of this terrible factor in human life without the assistance of the older poets,—the poets of the past. And in this we may notice, by the way, one distinct value of the study of the classics,— that the great ideas and facts about human life which the superb ancients put into their poetry shall not be absolutely lost as are their arts. No doubt the world will flower again, and greater thoughts and more profound discoveries than those of the past will be the glory of the men of the future efflorescence; but until that far-off day comes we cannot prize too dearly the treasures left us.

There is one aspect of the question which seems at first sight positively to negative this mode of thought; and that is the suffering in the apparently purely physical body of the dumb beings,—young children, idiots, animals,—and their desperate need of the power which comes of any sort of knowledge to help them through their sufferings.

The difficulty which will arise in the mind with regard to this comes from the untenable idea of the separation of the soul from the body. It is supposed by all those who look only at material life (and especially by the physicians of the flesh) that the body and the brain are a pair of partners who live together hand in hand and react one upon another. Beyond that they recognise no cause and therefore allow of none. They forget that the brain and the body are as evidently mere mechanism as the hand or the foot. There is the inner man—the soul—behind, using all these mechanisms; and this is as evidently the truth with regard to all the existences we know of as with regard to man himself. We cannot find any point in the scale of being at which soul-causation ceases or can cease. The dull oyster must have that in him which makes him choose the inactive life he leads; none else can choose it for him but the soul behind, which makes him be. How else can he be where he is, or be at all? Only by the intervention of an impossible creator called by some name or other.

It is because man is so idle, so indisposed to assume or accept responsibility, that he falls back upon this temporary makeshift of a creator. It is temporary indeed, for it can only last during the activity of the particular brain power which finds its place among us. When the man drops this mental life behind him, he of necessity leaves with it its magic lantern and the pleasant illusions he has conjured up by its aid. That must be a very uncomfortable moment, and must produce a sense of nakedness not to be approached by any other sensation. It would seem as well to save one's self this disagreeable experience by refusing to accept unreal phantasms as things of flesh and blood and power. Upon the shoulders of the Creator man likes to thrust the responsibility not only of his capacity for sinning and the possibility of his salvation, but of his very life itself, his very consciousness. It is a poor Creator that he thus contents himself with,—one who is pleased with a universe of puppets, and amused by pulling their strings. If he is capable of such enjoyment, he must yet be in his infancy. Perhaps that is so, after all; the God within us is in his infancy, and refuses to recognise his high estate. If indeed the soul of man is subject to the laws of growth, of decay, and of re-birth as to its body, then there is no wonder at its blindness. But this is evidently not so; for the soul of man is of that order of life which causes shape and form, and is unaffected itself by these things,—of that order of life which like the pure, the abstract flame burns wherever it is lit. This cannot be changed or affected by time, and is of its very nature superior to growth and decay. It stands in that primeval place which is the only throne of God,—that place whence forms of life emerge and to which they return. That place is the central point of existence, where there is a permanent spot of life as there is in the midst of the heart of man. It is by the equal development of that,—first by the recognition of it, and then by its equal development upon the many radiating lines of experience,—that man is at last enabled to reach the Golden Gate and lift the latch. The process is the gradual recognition of the god in himself; the goal is reached when that godhood is consciously restored to its right glory.

III

The first thing which it is necessary for the soul of man to do in order to engage in this great endeavor of discovering true life is the same thing that the child first does in its desire for activity in the body,—he must be able to stand. It is clear that the power of standing, of equilibrium, of concentration, of uprightness, in the soul, is a quality of a marked character. The word that presents itself most readily as descriptive of this quality is "confidence."

To remain still amid life and its changes, and stand firmly on the chosen spot, is a feat which can only be accomplished by the man who has confidence in himself and in his destiny. Otherwise the hurrying forms of life, the rushing tide of men, the great floods of thought, must inevitably carry him with them, and then he will lose that place of consciousness whence it was possible to start on the great enterprise. For it *must* be done knowingly, and without pressure from without,—this act of the new-born man. All the great ones of the earth have possessed this confidence, and have stood firmly on that place which was to them the one solid spot in the universe. To each man this place is of necessity different. Each man must find his earth and his own heaven.

We have the instinctive desire to relieve pain, but we work in externals in this as in everything else. We simply alleviate it; and if we do more, and drive it from its first chosen stronghold, it reappears in some other place with reinforced vigor. If it is eventually driven off the physical plane by persistent and successful effort, it reappears on the mental or emotional planes where no man can touch it. That this is so is easily seen by those who connect the various planes of sensation, and who observe life with that additional illumination. Men habitually regard these different forms of feeling as actually separate, whereas in fact they are evidently only different sides of one centre,—the point of personality. If that which arises in the centre, the fount of life, demands some hindered action, and consequently causes pain, the force thus created being driven from one stronghold must find another; it cannot be driven out. And all the blendings of human life which cause emotion and distress exist for its use and purposes as well as for those of pleasure. Both have their home in man; both demand their expression of right. The marvellously delicate mechanism of the human frame is constructed to answer to their lightest touch; the extraordinary intricacies of human relations evolve themselves, as it were, for the satisfaction of these two great opposites of the soul.

Pain and pleasure stand apart and separate, as do the two sexes; and it is in the merging, the making the two into one, that joy and deep sensation and profound peace are obtained. Where there is neither male nor female neither pain nor pleasure, there is the god in man dominant, and then is life real.

To state the matter in this way may savor too much of the dogmatist who utters his assertions uncontradicted from a safe pulpit; but it is dogmatism only as a scientist's record of effort in a new direction is dogmatism. Unless the existence of the Gates of Gold can be proved to be real, and not the mere phantasmagoria of fanciful visionaries, then they are not worth talking about at all. In the nineteenth century hard facts or legitimate arguments alone appeal to men's minds; and so much the better. For unless the life we advance towards is increasingly real and actual, it is worthless, and time is wasted in going after it. Reality is man's greatest need, and he demands to have it at all hazards, at any price. Be it so. No one doubts he is right. Let us then go in search of reality.

IV

One definite lesson learned by all acute sufferers will be of the greatest service to us in this consideration. In intense pain a point is reached where it is indistinguishable from its opposite, pleasure. This is indeed so, but few have the heroism or the strength to suffer to such a far point. It is as difficult to reach it by the other road. Only a chosen few have the gigantic capacity for pleasure which will enable them to travel to its other side. Most have but enough strength to enjoy and to become the slave of the enjoyment. Yet man has undoubtedly within himself the heroism needed for the great journey; else how is it martyrs have smiled amid the torture? How is it that the profound sinner who lives for pleasure can at last feel stir within himself the divine afflatus?

In both these cases the possibility has arisen of finding the way; but too often that possibility is killed by the overbalance of the startled nature. The martyr has acquired a passion for pain and lives in the idea of heroic suffering; the sinner becomes blinded by the thought of virtue and worships it as an end, an object, a thing divine in itself; whereas it can only be divine as it is part of that infinite whole which includes vice as well as virtue. How is it possible to divide the infinite,—that which is one? It is as reasonable to lend divinity to any object as to take a cup of water from the sea and declare that in that is contained the ocean. You cannot separate the ocean; the salt water is part of the great sea and must be so; but nevertheless you do not hold the sea in your hand. Men so longingly desire personal power that they are ready to put infinity into a cup, the divine idea into a formula, in order that they may fancy themselves in possession of it. These only are those who cannot rise and approach the Gates of Gold, for the great breath of life confuses them; they are struck with horror to find how great it is. The idol-worshipper keeps an image of his idol in his heart and burns a candle always before it. It is his own, and he is pleased at that thought, even if he bow in reverence before it. In how many virtuous and religious men does not this same state exist? In the recesses of the soul the lamp is burning before a household god,—a thing possessed by its worshipper and subject to him. Men cling with desperate tenacity to these dogmas, these moral laws, these principles and modes of faith which are their household gods, their personal idols. Bid them burn the unceasing flame in reverence only to the infinite, and they turn from you. Whatever their manner of scorning your protest may be, within themselves it leaves a sense of aching void. For the noble soul of the man, that potential king which is within us all, knows full well that this household idol may be cast down and destroyed at any moment,—that it is without finality in itself, without any real and absolute life. And he has been content in his possession, forgetting that anything possessed can only by the immutable laws of life be held temporarily. He has forgotten that the infinite is his only friend; he has forgotten that in its glory is his only home,—that it alone can be his god. There he feels as if he is homeless; but that amid the sacrifices he offers to his own especial idol there is for him a brief resting-place; and for this he clings passionately to it.

Few have the courage even slowly to face the great desolateness which lies outside themselves, and must lie there so long as they cling to the person which they represent, the "I" which is to them the centre of the world, the cause of all life. In their longing for a God they find the reason for the existence of one; in their desire for a sense-body and a world to enjoy in, lies to them the cause of the universe. These beliefs may be hidden very deep beneath the surface, and be indeed scarcely accessible; but in the fact that they are there is the reason why the man holds himself upright. To himself he is himself the infinite and the God; he holds the ocean in a cup. In this delusion he nurtures the egoism which makes life pleasure and makes pain pleasant. In this profound egoism is the very cause and source of the existence of pleasure and of pain. For unless man vacillated between these two, and ceaselessly reminded himself by sensation that he exists, he would forget it. And in this fact lies the whole answer to the question, "Why does man create pain for his own discomfort?"

The strange and mysterious fact remains unexplained as yet, that man in so deluding himself is merely interpreting Nature backwards and putting into the words of death the meaning of life. For that man does indeed hold within him the infinite, and that the ocean is really in the cup, is an incontestable truth; but it is only so because the cup is absolutely non-existent. It is merely an experience of the infinite, having no permanence, liable to be shattered at any instant. It is in the claiming of reality and permanence for the four walls of his personality, that man makes the vast blunder which plunges him into a prolonged series of unfortunate incidents, and intensifies continually the existence of his favorite forms of sensation. Pleasure and pain become to him more real than the great ocean of which he is a part and where his home is; he perpetually knocks himself painfully against these walls where he feels, and his tiny self oscillates within his chosen prison.

CHAPTER V. THE SECRET OF STRENGTH

I

Strength to step forward is the primary need of him who has chosen his path. Where is this to be found? Looking round, it is not hard to see where other men find their strength. Its source is profound conviction. Through this great moral power is brought to birth in the natural life of the man that which enables him, however frail he may be, to go on and conquer. Conquer what? Not continents, not worlds, but himself. Through that supreme victory is obtained the entrance to the whole, where all that might be conquered and obtained by effort becomes at once not his, but himself.

To put on armor and go forth to war, taking the chances of death in the hurry of the fight, is an easy thing; to stand still amid the jangle of the world, to preserve stillness within the turmoil of the body, to hold silence amid the thousand cries of the senses and desires, and then, stripped of all armor and without hurry or excitement take the deadly serpent of self and kill it, is no easy thing. Yet that is what has to be done; and it can only be done in the moment of equilibrium when the enemy is disconcerted by the silence.

But there is needed for this supreme moment a strength such as no hero of the battlefield needs. A great soldier must be filled with the profound convictions of the justness of his cause and the rightness of his method. The man who wars against himself and wins the battle can do it only when he knows that in that war he is doing the one thing which is worth doing, and when he knows that in doing it he is winning heaven and hell as his servitors. Yes, he stands on both. He needs no heaven where pleasure comes as a long-promised reward; he fears no hell where pain waits to punish him for his sins. For he has conquered once for all that shifting serpent in himself which turns from side to side in its constant desire of contact, in its perpetual search after pleasure and pain. Never again (the victory once really won) can he tremble or grow exultant at any thought of that which the future holds. Those burning sensations which seemed to him to be the only proofs of his existence are his no longer. How, then, can he know that he lives? He knows it only by argument. And in time he does not care to argue about it. For him there is then peace; and he will find in that peace the power he has coveted. Then he will know what is that faith which can remove mountains.

II

Religion holds a man back from the path, prevents his stepping forward, for various very plain reasons. First it makes the vital mistake of distinguishing between good and evil. Nature knows no such distinction; and the moral and social laws set us by our religions are as temporary, as much a thing of our own special mode and form of existence, as are the moral and social laws of the ants or the bees. We pass out of that state in which these things appear to be final, and we forget them forever. This is easily shown, because a man of broad habits of thought and of intelligence must modify his code of life when he dwells among another people. These people among whom he is an alien have their own deep-rooted religions and hereditary convictions, against which he cannot offend. Unless his is an abjectly narrow and unthinking mind, he sees that their form of law and order is as good as his own. What then can he do but reconcile his conduct gradually to their rules? And then if he dwells among them many years the sharp edge of difference is worn away, and he forgets at last where their faith ends and his commences. Yet is it for his own people to say he has done wrong, if he has injured no man and remained just?

I am not attacking law and order; I do not speak of these things with rash dislike. In their place they are as vital and necessary as the code which governs the life of a beehive is to its successful conduct. What I wish to point out is that law and order in themselves are quite temporary and unsatisfactory. a man's soul passes away from its brief dwelling-place, thoughts of law and order do not accompany it. If it is strong, it is the ecstasy of true being and real life which it becomes possessed of, as all know who have watched by the dying. If the soul is weak, it faints and fades away, overcome by the first flush of the new life.

Am I speaking too positively? Only those who live in the active life of the moment, who have not watched beside the dead and dying, who have not walked the battlefield and looked in the faces of men in their last agony, will say so. The strong man goes forth from his body exultant.

Why? Because he is no longer held back and made to quiver by hesitation. In the strange moment of death he has had release given him; and with a sudden passion of delight he recognises that it is release. Had; he been sure of this before, he would have been a great sage, a man to rule the world, for he would have had the power to rule himself and his own body. That release from the chains of ordinary life can be obtained as easily during life as by death. It only needs a sufficiently profound conviction to enable the man to look on his body with the same emotions as he would look on the body of another man, or on the bodies of a thousand men. In contemplating a battlefield it is impossible to realize the agony of every sufferer; why, then, realize your own pain more keenly than another's? Mass the whole together, and look at it all from a wider standpoint than that of the individual life. That you actually feel your own physical wound is a weakness of your limitation. The man who is developed psychically feels the wound of another as keenly as his own, and does not feel his own at all if he is strong enough to will it so. Every one who has examined at all seriously into psychic conditions knows this to be a fact, more or less marked, according to the psychic development. In many instances, the psychic is more keenly and selfishly aware of his own pain than of any other person's; but that is when the development, marked perhaps so far as it has gone, only reaches a certain point. It is the power which carries the man to the margin of that consciousness which is profound peace and vital activity. It can carry him no further. But if he has reached its margin he is freed from the paltry dominion of his own self. That is the first great release. Look at the sufferings which come upon us from our narrow and limited experience and sympathy. We each stand quite alone, a solitary unit, a pygmy in the world. What good fortune can we expect? The great life of the world rushes by, and we are in danger each instant that it will overwhelm us or even utterly destroy us. There is no defence to be offered to it; no opposition army can be set up, because in this life every man fights his own battle against every other man, and no two can be united under the same banner. There is only one way of escape from this terrible danger which we battle against every hour. Turn round, and instead of standing against the forces, join them; become one with Nature, and go easily upon her path. Do not resist or resent the circumstances of life any more than the plants present the rain and the wind. Then suddenly, to your own amazement, you find you have time and strength to spare, to use in the great battle which it is inevitable every man must fight,—that in himself, that which leads to his own conquest.

Some might say, to his own destruction. And why? Because from the hour when he first tastes the splendid reality of living he forgets more and more his individual self. No longer does he fight for it, or pit its strength against the strength of others. No longer does he care to defend or to feed it. Yet when he is thus indifferent to its welfare, the individual self grows more stalwart and robust, like the prairie grasses and the trees of untrodden forests. It is a matter of indifference to him whether this is so or not. Only, if it is so, he has a fine instrument ready to his hand; and in due proportion to the completeness of his indifference to it is the strength and beauty of his personal self. This is readily seen; a garden flower becomes a mere degenerate copy of itself if it is simply neglected; a plant must be cultivated to the highest pitch, and benefit by the whole of the gardener's skill, or else it must be a pure savage, wild, and fed only by the earth and sky. Who cares for any intermediate states? What value or strength is there in the neglected garden rose which has the canker in every bud? For diseased or dwarfed blossoms are sure to result from an arbitrary change of condition, resulting from the neglect of the man who has hitherto been the providence of the plant in its unnatural life. But there are wind-blown plains where the daisies grow tall, with moon faces such as no cultivation can produce in them. Cultivate, then, to the very utmost; forget no inch of your garden ground, no smallest plant that grows in it; make no foolish pretence nor fond mistake in the fancy that you are ready to forget it, and so subject it to the frightful consequences of half-measures. The plant that is watered to-day and forgotten to-morrow must dwindle or decay. The plant that looks for no help but from Nature itself measures its strength at once, and either dies and is re-created or grows into a great tree whose boughs fill the sky. But make no mistake like the religionists and some philosophers; leave no part of yourself neglected while you know it to be yourself. While the ground is the gardener's it is his business to tend it; but some day a call may come to him from another country or from death itself, and in a moment he is no longer the gardener, his business is at an end, he has no more duty of that kind at all. Then his favorite plants suffer and die, and the delicate ones become one with the earth. But soon fierce Nature claims the place for her own, and covers it with thick grass or giant weeds, or nurses some sapling in it till its branches shade the ground. Be warned, and tend your garden to the utmost, till you can pass away utterly and let it return to Nature and become the wind-blown plain where the wild-flowers grow. Then, if you pass that way and look at it, whatever has happened will neither grieve nor elate you. For you will be able to say, "I am the rocky ground, I am the great tree, I am the strong daisies," indifferent which it is that flourishes where once your rose-trees grew. But you must have learned to study the stars to some purpose before you dare to neglect your roses, and omit to fill the air with their cultivated fragrance. You must know your way through the trackless air, and from thence to the pure ether; you must be ready to lift the bar of the Golden Gate.

Cultivate, I say, and neglect nothing. Only remember, all the while you tend and water, that you are impudently usurping the tasks of Nature herself. Having usurped her work, you must carry it through until you have reached a point when she has no power to punish you, when you are not afraid of her, but can with a bold front return her her own. She laughs in her sleeve, the mighty mother, watching you with covert, laughing eye, ready relentlessly to cast the whole of your work into the dust if you do but give her the chance, if you turn idler and grow careless. The idler is father of the madman in the sense that the child is the father of the.man. Nature has put her vast hand on him and crushed the whole edifice. The gardener and his rose-trees are alike broken and stricken by the great storm which her movement has created; they lie helpless till the sand is swept over them and they are buried in a weary wilderness. From this desert spot Nature herself will re-create, and will use the ashes of the man who dared to face her as indifferently as the withered leaves of his plants. His body, soul, and spirit are all alike claimed by her.

III

The man who is strong, who has resolved to find the unknown path, takes with the utmost care every step. He utters no idle word, he does no unconsidered action, he neglects no duty or office however homely or however difficult. But while his eyes and hands and feet are thus fulfilling their tasks, new eyes and hands and feet are being born within him. For his passionate and unceasing desire is to go that way on which the subtle organs only can guide him. The physical world he has learned, and knows how to use; gradually his power is passing on, and he recognises the psychic world. But he has to learn this world and know how to use it, and he dare not lose hold of the life he is familiar with till he has taken hold of that with which he is unfamiliar. When he has acquired such power with his psychic organs as the infant has with its physical organs when it first opens its lungs, then is the hour for the great adventure. How little is needed—yet how much that is! The man does but need the psychic body to be formed in all parts, as is an infant's; he does but need the profound and unshakable conviction which impels the infant, that the new life is desirable. Once those conditions gained and he may let himself live in the new atmosphere and look up to the new sun. But then his must remember to check his new experience by the old. He is breathing still, though differently; he draws air into his lungs, and takes life from the sun. He has been born into the psychic world, and depends now on the psychic air and light. His goal is not here: this is but a subtle repetition of physical life; he has to pass through it according to similar laws. He must study, learn, grow, and conquer; never forgetting the while that his goal is that place where there is no air nor any sun or moon.

Do not imagine that in this line of progress the man himself is being moved or changing his place. Not so. The truest illustration of the process is that of cutting through layers of crust or skin. The man, having learned his lesson fully, casts off the physical life; having learned his lesson fully, casts off the psychic life; having learned his lesson fully, casts off the contemplative life, or life of adoration.

All are cast aside at last, and he enters the great temple where any memory of self or sensation is left outside as the shoes are cast from the feet of the worshipper. That temple is the place of his own pure divinity, the central flame which, however obscured, has animated him through all these struggles. And having found this sublime home he is sure as the heavens themselves. He remains still, filled with all knowledge and power. The outer man, the adoring, the acting, the living personification, goes its own way hand in hand with Nature, and shows all the superb strength of the savage growth of the earth, lit by that instinct which contains knowledge. For in the inmost sanctuary, in the actual temple, the man has found the subtle essence of Nature herself. No longer can there be any difference between them or any half-measures. And now comes the hour of action and power. In that inmost sanctuary all is to be found: God and his creatures, the fiends who prey on them, those among men who have been loved, those who have been hated. Difference between them exists no longer. Then the soul of man laughs in its strength and fearlessness, and goes forth into the world in which its actions are needed, and causes these actions to take place without apprehension, alarm, fear, regret, or joy.

This state is possible to man while yet he lives in the physical; for men have attained it while living. It alone can make actions in the physical divine and true.

Life among objects of sense must forever be an outer shape to the sublime soul,—it can only become powerful life, the life of accomplishment, when it is animated by the crowned and indifferent god that sits in the sanctuary.

The obtaining of this condition is so supremely desirable because from the moment it is entered there is no more trouble, no more anxiety, no more doubt or hesitation. As a great artist paints his picture fearlessly and never committing any error which causes him regret, so the man who has formed his inner self deals with his life.

But that is when the condition is entered. That which we who look towards the mountains hunger to know is the mode of entrance and the way to the Gate. The Gate is that Gate of Gold barred by a heavy bar of iron. The way to the threshold of it turns a man giddy and sick. It seems no path, it seems to end perpetually, its way lies along hideous precipices, it loses itself in deep waters.

Once crossed and the way found it appears wonderful that the difficulty should have looked; so great. For the path where it disappears does but turn abruptly, its line upon the precipice edge is wide enough for the feet, and across the deep waters that look so treacherous there, is always a ford and a ferry. So it happens in all profound experiences of human nature. When the first grief tears the heart asunder it seems that the path has ended and a blank darkness taken the place of the sky. And yet by groping the soul passes on, and that difficult and seemingly hopeless turn in the road is passed.

So with many another form or human torture. Sometimes throughout a long period or a whole lifetime the path of existence is perpetually checked by what seem like insurmountable obstacles. Grief, pain, suffering, the loss of all that is beloved or valued, rise up before the terrified soul and check it at every turn. Who places those obstacles there? The reason shrinks at the childish dramatic picture which the religionists place before it,—God permitting the Devil to torment His creatures for their ultimate good! When will that ultimate good be attained? The idea involved in this picture supposes an end, a goal. There is none. We can any one of us safely assent to that; for as far as human observation, reason, thought, intellect, or instinct can reach towards grasping the mystery of life, all data obtained show that the path is endless and that eternity cannot be blinked and converted by the idling soul into a million years.

In man, taken individually or as a whole, there clearly exists a double constitution. I am speaking roughly now, being well aware that the various schools of philosophy cut him up and subdivide him according to their several theories. What I mean is this: that two great tides of emotion sweep through his nature, two great forces guide his life; the one makes him an animal, and the other makes him a god. No brute of the earth is so brutal as the man who subjects his godly power to his animal power. This is a matter of course, because the whole force of the double nature is then used in one direction. The animal pure and simple obeys his instincts only and desires no more than to gratify his love of pleasure; he pays but little regard to the existence of other beings except in so far as they offer him pleasure or pain; he knows nothing of the abstract love of cruelty or of any of those vicious tendencies of the human being which have in themselves their own gratification. Thus the man who becomes a beast has a million times the grasp of life over the natural beast, and that which in the pure animal is sufficiently innocent enjoyment, uninterrupted by an arbitrary moral standard, becomes in him vice, because it is gratified on principle. Moreover he turns all the divine powers of his being into this channel, and degrades his soul by making it the slave of his senses. The god, deformed and disguised, waits on the animal and feeds it.

Consider then whether it is not possible to change the situation. The man himself is king of the country in which this strange spectacle is seen. He allows the beast to usurp the place of the god because for the moment the beast pleases his capricious royal fancy the most. This cannot last always; why let it last any longer? So long as the animal rules there will be the keenest sufferings in consequence of change, of the vibration between pleasure and pain, of the desire for prolonged and pleasant physical life. And the god in his capacity of servant adds a thousand-fold to all this, by making physical life so much more filled with keenness of pleasure,—rare, voluptuous, aesthetic pleasure,—and by intensity of pain so passionate that one knows not where it ends and where pleasure commences. So long as the god serves, so long the life of the animal will be enriched and increasingly valuable. But let the king resolve to change the face of his court and forcibly evict the animal from the chair of state, restoring the god to the place of divinity.

Ah, the profound peace that falls upon the palace! All is indeed changed. No longer is there the fever of personal longings or desires, no longer is there any rebellion or distress, no longer any hunger for pleasure or dread of pain. It is like a great calm descending on a stormy ocean; it is like the soft rain of summer falling on parched ground; it is like the deep pool found amidst the weary, thirsty labyrinths of the unfriendly forest.

But there is much more than this. Not only is man more than an animal because there is the god in him, but he is more than a god because there is the animal in him.

Once force the animal into his rightful place, that of the inferior, and you find yourself in possession of a great force hitherto unsuspected and unknown. The god as servant adds a thousand-fold to the pleasures of the animal; the animal as servant adds a thousand-fold to the powers of the god. And it is upon the union, the right relation of these two forces in himself, that man stands as a strong king, and is enabled to raise his hand and lift the bar of the Golden Gate. When these forces are unfitly related, then the king is but a crowned voluptuary, without power, and whose dignity does but mock him; for the animals, undivine, at least know peace and are not torn by vice and despair.

That is the whole secret. That is what makes man strong, powerful, able to grasp heaven and earth in his hands. Do not fancy it is easily done. Do not be deluded into the idea that the religious or the virtuous man does it! Not so. They do no more than fix a standard, a routine, a law, by which they hold the animal in check. The god is compelled to serve him in a certain way, and does so, pleasing him with the beliefs and cherished fantasies of the religious, with the lofty sense of personal pride which makes the joy of the virtuous. These special and canonized vices are things too low and base to be possible to the pure animal, whose only inspirer is Nature herself, always fresh as the dawn. The god in man, degraded, is a thing unspeakable in its infamous power of production.

The animal in man, elevated, is a thing unimaginable in its great powers of service and of strength.

You forget, you who let your animal self live on, merely checked and held within certain bounds, that it is a great force, an integral portion of the animal life of the world you live in. With it you can sway men, and influence the very world itself, more or less perceptibly according to your strength. The god, given his right place, will so inspire and guide this extraordinary creature, so educate and develope it, so force it into action and recognition of its kind, that it will make you tremble when you recognise the power that has awakened within you. The animal in yourself will then be a king among the animals of the world.

This is the secret of the old-world magicians who made Nature serve them and work miracles every day for their convenience. This is the secret of the coming race which Lord Lytton foreshadowed for us.

But this power can only be attained by giving the god the sovereignty. Make your animal ruler over yourself, and he will never rule others.

EPILOGUE

Secreted and hidden in the heart of the world and in the heart of man is the light which can illumine all life, the future and the past. Shall we not search for it? Surely some must do so. And then perhaps those will add what is needed to this poor fragment of thought.

THROUGH THE GATES OF GOLD

From *The Path*, March, 1887

The most notable book for guidance in Mysticism which has appeared since *Light on the Path* was written has just been published under the significant title of *Through the Gates of Gold*. Though the author's name is withheld, the occult student will quickly discern that it must proceed from a very high source. In certain respects the book may be regarded as a commentary on *Light on the Path*. The reader would do well to bear this in mind. Many things in that book will be made clear by the reading of this one, and one will be constantly reminded of that work, which has already become a classic in our literature. *Through the Gates of Gold* is a work to be kept constantly at hand for reference and study. It will surely take rank as one of the standard books of Theosophy.

The "Gates of Gold" represent the entrance to that realm of the soul unknowable through the physical perceptions, and the purpose of this work is to indicate some of the steps necessary to reach their threshold. Through its extraordinary beauty of style and the clearness of its statement it will appeal to a wider portion of the public than most works of a Theosophical character. It speaks to the Western World in its own language, and in this fact lies much of its value.

Those of us who have been longing for something "practical" will find it here, while it will probably come into the hands of thousands who know little or nothing of Theosophy, and thus meet wants deeply felt though unexpressed. There are also doubtless many, we fancy, who will be carried far along in its pages by its resistless logic until they encounter something which will give a rude shock to some of their old conceptions, which they have imagined as firmly based as upon a rock—a shock which may cause them to draw back in alarm, but from which they will not find it so easy to recover, and which will be likely to set them thinking seriously.

The titles of the five chapters of the book are, respectively, "The Search for Pleasure," "The Mystery of Threshold," "The Initial Effort," "The Meaning of Pain," and "The Secret of Strength." Instead of speculating upon mysteries that lie at the very end of man's destiny, and which cannot be approached by any manner of conjecture, the work very sensibly takes up that which lies next at hand, that which constitutes the first step to be taken if we are ever to take a second one, and teaches us its significance. At the outset we must cope with sensation and learn its nature and meaning. An important teaching of *Light on the Path* has been misread by many. We are not enjoined to kill out sensation, but to "kill out *desire* for sensation," which is something quite different. "Sensation, as we obtain it through the physical body, affords us all that induces us to live in that shape," says this work. The problem is, to extract the meaning which it holds for us. That is what existence is for. "If men will but pause and consider what lessons they have learned from pleasure and pain, much might be guessed of that strange thing which causes these effects."

"The question concerning results seemingly unknowable, that concerning the life beyond the Gates," is presented as one that has been asked throughout the ages, coming at the hour "when the flower of civilization had blown to its full, and when its petals are but slackly held together," the period when man reaches the greatest physical development of his cycle. It is then that in the distance a great glittering is seen, before which many drop their eyes bewildered and dazzled, though now and then one is found brave enough to gaze fixedly on this glittering, and to decipher something of the shape within it. "Poets and philosophers, thinkers and teachers, all those who are the 'elder brothers of the race'—have beheld this sight from time to time, and some among them have recognized in the bewildering glitter the outlines of the Gates of Gold."

Those Gates admit us to the sanctuary of man's own nature, to the place whence his life-power comes, and where he is priest of the shrine of life. It needs but a strong hand to push them open, we are told. "The courage to enter them is the courage to search the recesses of one's own nature without fear and without shame. In the fine part, the essence, the flavor of the man, is found the key which unlocks those great Gates."

The necessity of killing out the sense of separateness is profoundly emphasized as one of the most important factors in this process. We must divest ourselves of the illusions of the material life. "When we desire to speak with those who have tried the Golden Gates and pushed them open, then it is very necessary—in fact it is essential—to discriminate, and not bring into our life the confusions of our sleep. If we do, we are reckoned as madmen, and fall back into the darkness where there is no friend but chaos. This chaos has followed every effort of man that is written in history; after civilization has flowered, the flower falls and dies, and winter and darkness destroy it." In this last sentence is indicated the purpose of civilization. It is the blossoming of a race, with the purpose of producing a certain spiritual fruit; this fruit having ripened, then the degeneration of the great residuum begins, to be worked over and over again in the grand fermenting processes of reincarnation. Our great civilization is now flowering and in this fact we may read the reason for the extraordinary efforts to sow the seed of the Mystic Teachings wherever the mind of man may be ready to receive it.

In the "Mystery of Threshold," we are told that "only a man who has the potentialities in him both of the voluptuary and the stoic has any chance of entering the Golden Gates. He must be capable of testing and valuing to its most delicate fraction every joy existence has to give; and he must be capable of denying himself all pleasure, and that without suffering from the denial."

The fact that the way is different for each individual is finely set forth in "The Initial Effort," in the words that man "may burst the shell that holds him in darkness, tear the veil that hides him from the eternal, at any moment where it is easiest for him to do so; and most often this point will be where he least expects to find it." By this we may see the uselessness of laying down arbitrary laws in the matter.

The meaning of those important words, "All steps are necessary to make up the ladder," finds a wealth of illustration here. These sentences are particularly pregnant: "Spirit is not a gas created by matter, and we cannot create our future by forcibly using one material agent and leaving out the rest. Spirit is the great life on which matter rests, as does the rocky world on the free and fluid ether; whenever we can break our limitations we find ourselves on that marvellous shore where Wordsworth once saw the gleam of the gold." Virtue, being of the material life, man has not the power to carry it with him, "yet the aroma of his good deeds is a far sweeter sacrifice than the odor of crime and cruelty."

"To the one who has lifted the golden latch the spring of sweet waters, the fountain itself whence all softness arises, is opened and becomes part of his heritage. But before this can be reached a heavy weight has to be lifted from the heart, an iron bar which holds it down and prevents it from arising in its strength."

The author here wishes to show that there is sweetness and light in occultism, and not merely a wide dry level of dreadful Karma, such as some Theosophists are prone to dwell on. And this sweetness and light may be reached when we discover the iron bar and raising it shall permit the heart to be free. This iron bar is what the Hindus call "the knot of the heart"! In their scriptures they talk of unloosing this knot, and say that when that is accomplished freedom is near. But what is the iron bar and the knot? is the question we must answer. It is the astringent power of self—of egotism—of the idea of separateness. This idea has many strongholds. It holds its most secret court and deepest counsels near the far removed depths and centre of the heart. But it manifests itself first, in that place which is nearest to our ignorant perceptions, where we see it first after beginning the search. When we assault and conquer it there it disappears. It has only retreated to the next row of outworks where for a time it appears not to our sight, and we imagine it killed, while it is laughing at our imaginary conquests and security. Soon again we find it and conquer again, only to have it again retreat. So we must follow it up if we wish to grasp it at last in its final stand just near the "kernel of the heart." There it has become "an iron bar that holds down the heart," and there only can the fight be really won. That disciple is fortunate who is able to sink past all the pretended outer citadels and seize at once this *personal devil* who holds the bar of iron, and there wage the battle. If won there, it is easy to return to the outermost places and take them by capitulation. This is very difficult, for many reasons. It is not a mere juggle of words to speak of this trial. It is a living tangible thing that can be met by any real student. The great difficulty of rushing at once to the centre lies in the unimaginable terrors which assault the soul on its short journey there. This being so it is better to begin the battle on the outside in just the way pointed out in this book and *Light on the Path*, by testing experience and learning from it.

In the lines quoted the author attempts to direct the eyes of a very materialistic age to the fact which is an accepted one by all true students of occultism, that the true heart of a man—which is visibly represented by the muscular heart—is the focus point for spirit, for knowledge, for power; and that from that point the converged rays begin to spread out fan-like, until they embrace the Universe. So it is the Gate. And it is just at that neutral spot of concentration that the pillars and the doors are fixed. It is beyond it that the glorious golden light burns, and throws up a "burnished glow." We find in this the same teachings as in the Upanishads. The latter speaks of "the ether which is within the heart," and also says that we must pass across that ether.

"The Meaning of Pain" is considered in a way which throws a great light on the existence of that which for ages has puzzled many learned men. "Pain arouses, softens, breaks, and destroys. Regarded from a sufficiently removed standpoint, it appears as a medicine, as a knife, as a weapon, as a poison, in turn. It is an implement, a thing which is used, evidently. What we desire to discover is, who is the user; what part of ourselves is it that demands the presence of this thing so hateful to the rest?"

The task is, to rise above both pain and pleasure and unite them to our service. "Pain and pleasure stand apart and separate, as do the two sexes; and it is in the merging, the making the two into one, that joy and deep sensation and profound peace are obtained. Where there is neither male nor female, neither pain nor pleasure, there is the god in man dominant, and then is life real."

The following passage can hardly fail to startle many good people: "Destiny, the inevitable, does indeed exist for the race and for the individual; but who can ordain this save the man himself? There is no clew in heaven or earth to the existence of any ordainer other than the man who suffers or enjoys that which is ordained." But can any earnest student of Theosophy deny, or object to this? Is it not a pure statement of the law of Karma? Does it not agree perfectly with the teaching of the Bhagavat-Gita? There is surely no power which sits apart like a judge in court, and fines us or rewards us for this misstep or that merit; it is we who shape, or ordain, our own future.

God is not denied. The seeming paradox that a God exists within each man is made clear when we perceive that our separate existence is an illusion; the physical, which makes us separate individuals, must eventually fall away, leaving each man one with all men, and with God, who is the Infinite.

And the passage which will surely be widely misunderstood is that in "The Secret of Strength." "Religion holds a man back from the path, prevents his stepping forward, for various very plain reasons. First, it makes the vital mistake of distinguishing between good and evil. Nature knows no such distinctions." Religion is always man-made. It cannot therefore be the whole truth. It is a good thing for the ordinary and outside man, but surely it will never bring him to the Gates of Gold. If religion be of God how is it that we find that same God in his own works and acts violating the precepts of religion? He kills each man once in life; every day the fierce elements and strange circumstances which he is said to be the author of, bring on famine, cold and innumerable untimely deaths; where then, in The True, can there be any room for such distinctions as right and wrong? The disciple, must as he walks on the path, abide by law and order, but if he pins his faith on any religion whatever he will stop at once, and it makes no matter whether he sets up Mahatmas, Gods, Krishna, Vedas or mysterious acts of grace, each of these will stop him and throw him into a rut from which even heavenly death will not release him. Religion can only teach morals and ethics. It cannot answer the question "what am I?" The Buddhist ascetic holds a fan before his eyes to keep away the sight of objects condemned by his religion. But he thereby gains no knowledge, for that part of him which is affected by the improper sights has to be known by the man himself, and it is by experience alone that the knowledge can be possessed and assimilated.

The book closes gloriously, with some hints that have been much needed. Too many, even of the sincerest students of occultism, have sought to ignore that one-half of their nature, which is here taught to be necessary. Instead of crushing out the animal nature, we have here the high and wise teaching that we must learn to fully understand the animal and subordinate it to the spiritual. "The god in man, degraded, is a thing unspeakable in its infamous power of production. The animal in man, elevated, is a thing unimaginable in its great powers of service and of strength," and we [are] told that our animal self is a great force, the secret of the old-world magicians, and of the coming race which Lord Lytton foreshadowed. "But this power can only be attained by giving the god the sovereignty. Make your animal ruler over your self, and he will never rule others."

This teaching will be seen to be identical with that of the closing words of *The Idyll of the White Lotus*: "He will learn how to expound spiritual truths, and to enter into the life of his highest self, and he can learn also to hold within him the glory of that higher self, and yet to retain life upon this planet so long as it shall last, if need be; to retain life in the vigor of manhood, till his entire work is completed, and he has taught the three truths to all who look for light."

There are three sentences in the book which ought to be imprinted in the reader's mind, and we present them inversely:

"Secreted and hidden in the heart of the world and the heart of man is the light which can illumine all life, the future and the past."

"On the mental steps of a million men Buddha passed through the Gates of Gold; and because a great crowd pressed about the threshold he was able to leave behind him words which prove that those gates will open."

"This is one of the most important factors in the development of man, the recognition—profound and complete recognition—of the law of universal unity and coherence."

THE END

BOOK FOUR.
A CRY FROM AFAR

To Students of "Light on the Path."

CHAPTER I

The opening sentences of "Light on the Path" are the far cry from beyond the incarnations to those who are struggling in them. While man is embodied he is incapable of apprehending the state which is indicated by these sentences, for he is actually passing through the vale of tears, he is subject to pain, he is unable to live without causing pain, and it is by the power of his living heart that he attains complete experience, and unites himself consciously with the whole.

The keynote to the mystery, the stupendous promise of the far future, which makes the pilgrimage endurable, is given in these first sentences. They stand at the beginning of the path, the ray of light that comes from the very end of it, where full light is; the ray of light which illumines its whole course and guides the pilgrim and cheers him on the bitter way.

No human eyes can be incapable of tears, even those of the Master in life, the adept or the teacher. From the time that illusion and ignorance begin to pass away from the soul, and enlightenment takes the place of darkness, the disciple dwells in present sorrow, for he sees ignorance and consequent suffering on all sides. Tears are as the dew on the dried ground; his being would wither in the dryness of the material world, if there did not arise from himself that tenderness which is tears, and which dissolves, from within, the iron bondage of separateness. Let no man look for the time when his eyes shall be incapable of tears; if that state should come upon him while he is still that which we now call man he would have become a partner in the dark company which is fighting for the ruin of the race. Infinite pity, the capacity for profound sorrow and compassion, characterize the enlightened man, are an intrinsic part pf the nature of the Saviours of the race, and are only to be laid down at the far gate of eternal life when these saviours and shepherds have guided all their flocks safely to it and though it. But it is right and necessary for the disciple to know that there is in the future an Hour when all tears shall have been wiped away never to well up again; when all sources of sorrow shall be at an end, the whole enslaved nature of man having been freed and having escaped for ever from the pangs of desire. It will then no longer be human nature, and in the condition into which it will be born that which is known now to us as sorrow will be inconceivable. None can pass that gate till all can pass it; for the purified and perfected soul which is ready to go through and enter the new life is unable to do so because of the bond of sympathy between him and all those others who are to him much dearer than himself; because of the deep yearnings of compassion, and the welling up of the tears which are a mark of humanity, and one of its chief glories. The ethereal being within man's physical body sheds many tears of too subtle and fine a nature to be shed by the physical eyes; and the spirit weeps when it stands upon the threshold of matter and is drawn into its darkness by the laws of life and love and the bonds of kinship and association. Thus the whole being is softened and suffused with the dew of its own tenderness. All men must be thus softened and suffused ere they are fitted to enter upon that state in which they are incapable of tears. Then the eyes of the pure spirit will see that which has for us now neither shape nor colour because it is invisible, and can only be apprehended by faith. The capacity for faith is the first essential quality for the disciple who has heard the far cry and would enter upon the path which shall eventually bring him to that state in which he will be able to see.

That which is called the hearing of the ear of the emancipated and redeemed being is a complete consciousness of all that is, without any difficulty in separating one sound from another, or any necessity to do so. The whole makes itself known, in its living activity, to the ceaseless apprehension of the one who is able to hear. This hearing is only possible when the senses have not only been subdued but entirely laid aside, with the vestures to which they belong. The apprehension through the medium of the senses must have ceased altogether before the released and purified spirit can obtain consciousness of the whole by means of attention.

The intensity of sensitiveness must be increased with every successive incarnation in order that the spirit shall acquire knowledge and experience, and so progress and ripen and make the required advance towards that condition in which direct consciousness is possible. No sound, no smallest cry, no trumpet call can be ignored or avoided with impunity; because that of which the spirit prefers to remain ignorant it will have to learn in later and more severe lessons. All teaching and experience increase in severity with the progress of the soul and the advancement of the race as we see these take place in time; only so can the race be ushered into the eternal state and induced to cross the threshold of birth into complete being.

The far cry from the Master to the disciple conveys an even greater command in respect to the power of speech than in respect to sight and hearing. Speech is the creative power and the spoken word can be uttered only by the perfected being which has taken on the attributes of the divine power. By the spoken word were the heavens and the earth made, for the development and the education of the soul of man, and by the spoken word will innumerable heavens and earths be made yet, for the races which need the experience of dwelling within them.

The disciple who has conquered self and yielded his being to the whole, has obtained within himself the germ of each of the necessary powers of the purified and perfected being. He has that confidence which comes of the surrender of the personal desire and the consciousness of the whole; he has that hearing which brings to him the sound of many voices whether of suffering or joy; he has that sight, which shows him other men's lives, other men's woes and hopes, and enables him to penetrate into the heart of those with whom he associates; he has obtained such knowledge of men that his presence among them develops and attracts the creative force and develops the power of love. The disciple who has so far attained, who has beheld the wonder of his own living soul, is able to read the future of man. He knows the meaning of the "far cry" which he has heard, the voice that has come to him in the silence, from the pioneers of the race who stand at the gate of eternal life and call to him. He can enter the Hall of Learning and see written there the words which contain within them the fate and future of the race. The lessons which man has to learn are there set forth, and it is those lessons which shape the future. It is only the slowness of the individual man to enter into the life of the whole and to surrender his personal desires, which hinders the progress of the whole race. The steps are set plainly before all men and each man, and have to be taken in their due course. The pioneers who have climbed to the highest must linger there for the laggards, and even descend to help them up; for the spirit of humanity is an indivisible whole.

Faith, hope and love are the three first qualities essential to all who move towards the light. Faith, which is the perfect trust in that which though known, cannot be expressed; that entire confidence in the evolution of the whole which enables the disciple to stand calm amid all conflicts, and to fight unflinchingly against the heaviest odds; and that love which embraces all and forgives all.

The invisible, for the recognition of which faith is essential, surrounds us and presses upon us at all points, and the man who does not recognise it dwells in a cage formed of his own personality. There is ethereal and spiritual continuity, a linking of all parts, which passes through man's physical being in the same way that light passes through a transparent substance. It passes through it and is not arrested by it. Thought passes through other men's minds, emotion passes through men's hearts, in such a manner as to be almost visible in their action. Faith is scarcely needed for the apprehension of the fact that thought and feeling pass through men in waves; occasions of great and universal interest have made this plain. But it is only recognised in connection with events of unusual importance such as simultaneous discoveries, and religious revivals, outbreaks of rebellion or war-like demonstrations. That which is evident at these times of excitement is true at all times. Much that is supposed to be due to what is called instinct, and to be inborn, is due to the tides of thought and feeling which ceaselessly pass through the human race. Thought power is known in the present century and to a certain extent understood; but even those who consciously use it are frequently under the misapprehension that the thoughts by which they influence others originate in their own minds. This is an impossibility, as thought is a flowing tide, set in motion on the threshold of the material world and inspired by powers beyond and outside this limited condition. As the waves of light pass through all things, and each thing receives and reflects such rays as it is capable of receiving and reflecting, so with the waves of thought. They pass through all men's souls, and each soul apprehends that which it is capable of apprehending, and gives that to the world. They are the inspiring tide of man's life, and they become in him that which is called good or bad, in accordance with is own capacity. The disciple who has faith opens his soul to the fulness of the tide, and his soul becomes white as do the white flowers which reflect all the rays of light instead of selecting among them. He knows that in this tide that exists which is brotherhood. Men do not need to aim at unity of thought, or to set thought forces in motion. They need to be able to apprehend the full tide of thought that sweeps ceaselessly through the collective mind of the race, and those who are capable of this have attained to that condition which places them inalienably among the White Brotherhood. Then they know the power of the Brotherhood, and each leans upon the other equally, without need of speech or contact. The iron bar of separateness is for them pushed back, and the golden gate is set ajar. The disciple who has pushed this iron bar back knows that the criminal and evil-doer err because of limitation, and because of inability to apprehend. He knows that there is no punishment for sin save forgiveness, because the love which gave the great opportunity that is contained in the pilgrimage through matter, desires only that every man shall so grow and develop that he shall be able to accomplish this pilgrimage, and so help to release and redeem the race and free it for ever from material conditions. The emotions of the heart appear, to the man who dwells within his separate personality, to be his own, born within himself. They are his, and they are not his, in the same sense that the air he breathes, and the winds which stir that air, are, and are not, the possession of his physical body. They pass through him, and he shares them with all others who come within their range of action. In studying his own heart the disciple obtains illumination and perceives aright the hearts of other men, because his discipleship makes him aware of the flow of emotion which passes through him and them, and enables him to understand that it is necessary to have experienced all feeling, to have responded to every wave of emotion possible to man, before it is given to him to enter the condition in which sensitiveness can be laid aside. The criminal and evil-doer are misguided by being only able to feel in a portion of their being; sensitiveness is awakened only in the lowest and most possessive part of the nature and all the divine part is numb and without sensation. Thus they are not merely separated from the brotherhood of love, but separated from the race to which they physically belong. But the sensitiveness increases, following the law of growth under which man exists; and in the course of the incarnations the whole heart becomes capable of responding to the whole tide of human emotion, and that part of it which made the sinner to sin drops into its place as a part of a whole which in its completeness makes man divine. And only when this is accomplished to the uttermost can sensitiveness be laid aside, and the soul stand in the blood of its human heart, made to flow by the thrust of its own sword. For each purified spirit, when the whole race is freed and redeemed, will destroy within itself that germ which has caused it to be aware of pleasure, and God will then wipe away all his tears, and he will become incapable of shedding any more. Then will he be able to see, and be able to stand. Then will the "far cry" have been heard and answered.

CHAPTER II.

The ambition which hurls the souls of men into the abysses, is not the simple form of desire for success which is called by that name in ordinary life. Until old age is reached this is a necessary spur without which a deadly apathy would fall upon the race. For this reason the disciple is told to work as those work who are ambitious, for it is necessary for him to stand side by side with the toilers and the strugglers, so long as he is in the activity of the world. He must fight in their ranks if he is to be among them. And while he is still human it is essential that he share in the desire for success which is the natural stimulant to effort. The rewards which ordinary men accept as the proof of success are of no value to him; the ordinary man looks for them because he desires possessions for himself and is willing to win them from the others by his work. The disciple is in no danger of desiring such rewards, and if the loom of fate weaves them into his career, he estimates them at their true value as temporary burdens and responsibilities. The emulation in effort must be his as much as it is any other man's; effort surpassing that which is possible to other men is expected of him whenever it is required for the advancement of the race. He works better than the ordinary man who is ambitious, just as the willing horse works better than the horse that needs the spur.

It is not on the planes of mental or physical activities that the disciple has to kill out ambition. The great danger to him, throughout his pilgrimage, is lest a seed of spiritual pride shall germinate within him and stifle his higher nature before he is aware of its growth. For it grows as weeds do in rich soil. Some unexpected incident will reveal the man to himself in a new light; instead of being the humble disciple he believed himself to be, he finds himself filled with pride in his own capacities and gifts, and unable to ask for help from the divine forces that pass through him because he has permitted himself to believe that he has power within himself by right of his spiritual personality. Then ambition may seize upon him and he will endeavour to scale the heights of power and to assume prerogatives which can be given safely only by the hand of a Master to a tried and tested disciple. The attainment of power is one of the first aims of the disciple; it is aimed at continuously throughout his whole path of progress, and it is still his aim when he reaches the end of the pilgrimage and is ready to pass the threshold. The power he endeavours to obtain gives him no personal dignity or glory or position; he cannot influence men in order to secure any personal ends. That possibility is taken from him at his very first step on the true path, and is never again put into his hands. The ambition which is born of spiritual pride, and which assails him when he is well advanced upon the way, does not bring personal power to him; he has surrendered that desire of man when he became a disciple; and when the lust for it returns with sevenfold force upon a much higher plane of being the sole result is that he is hurled into the abysses, from which he will have to be saved by great efforts of his own and of the Saviours of the world. But the true power, the power of the brotherhood of love, born of the brooding spirit of the Divine in man, this is to be desired most ardently from the first moment of discipleship, and that desire must never cease. This desire is what makes the disciple at once a partner in the great task of redeeming the race. His sphere of action steadily increases with his growth, until the man who has by the purity of his desire to help a single friend been enabled to do so is entrusted with the guidance of a whole nation of beings or a whole school of thought. The principle of development on this pilgrimage in which we are engaged, involves associations of men; the first form of this is the family life which is a natural condition of the natural man. Out of this arise innumerable orders, more or less selfish or unselfish according to the character of the men who belong to them. One of the tasks of the disciple is to lead and guide the associations of men into paths of effort for the good of the race. He is led to take his part in the movements which are initiated by the masters and guides, and his business is to use the power of the brotherhood to which he belongs for the purification of the motives and actions of the associations of men in which he takes part. The infinite resources of the power behind him, upon which he draws ceaselessly so long as his soul is set in its true course, soon make themselves apparent, and a great impetus is given to the movement with which he has associated himself. But this does not alter his condition of personal obscurity; it will probably increase it. If he is drawn from that obscurity and attention is attracted to his personality, the effect will be to make him loved of a few but hated of many. This hatred arises from the opposition to the brotherhood of love and to the efforts of the Saviours of the world, which is an inherent part of the nature of the animal and personal man. It is, therefore, far better for the work in which he is taking part that the man himself should remain in the greatest obscurity possible. The quality of discipleship arouses the evil passions of other men, and the work is helped on more effectively if this quality is kept in abeyance on the physical plane and its power exercised in its fulness only upon the mental and ethereal natures of the men by whom a disciple is surrounded in the world. The animal nature of man will fight more fiercely now for ascendancy than in the past, for the advance and progress of the whole makes its power more insecure. It is, therefore, more necessary than in past ages that the presence of disciples among associations of men should be felt only in the general uplifting of those associations, not in the leadership of the disciples themselves. This disarms and baffles the animal part of the men who find themselves impelled to unusual actions, and guided by higher motives than habitually enter into their consciousness. The task set the disciple in thus guiding the movement in which he is taking part is much more severe than if he were permitted to lead by personal influence and external guidance, as he has to affect the natures of the men amongst whom he is working, as well as their actions. The ordinary man, one who has not yet entered upon the path or even become aware of it, must experience a change in himself after being associated with a disciple in any public work or mutual effort. He is not conscious of it at the time, because the action of the invisible power is subtle; but when he looks back over his life he will perceive a time when his motives became elevated and he will recognise that this was due to a certain association; though even then he may not guess which man among those he worked with was the medium for the divine influences.

When the disciple first begins to find he has this power of affecting the men amongst whom he works, without the use of physical speech, spiritual ambition (that deepest and most deadly enemy) assails him for the first time. The ordinary man, who has not yet set foot upon the path, cannot even imagine the force of this temptation. It is so strong that it intoxicates the soul; it is so insidious that it deludes the mind. Bewildered by the possibilities of his own being the disciple stands amazed and dazzled. He has desired power for good, and it has come to him; he has asked to be as the gods, and one of their qualities is his. It seems to him that now surely he may act like a god, and order the fates of men. He forgets that this power which has come to him is only one of the qualities of the gods; that in their long development by means of a suffering and pain as well as joy and splendour, a whole circlet of powers and gifts have become theirs, each tempering the others, and blending with them. The four rules which appear in the opening sentences of Light on the Path indicate four qualities which must be attained by the purified spirit before it can be released, and these must be attained equally. The power of helping others (or the power of speech) is only one of them, and by itself exposes the spirit to the greatest danger.

CHAPTER III.

Desire of life is that which prevents the spirit from giving that sword thrust which will make the blood of the human heart pour forth. It is not the narrow craving to continue one personal career, one incarnation, because of the fear that there is nothing to replace it, a craving experienced by atheists and materialists when old age comes upon them, and which brings its own punishment with it. The certainty that by no manner of means can this desire be gratified converts it into a torture from the very first. It is no petty passion which grows in a diseased or dwarfed mind, that is referred to in the phrase "Kill out desire of life." It is the great dominant emotion in the souls of men, which has made them into human beings, which has given them the capacity to endure incarnation after incarnation of experience in the bewildering and exhausting conditions of time and space, pleasure and pain. Animated by this overwhelming emotion the souls of men throng the threshold of the material world, eagerly looking for places of incarnation, and for bodies in which to incarnate and enter upon what man calls life -- that is, human life. The angels who have perfected being, and dwell in equilibrium, freed from the vicissitudes of physical and mental sensation, gaze in awe and that is referred to in the phrase "Kill out desire of life." It is the great dominant emotion in the souls of men, which has made them into human beings, which has given them the capacity to endure incarnation after incarnation of experience in the bewildering and exhausting conditions of time and space, pleasure and pain. Animated by this overwhelming emotion the souls of men throng the threshold of the material world, eagerly looking for places of incarnation, and for bodies in which to incarnate and enter upon what man calls life -- that is, human life. The angels who have perfected being, and dwell in equilibrium, freed from the vicissitudes of physical and mental sensation, gaze in awe and wonder upon the souls that press in upon this terrible experience of human life, blinded by the passion for it which possesses them. That awe and wonder is felt in respect to the divine power which is able to impart an emotion of so stupendous a nature that it can impel a whole race of beings to enter upon a bitter and terrible path full of danger and vicissitude. The longing for physical life comes upon the souls in a wave so overpowering that all other hopes and aims are lost sight of, and in great crowds they come towards the material universe and press upon it from all sides, eager to enter, willing to take any mode of entrance rather than brook delay.

This wave of emotion began to take effect as soon as the material universe was created, in order that scholars should willingly enter the school; and it has persisted from then till now, and will persist until the race approaches its release. It is that which brings souls back again and again to the threshold of material life, when again and again they have found that pain recurs and pleasure perishes. No matter how deeply they have learned this lesson they still crave with an overwhelming longing for the experience. It is only the disciples who are far advanced on the path who are able to regard this emotion as a thing outside themselves, as a man regards the sea when he swims in it. They know that it is this longing for physical life which brings them into the world where the path of the pilgrimage has been laid; they know that this path must be trodden, and they submit to be brought hither again and again, yielding to the longing for sense experience, knowing that in time they will be freed from it. And while they thus yield and labour with ardour in all the fields of effort open to men they seek in their own higher nature to destroy the personal element which makes man the slave of the desire of life. Like all other passions it must be subject to the higher self, and be steadily, if slowly, eliminated from the nature. The disciple who has heard the far cry will one day be able to kill out all desire for physical experience and, without any personal craving whatsoever, will enter into physical life, or act upon it from the ethereal plane, a free spirit. These free spirits, untouched by selfishness, entering into material life solely to help others, drawn hither by links of love and pity and sympathy, are the splendour and glory of the human race, and are a source from which it obtains power. They are the links between the masses of men and the Masters who send forth the Far Cry, which is intended to draw all souls out of the darkness. It is only the disciple who hears the Far Cry; but he is given the means by which to pass it on as a message adapted to the apprehension of those with whom he comes in contact. This is his duty, more now than ever before.

The whole race is more capable of attention than it has been in the past this is perceived by those who regard it from the ethereal world. That is a step taken; and the utmost has to be made of every step, for the time is waning. With the passing away of Time -- the opportunity given in this especial pilgrimage will be gone. Every member of the race has to be taken through the gate at last; and all will wait at the Portal for the last laggard, who will be drawn upwards by innumerable hands of love stretched out towards him. But the manner in which this opportunity is used by man as a whole affects the status of the spirit of the race in the great future. This is a mystery, too vast for the comprehension of the disciple; but the masters and pioneers know it, and therefore the Far Cry goes forth unceasingly to those who have ears to hear. Work and strive, and live and love more intensely and persistently than other men; but in your higher nature kill out those germs of spiritual desire which make the souls of men long for activity and pre-eminence in the narrow limits of time and space, under the dominion of pleasure and pain. The stupendous effort is more possible than it seems at first sight, for the forces, visible and invisible, which surround man and hold him in his place, are all directed towards his assistance. They are his allies, given to him by the same beneficent power that gives him opportunity. In whatever direction a man's nature leads him he finds these forces ready to give him aid. If his tendency is evil he is assisted by the very elements, which readily adapt themselves to his plan and plot. It is necessary for him that this should be so. Alone, without these helpers, he could not work either good or ill in this bewildering state of human life. So soon as he sets his feet in the path that leads to freedom, these same forces, which have helped him to garner the experience of the evildoer, or the apathetic dweller in sloth, or the seeker after pure pleasure, collect around him with renewed and redoubled power to aid and hasten him on his way. As man he must stand alone, and give help; as spirit he is bound up with the whole brotherhood of love and held by up the impelling force of the spiritual life of the universe. The universe exists only that he shall obtain freedom; and the physical and material part of the world he dwells in is pledged to its Creator to assist him to that end. For this was it created in material shape. We perceive that man is surrounded by innumerable creatures and substances, all of which have their appointed place in the universe and are pursuing their appointed path, to all appearance quite independent of man. The connection between the whole material universe is a subtle one, not to be perceived by human intelligence. The dweller in the ethereal spaces is aware of it and is able to utilize his knowledge of it for the assistance of embodied man. The immense number of conscious beings who are united in the material universe, and surround man, are held together in this condition by a deep bond which has its source in the Divine Breath. Escape from this condition is very easy for them, because their bondage here is not the bondage of pilgrimage but of willing association. Not only the beings whom we recognise as conscious, but also the beings which unite to hold together the bodies in which other beings dwell, the beings which have subjected themselves to the laws which order the composition of what we call material atoms, all alike are united in the maintenance of a physical life which is the school for the souls of men. The dominion given to man over them is of a very different character from what he supposes it to be. He makes mistakes continually in his conduct in relation to them, and these errors have all to be corrected before his lesson is complete. He drives from him the forces which are pledged to aid and uphold him, and increases the dreariness of his position and the sense of its insecurity, by so doing.

That great passion, desire of life, brings the souls of men into intimate relationship with the beings who form the universe which enables him to gratify it. He is blind to the fact that he is indebted to them for this gratification. He fancies the elements and the substances exist without effort.

Not so. There is a continuous and beneficent effort made on his behalf, and it is necessary for him to learn to acknowledge this and to repay it by right conduct. The perfected man conducts himself rightly towards all things; whether his perception enables him to perceive them as animate or not. That which he imagines to be inanimate because its consciousness is so far removed from his own, is the most necessary to him of all his surroundings, and as his development advances he becomes aware of this, and recoginses his debt. He knows then that in destroying within himself the desire of life he is releasing legions of beings from a task undertaken by them for his benefit.

CHAPTER IV.

When the flower has bloomed, and the silence that is peace has followed the storm, the disciple has entered that high grade which makes him an adept in life, one of the pioneers of the race. The storm of personal life is at -- end for him for ever; never again will he strive for the small ends to which men devote themselves, never again will his spirit rebel against its creator because of personal deprivations or losses. For him there is peace. And in that calm comes the new commands. The disciple may not remain in the stillness of the peace he has obtained at so high a price. He must take the peace with him and go forth; it is the reward he reaps for the surrender of the self. He must now go to sow the seeds of knowledge in the souls of other men. Encompassed by the peace which he has obtained he can return to the battlefield of life and fight for the great issues which hitherto he has scarcely been able to recognise, blinded as he has been by his own personality. He will thus fight as no mere man can fight, and yet stand aside in the battle. The warrior is the divine part in himself which is entirely impersonal, entirely devoted to the Supreme, entirely at the service of the whole brotherhood. The coming battle is no battle for conquest of the self; that is over and past, unless the disciple lose his footing and fall from his place. The battlefield Oil which he now takes his place is not that on which the souls of men struggle with the animal part that would control them, nor that on which the spirits of men fight with their own ambitious natures. It is the arena in which the spirit of the race, the indivisible spirit of Humanity, fights for the final conquest that shall raise it to the high estate for which it is destined. Sooner or later this battle must be won; the warrior is incapable of defeat. But it is the task of the adepts in life to shorten the bitterness of the way and hasten the great day of victory.

The song of life is heard only when the adept is able to enter upon this great impersonal effort. Then the 'mystic' beauty and harmony of the whole is made plain to him, and the discords which have oppressed him while he was still only in possession of the apprehension of man disappear. The pain and darkness and confusion of mortal life arise entirely from the limited capacity and partial apprehension of mortal man; as he grows into the immortal conditions and recognises more and more of that which surrounds him, he becomes capable of perceiving hitherto invisible forms and colours, and of hearing hitherto inaudible sounds, which make all discord into harmony, all darkness into light, all incompleteness into perfection.

THE END.

BOOK FIVE.
THE IDYLL OF THE WHITE LOTUS

TO THE TRUE AUTHOR,
THE INSPIRER OF THIS WORK,
IT IS DEDICATED.

PREFACE

We are pleased to announce this reprint of a work which, though written in the form of a novel, has a deep spiritual meaning underlying it.

It is a story told in all ages, and among every people. It is the tragedy of the soul. Attracted by desire, it stoops to sin; brought to itself by suffering, it turns for help to the redeeming spirit within and in the final sacrifice achieves its apotheosis and sheds a blessing on mankind. It is a story of initiation written in tender and beautiful language, and bears on its face the stamp of verdicity in simplicity and dignity. -- THE PUBLISHERS.

PROLOGUE.

Behold I stood alone, one among many, an isolated individual in the midst of a united crowd. And I was alone, because, among all the men my brethren who knew, I alone was the man who both knew and taught. I taught the believers at the gate, and was driven to do this by the power that dwelleth in the sanctuary. I had no escape, for in that deep darkness of the most sacred shrine, I beheld the light of the inner life, and was driven to reveal it, and by it was I upheld and made strong. For indeed, although I died, it took ten priests of the temple to accomplish my death, and even then they but ignorantly thought themselves powerful.

PART I.

CHAPTER I.

Ere my beard had become a soft down upon my chin I entered the gates of the temple to begin my noviciate in the order of the priesthood.

My parents were shepherds outside the city. I had never but once entered within the city walls until the day my mother took me to the gate of the temple. It as a feast day in the city, and my mother, a frugal and industrious woman thus fulfilled two purposes by her journey. She took me to my destination, and then she departed to enjoy a brief holiday amid the sights and scenes of the city.

I was enthralled by the crowds and noises of the streets. I think my nature was always one that strove to yield itself to the great whole of which it was such a small part -- and by yielding itself, to draw back into it the sustenance of life.

But out of the bustling throng we soon turned. We entered upon a broad, green plain upon the further side of which ran our sacred, beloved river. How plainly I behold that scene still! On the banks of the water I saw the sculptured roofs and glittering ornaments of the temple and its surrounding buildings shining in the clear morning air. I had no fear, for I had no definite expectations. But I wondered much whether life within those gates was as beautiful a thing as it seemed to me it must be.

At the gate stood a black-robed novice speaking to a woman from the city, who carried flasks of water which she urgently prayed one of the priests to bless. She would then have for sale a precious burden -- a thing paid dearly for by the superstitious populace.

I peeped through the gate as we stood waiting for our turn of speech, and beheld a sight that struck me with awe. That awe lasted a long time, even when I had entered into almost hourly familiarity with the figure which so impressed me.

It was one of the white-robed priests, pacing slowly down the broad avenue towards the gate. I had never seen one of those white-robed priests before, save on the single occasion when I had before visited the city. I then had seen several upon the sacred boat in the midst of a river procession.

But now this figure was near me, approaching me -- I held my breath.

The air was indeed very still, but those stately white garments looked, as the priest moved beneath the shadow of the avenue, as if no earthly breeze could stir them. His step had the same equable character. He moved, but it seemed scarcely as though he walked in the fashion that other and impetuous mortals walk. His eyes were bent on the ground, so that I could not see them; and, indeed, I dreaded the raising of those drooping lids. His complexion was fair, and his hair of a dull gold color. His beard was long and full, but it had the same strangely immovable, almost carven look, to my fancy. I could not imagine it blown aside. It seemed as though cut in gold, and made firm for eternity. The whole man impressed me thus -- as a being altogether removed from the ordinary life of man.

The novice looked around, his notice attracted probably by my intense gaze, for no sound reached my ears from the priest's footfall. "Ah!" he said, "here is the holy priest Agmahd, I will ask him."

Closing the gate behind him, he drew back, and we saw him speak to the priest, who bowed his head slightly. The man returned, and taking the water flasks from the woman carried them to the priest, who laid his hand for a second upon them.

She took them again with profuse thanks, and then we were asked our business.

I was soon left alone with the black-robed novice. I was not sorry though considerably awed. I had never cared much for my old task of tending my father's sheep, and of course I was already filled with the idea that I was about to become something different from the common herd of men. This idea will carry poor human nature through severer trials even than that of leaving one's home forever and entering finally upon a new and untried course of life.

The gate swung to behind me, and the black-robed man locked it with a great key that hung to his waist. But the action gave me no sense of imprisonment, -- only a consciousness of seclusion and separateness. Who could associate imprisonment with a scene such as that which lay before me?

The temple doors were facing the gate, at the other end of a broad and beautiful avenue. It was not a natural avenue formed by trees planted in the ground, and luxuriating in a growth of their own choosing. It was formed by great tubs of stone, in which were planted shrubs of enormous size, but evidently trimmed and guided most carefully into the strange shapes they formed. Between each shrub was a square block of stone, upon which was a carven figure. Those figures nearest the gate I saw to be sphinxes and great animals with human heads but afterwards I did not dare raise my eyes to gaze curiously upon them; for I saw again approaching us, in the course of his regular walk to and fro, the golden-bearded priest Agmahd.

Walking on by the side of my guide, I kept my eyes upon the ground. When he paused I paused, and found that my eyes fell upon the hem of the priest's white robe. That hem was delicately embroidered with golden characters: it was enough to absorb my attention and fill me with wonder for a while.

"A new novice?" I heard a very quiet and sweet voice say. "Well, take him into the school; he is but a youth yet. Look up, boy; do not fear."

I looked up, thus encouraged, and encountered the gaze of the priest. His eyes, I saw, even then in my embarrassment, were of changing color --

blue and gray. But, soft-hued though they were, they did not give me the encouragement which I had heard in his voice. They were calm indeed: full of knowledge: but they made me tremble.

He dismissed us with a movement of his hand, and pursued his even walk down the grand avenue; while I, more disposed to tremble than I had been before, followed silently my silent guide. We entered the great central doorway of the temple, the sides of which were formed of immense blocks of uncut stone. I suppose a fit of something like fear must have come upon me, after the inquisition of the holy priest's eyes; for I regarded these blocks of stone with a vague sense of terror.

Within I saw that from the central doorway, a passage proceeded in a long direct line with the avenue through the building. But that was not our way. We turned aside and entered upon a network of smaller corridors, and passed through some small bare rooms upon our way.

We entered at last a large and beautiful room. I say beautiful, though it was entirely bare and unfurnished, save for a table at one corner. But its proportions were so grand, and its structure so elegant, that even my eye, unaccustomed to discern architectural beauties, was strangely impressed, with a sense of satisfaction.

At the table in the corner sat two other youths, copying or drawing, I could not quite see what. At all events I saw they were very busy, and I wondered that they scarcely raised their heads to observe our entrance. But, advancing, I perceived that behind one of the great stone projections of the wall, there sat an aged white-robed priest, looking at a book which lay upon his knee.

He did not notice us until my guide stood deferentially bowing right in front of him.

"A new pupil?" he said, and looked keenly at me out of his dim, bleared-looking eyes. "What can he do?"

"Not much I fancy," said my guide, speaking of me in an easy tone of contempt. "He has been but a shepherd lad."

"A shepherd lad," echoed the old priest; "he will be no use here, then. He had best work in the garden. Have you ever learned to draw or copy writing?" he asked, turning upon me.

I had been taught these things as far as might be, but such accomplishments were rare, except in the priestly schools and among the small cultivated classes outside the priesthood.

The old priest looked at my hands, and turned back to his book.

"He must learn some time," he said; "but I am too full of work now to teach him. I want more to help me in my work; but with these sacred writings that have to be closed now, I cannot stay to instruct the ignorant. Take him to the garden for a while at least, and I will see about him by-and-by."

My guide turned away and walked out of the room. With a last look around, at its beautiful appearance, I followed him.

I followed him down a long, long passage, which was cool and refreshing in its darkness. At the end was a gate instead of a door, and here my guide rang a loud bell.

We waited in silence after the bell had rung. No one came, and presently my guide rang the bell again. But I was in no hurry. With my face pressed against the bars of the gate, I looked forth into a world so logical, that I thought to myself, "It will be no ill to me if the blear-eyed priest does not want to take me from the garden yet a while!"

It had been a dusty hot walk from our home to the city, and there the paved streets had seemed to my country-bred feet infinitely wearisome. Within the gates of the temple I had as yet only passed down the grand avenue, where everything filled me so deeply, with awe, that I scarce dared look upon it. But here was a world of delicate and refreshing glory. Never had I seen a garden like this. There was greenness, deep greenness; there was a sound of water, the murmuring of gentle water under control, ready to do service for man and refresh in the midst of the burning heat which called the magnificence of color and grand development of form into the garden.

A third time the bell rang -- and then I saw, coming from among the great green leaves, a black-robed figure. How strangely out of place did the black dress look here! and I thought with consternation that I should also be clothed in those garments before long, and should wander among the voluptuous beauties of this magical place like a strayed creature from a sphere of darkness.

The figure approached, brushing, with its coarse . . ., like the delicate foliage. I gazed with a sudden awakening of interest upon the face of the man who drew near, and into whose charge I supposed I was to be committed. And well I might; for it was a face to awake interest in any human breast.

CHAPTER II.

"What is it?" asked the man querulously, as he looked at us through the gate. "I sent fruit and to spare into the kitchen this morning. And I can give you no more flowers to-day; all I have to pluck will be wanted for the procession to-morrow."

"I am not wanting your fruit or your flowers," said my guide, who seemed fond of adopting a lofty tone. "I have brought you a new pupil, that's all."

He unlocked the gate, motioned me to pass through, and shutting it behind me, walked away down the long corridor (which now, looking back from the garden seemed so dark) without another word.

"A new pupil for me! And what am I to teach you, child of the country?" I gazed upon the strange man in silence. How could I tell what he was to teach me?

"Is it the mysteries of the growth of the plants you are to learn? -- or the mysteries of the growth of sin and deceit? Nay, child, look not so upon me, but ponder my words and you will by-and-by understand them. Now, come with me, and fear not."

He took my hand and led me under the tall-leaved plants towards the sound of water. How exquisite it seemed to my ears, that soft, bright, musical rhythm!

"Here is the home of our Lady the Lotus," said the man. "Sit down here and look upon her beauty while I work; for I have much to do that you cannot help me in."

Nothing loth, indeed, was I to sink upon the green grass and only look -- look in amazement -- in wonder -- in awe!

That water -- that delicate-voiced water -- lived only to feed the queen of flowers. I said to myself, thou art indeed the Queen of all flowers imaginable.

THE WHITE LOTUS.

And as I gazed dreamily in my youthful enthusiasm upon this white bloom which seemed to me, with its soft, gold-dusted heart, the very emblem of pure, romantic love -- as I gazed the flower seemed to change in shape -- to expand -- to rise towards me. And lo, drinking at the stream of sweet sounding water, stooping to take its refreshing drops upon her lips, I beheld a woman of fair skin with hair like the dust of gold. Amazed, I looked and strove to move towards her, but ere I could make any effort my whole consciousness left me, and, I suppose, I must have swooned away. For, indeed, the next that I can recall I lay upon the grass, with the sense of cool water upon my face, and opening my eyes, I beheld the black-robed, strange faced gardener leaning over me.

"Was the heat too much for thee?" he asked, his brow knit in perplexity. "Thou lookest a strong lad to faint for the heat, and that, moreover, in a cool place like this."

"Where is she?" was my only reply, as I attempted to rise upon my elbow and look towards the lily bed.

"What!" cried the man his whole countenance changing, and assuming a look of sweetness that I should never have supposed could appear upon a face so naturally unbeautiful. "Hast thou seen her? But no -- I am hasty in supposing it. What have you seen boy? -- do not hesitate to tell me."

The gentleness of his expression helped my scattered and startled senses to collect themselves. I told him what I had seen and, as I spoke, I looked towards the lily bed, hoping, indeed, that the fair woman might again stoop to slake her thirst at the streamlet.

The manner of my strange teacher gradually changed as I spoke to him. When I ceased describing the beautiful woman with the enthusiasm of a boy who has never seen any but his own dusky-skinned race, he fell upon his knees beside me.

"Thou hast seen her!" he said in a voice of deep excitement. "All hail! for thou art destined to be a teacher among us -- a help to the people -- thou art a seer!"

Bewildered by his words, I only looked upon him in silence. After a moment I grew terrified, for I began to think he must be mad. I looked around, wondering whether I could return to the temple and escape from him. But even as I debated within myself whether to venture upon this, he rose and turned upon me with the singular sweet smile, which appeared to cover and hide the ugliness of his strongly marked features.

"Come with me," he said; and I rose and followed him. We passed through the garden which was so full of attractions for my wandering eyes that I loitered on my path behind him. Ah, such sweet flowers; such rich purples and deep-hearted crimson. Difficult I found it not to pause and inhale the sweetness of each fair-faced blossom, though still they seemed to me, in my so recent adoration of its beauty, to but reflect the supreme exquisiteness of the white lotus flower.

We went towards a gate in the temple: a different one from that by which I had entered the garden. As we approached it, there issued forth two priests clad in the same white linen robes as I had seen worn by the golden-bearded priest Agmahd. These men were dark; and though they moved with a similar stateliness and equilibrium, as though indeed, they were the most firmly rooted growth of the earth, yet to my eyes they lacked a something which the priest Agmahd possessed -- a certain perfection of calm and assuredness. They were younger than he, I soon saw; perhaps therein lay the difference. My dark-visaged teacher drew them aside, leaving me to stand in the pleasant shadow of the deep-arched doorway. He spoke to them excitedly, though evidently with reverence; while they, listening with quick interest, glanced ever and anon towards me.

Presently they came to me, and the black-robed man turned and moved over the grass, as though returning on the way we had come together. The white-clad priests, advancing under the doorway, spoke together in low whispers. When they reached me they motioned me to follow them, and I did so: passing through cool, high-roofed corridors and gazing idly, as was always a foolish habit of mine, upon everything I passed; while they, still whispering together as they preceded me, would now and then cast looks upon me, the meaning of which I could not understand.

Presently they turned out of the corridors, and entered into a large room similar to the one I had already seen where the old priest was instructing his copyists. This was divided by an embroidered curtain which fell in majestic folds from the lofty roof to the ground. I always loved beautiful things, and I noticed how, as it touched the ground, it stood firm with the stiffness of the rich gold work upon it.

One of the priests advanced, and drawing back one side of the curtain a little, I heard him say --

"My lord, may I enter?"

And now I began to tremble a little again. They had not looked unkindly upon me, yet how could I tell what ordeal awaited me? I looked in fear upon the beautiful curtain and wondered, in some natural fear, who sat behind it.

I had not overlong in which to tremble and be afraid of I knew not what. Before long the priest who had entered returned, and accompanying him I saw was the golden-bearded priest Agmahd.

He did not speak to me, but said to the others --

"Wait thou here with him, while I go to my brother Kamen Baka."

And saying this, he left us alone again in the great stone room.

My fears returned trebly upon me. Had but the stately priest given me a glance which held kindness in it, I had not so yielded to them, but now I was again plunged in vague terrors of what next should come upon me; and I was weakened also by the swoon which had but so recently prostrated me. Trembling, I sank upon a stone bench, which ran around the wall; while the two dark-haired priests talked together.

I think the suspense would soon hove brought another lapse into unconsciousness upon me, but suddenly I was again awakened to the doubts and possibilities of my position by the entrance of Agmahd, accompanied by another priest of most noble appearance. He was fair-skinned and fair-haired, though not so fair in either as Agmahd; he shared with him the stately immobility of appearance which made Agmahd an object of the deepest awe to me; and in his dark eyes there was a benevolence which I had not yet seen in any of the priests' countenances. I felt less fearful as I looked upon him.

"This is he," said Agmahd, in his musically cold voice.

Why, I wondered, was I thus spoken of? I was but a new novice, and had already been handed over to my teacher.

"Brethren" cried Kamen Baka, "is it not best that he should be clothed in the white garment of the seer? Take him to the baths; let him bathe and be anointed. Then will I and Agmahd my brother put upon him the white robe. We will then leave him to repose, while we report to the company of the high priests. Bring him back here when he has bathed."

The two younger priests led me from the room. I began to see that they belonged to an inferior order in the priesthood, and, looking on them now, I saw that their white robes had not the beautiful golden embroidery upon them, but were marked with black lines and stitchings around the edges.

How delicious, after all my weariness, was the scented bath which they led me to! It soothed and eased my very spirit. When I left it I was rubbed with a soft and sweet oil, and then they wrapped me in a linen sheet, and brought me refreshment -- fruits, oiled cakes, and a fragrant draught that seemed to both strengthen and stimulate me. Then I was led forth again to the chamber in which the two priests awaited me.

They were there, with another priest of the inferior order, who held in his hands a fine linen garment of pure white. The two priests took this, and, as the others drew away the sheet from my form, they together put it upon me. And when they had done so, they joined their hands upon my head, while the other priests knelt down where they stood.

I knew not what all this meant -- I was again becoming alarmed. But the bodily refreshment had done much to soothe my soul, and when without further ceremony, they sent me away again with the two inferior priests, with whom I felt a little familiarized, my spirits arose, and my step became light.

They took me to a small room, in which was a long, low divan covered with a linen sheet. There was nothing else in the room, and indeed I felt as if my eyes and brain might well remain without interest for a while; for how much had I not seen since I entered the temple in the morning! How long it seemed since I had let go my mother's hand at the gate!

"Rest in peace," said one of the priests. "Take your fill of sleep, for you will be awakened in the first cool hours of the night!"

And so they left me.

CHAPTER III.

I lay upon my couch, which was soft enough to make it very welcome to my weary limbs, and before long I was buried in profound sleep, notwithstanding the strangeness of my surroundings. The health and faith of youth enabled me to forget all the newness of my position in the temporary luxury of complete rest. Not long afterwards I have entered that cell to gaze upon that couch, and marvel where the peace of mind had flown that had been mine in my ignorant boyhood.

When I awoke it was quite dark, and I started suddenly to a sitting posture, vividly conscious of a human presence in the room. My wits were scattered by my sudden awakening. I thought myself to be at home, and that it was my mother who was silently watching beside me.

"Mother," I cried out, "what is the matter? Why are you here? Are you ill? Are the sheep astray?"

For a moment there was no answer, and my heart began to beat rapidly as I realized in the midst of the blank darkness that I was not at home -- that I was indeed in a new place -- that I knew not who it might be that thus silently watched in my room. For the first time I longed for my little homely chamber -- for the sound of my mother's voice. And, though I think I was a brave lad, and one not given to womanish weakness, I lay down again and wept aloud.

"Bring lights," said a quiet voice; "he is awake."

I heard sounds, and then a strong fragrance crept to my nostrils. Immediately afterwards two young novices entered at the door, bearing silver lamps, which threw a sudden and vivid light into the room. Then I saw -- and the sight so startled me that I ceased to weep and, forgot my home-sickness -- I saw that my room was quite full of white-robed priests, all standing motionless. No wonder, indeed, that I had been overpowered by the sense of a human presence in my room. I was surrounded by a silent and statuesque crowd of men whose eyes were bent upon the ground, whose hands were crossed upon their breasts. I sank back again upon my couch and covered my face; the lights, the crowd of faces, overpowered me; and I felt strongly disposed, when I had recovered from my astonishment, to begin weeping again from sheer bewilderment of ideas. The fragrance grew stronger and more intense, the room seemed filled with burning incense; and, opening my eyes, I saw that a young priest on each side of me held the vases which contained it. The room, as I have said, was full of priests; but there was an inner circle close about my couch. Upon the faces of these men I gazed with awe. Among them were Agmahd and Kamen and the others shared with them the strange immobility of expression which had affected me so deeply. I glanced from face to face and covered my eyes again trembling. I felt as though walled in by an impenetrable barrier; I was imprisoned, with these men around me, by something infinitely more impassable than stone walls. The silence was broken at last. Agmahd spoke.

"Arise, child," he said, "and come with us." I arose obediently, though truly I would rather have remained alone in my dark chamber than have accompanied this strange and silent crowd. But I had no choice save silent compliance when I encountered the cold, impenetrable blue eyes which Agmahd turned upon me. I arose, and found that when I moved I was enclosed by the same inner circle. Before, behind, and at the side of me they walked, the others moving in orderly fashion outside the centre. We passed down a long corridor until we reached the great entrance door of the temple. It stood open and I felt refreshed as by the face of an old friend by the glimpse I got of the starlit dome without. But the glimpse was brief. We halted just inside the great doors, and some of the priests closed and barred them; we then turned towards the great central corridor which I had observed on my first entrance. I noticed now that, though so spacious and beautiful, no doors opened into it, save one deep arched one right at the end, facing the great temple avenue. I wondered idly where this solitary door would lead.

They brought a little chair, and placed it in the midst of the corridor. On this I was told to sit, facing the door at the far end. I did so, silent and alarmed; -- what meant this strange thing? Why was I to sit thus, with the high priests standing around me? What ordeal was before me? But I resolved to be brave, to have no fear. Was not I already clothed in a pure white linen garment? Truly it was not embroidered in gold; but yet it was not stitched with black, like that of the younger priests. It was pure white; and priding myself that this must mean some sort of distinction. I tried to sustain my failing courage by this idea.

The incense grew so strong that it made my head confused. I was unaccustomed to the scents which the priests so lavishly scattered.

Suddenly -- without word or any sign of preparation -- the lights were extinguished, and I found myself once more in the dark, surrounded by a strange and silent crowd.

I tried to collect myself and realize where I was. I remembered that the mass of the crowd was behind me, that in front of me the priests had parted, so that, though the inner circle still separated me from the others, I was looking, when the lights were put out, straight down the corridor towards the deep-arched door way.

I was alarmed and miserable. I curled myself together on my seat, intending to be brave, if need be, but in the meantime to remain as silent and unobtrusive as possible. Much did I check the calm faces of those high priests whom I knew to be standing immovably beside me. The absolute silence of the crowd behind filled me with terror and awe. I was at some moments so full of alarm that I wondered whether, if I arose and moved straight down the corridor, I could escape from between the priests unnoticed. But I dared not try it; and indeed the incense combined with the effects of the subtle drink and the quiet were producing an unaccustomed drowsiness.

My eyes were half closed, and I think I might soon have fallen asleep, but my curiosity was suddenly aroused by perceiving that a line of light showed around the edges of the doorway at the far end of the corridor. I opened my eyes wide to look, and soon saw that slowly, very slowly, the door was being opened. At last it stood half-way open and a dim suffused kind of light came forth from it. But at our end of the corridor the darkness remained total and unrelieved, and I heard no sound or sign of life, save a low, subdued breathing from the men who surrounded me.

I closed my eyes after a few moments; for I was gazing so intently out of the darkness that my eyes grew wearied. When I opened them again I saw that there stood a figure just outside the doorway. Its outline was distinct, but the form and face were dim, by reason of the light being behind; yet, unreasonable as it was, I was filled with a sudden horror -- my flesh creeped, and I had to use a kind of physical repressive force in order to prevent myself from screaming aloud. This intolerable sense of fear momently increased; for the figure advanced towards me, slowly, and with a kind of gliding motion that was unearthly. I saw now, as it neared, that it was robed in some kind of dark garment, which almost entirely veiled form and face. But I could not see very clearly, for the light from the doorway only faintly reached out from it. But my agony of fear was suddenly augmented by observing that, when the gliding figure nearly approached me, it kindled some kind of light which it held, and which illumined its dim drapery. But this light made nothing else visible. By a gigantic effort I removed my fascinated gaze from the mysterious figure, and turned my head, hoping to see the forms of the priests beside me. But their forms were not to be seen -- all was a total blank of darkness. This released the spell of horror that was on me, and I cried out -- a cry of agony and fear -- and bowed my head in my hands.

The voice of Agmahd fell upon my ear. "Fear not, my child," he said in his melodious, undisturbed accents.

I made an effort to control myself, helped by this sound which savored at least of something less unfamiliar and terrible than the veiled figure which stood before me. It was there -- not close, but close enough to fill my soul with a kind of unearthly terror.

"Speak, child," said again the voice of Agmahd, "and tell us what alarms thee?"

I dared not disobey, though my tongue clove to the roof of my mouth; and, indeed, a new surprise enabled me to speak more easily than otherwise I could have done.

"What," I exclaimed, "do you not see the light from the doorway, and the veiled figure? Oh! send it away; it frightens me!"

A low, subdued murmur seemed to come from all the crowd at once evidently my words excited them. Then the calm voice of Agmahd again spoke: --

"Our queen is welcome, and we do her all reverence."

The veiled figure bowed its head, and then advanced nearer. Agmahd spoke once more, after a pause of total silence --

"Cannot our lady make her subjects more open-eyed, and give them commands as before?"

The figure stooped, and seemed to trace something on the ground. I looked and saw the words in letters of fire, which vanished as they came --

"Yes; but the child must enter my sanctuary alone with me."

I saw the words, I say, and my very flesh trembled with horror. The unintelligible dread of this veiled form was so powerful that I would rather have died than fulfill such a command. The priests were silent, and I guessed that, as the figure, so the fiery letters were invisible to them. Immediately I reflected that if, strange and incredible as it seemed, it were so, they would not know of the command. Terrified as I was, how could I bring myself to frame the words which should bring upon me an ordeal so utterly dreadful?

I remained silent. The figure turned suddenly towards me and seemed to look on me. Then again it traced, in the swiftly vanishing, fiery letters -- "Pass on my message."

But I could not; indeed, horror had now made it physically impossible. My tongue was swollen and seemed to fill my mouth.

The figure turned to me with a gesture of fierce anger. With a quick, gliding movement, it darted towards me, and drew the veil from its face.

My eyes seemed to start from their sockets, as that face was upturned close to mine. It was not hideous, though the eyes were full of an icy anger -- in anger that flashed not, but froze. It was not hideous, yet it filled me with such loathing and fear as I had never imagined possible, and the horror of it lay in the fearful unnaturalness of the countenance. It seemed to be formed of the elements of flesh and blood, yet it impressed me as being only a mask of humanity -- a fearful, corporeal unreality -- a thing made up of flesh and blood, without the life of flesh and blood. Into a second were crowded these horrors. Then with a piercing shriek I swooned for the second time in that day -- my first day in the temple.

CHAPTER IV.

When I awoke I felt my body to be covered with a cold dew, and my limbs seemed lifeless. I lay helplessly wondering where I was.

It was still and dark, and at best the sense of solitary quiet was delightful. But soon my mind began to review the events which had made the past day seem like a year to me. The vision of the white Lotus-flower grew strong in my eyes, but waned as my terrified soul flew on to the recollection of that later and most horrible sight -- that which, indeed, had been the last before them, until now when I awoke in the darkness.

Again I saw it: again, in my imagination, I saw that uplifted face -- its ghastly unreality, the cold glare of its cruel eyes. I was unstrung, unnerved, exhausted -- and again though now the vision seemed but my own imagination I cried aloud in terror.

Immediately I saw a light approach the doorway of the room, and a priest entered, carrying a silver lamp.

I saw by its rays, that I was in a chamber which I had not before entered. It seemed full of comfort. I saw that soft falling curtains made it secluded, and I felt that the air was full of a pleasant fragrance.

The priest approached, and as he neared me he bowed his head.

"What needs my lord?" he said. "Shall I bring fresh water if thou art thirsty!"

"I am not thirsty," I answered; "I am afraid -- afraid of the horrible thing which I have seen."

"Nay," he answered, "it is but thy youth that makes thee afraid. The gaze of our all-powerful lady is at all times enough to make a man swoon. Fear not, for thou art honored in that thine eyes have vision. What shall I bring to give thee ease?"

"Is it night?" I said, restlessly turning upon my soft couch.

"It is near morning now," answered the priest. "Oh that the day would come!" I exclaimed; "that the blessed sun should blot from my eyes the thing that makes me shudder! I am afraid of the darkness, for the darkness is the evil face!"

"I will stay beside your bed," said the priest quietly. He placed the silver lamp upon a stand and sat down near me. His face relapsed into instant composure, and ere he had been there a moment he seemed to me naught but a carven statue. His eyes were cold: his speech, though full of kind words, had no warmth in it. I shrank away from him; for as I looked on him the vision of the corridor seemed to rise between us. I bore this a while, trying to find comfort in his presence; but at length I burst forth in words, forgetting my fear of giving offence, which had kept me until now so obediently quiet.

"Oh, I cannot bear it!" I cried. "Let me go away; let me go out -- into the garden -- anywhere! The whole place is full of the vision. I see it everywhere. I cannot shut my eyes against it! Oh, let me -- let me go away!"

"Rebel not against the vision" answered the priest. "It came to thee from the sanctuary -- from the most sacred shrine. It has marked thee as one different from others, one who will be honored and eared for among us. But thou must subdue the rebellion of thy heart."

I was silent. The words sank like cold icicles upon my soul. I did not grasp their meaning -- indeed, it was impossible that I should; but was sensitively alive to the chill of the speech. After a long pause, in which I tried hard to put thought out of my mind, and so obtain release from my fears, a sudden recollection seized me with an agreeable sense of relief.

"Where," I said, "is the black man whom I saw in the garden yesterday?"

"What? -- the gardener, Seboua! He will be sleeping in his chamber. But when the days breaks he rise and go out into the garden."

"May I go with him?" I asked, with feverish anxiety, even clasping my hands as in prayer, so distressed was I lest I should be refused.

"Into the garden? If you are restless, it will soothe the fever that is upon your frame, to go among the morning dews and the fresh flowers. I will call Seboua to fetch you, when I see the dawn breaking."

I heaved a deep sigh of relief at this easy assent to my prayer; and turning away from the priest, lay still with closed eyes, trying to keep all horrid sights or imaginings from me by the thought of the sense of delight which would soon be mine when I should leave the close, artificially perfumed chamber for the sweetness and free inbreathing of the outer air.

I said no word, waiting patiently; and the priest sat motionless beside me. At last, after what seemed to me hours of weary waiting, he arose and extinguished the silver lamp. I saw then that a dim gray light entered the room from the lofty windows.

"I will call Seboua," he said, turning to me, "and send him to you. Remember that this is your chamber, which is henceforth to belong to you. Return here before the morning ceremonies; there will be novices waiting with the bath and oil for your anointment."

"And how," said I, much terrified at the idea of being, by some strange destiny, so important a person -- "how shall I know when to return here?"

"You need not come till after the morning meal. A bell rings for that; and, moreover, Seboua will tell you." With these words he departed.

I was full of pleasure at the thought of the fresh air which would revive my unnaturally wearied body; and I longed to see Seboua's strange face, and the sweet smile which would now and then obliterate his ugliness. It seemed as though his had been the only human face I had seen since I parted with my mother.

I looked to see if I still wore my linen garment so that I was ready to go with him. Yes, it was on me, my pure white dress. I looked on it with a sense of pride, for I had never worn anything so finely woven before. I was so far restored to quietude by the idea of being again with Seboua that I lay looking idly at my dress, and wondering what my mother would have thought, seeing me clad in this fine and delicate linen.

It was not long before I heard a step which roused me from my dreaming; Seboua's strange visage appeared in the doorway; Seboua's black form advanced towards me. He was ugly -- yes; uncouth -- yes; black and without any fairness of appearance. Yet as he entered and looked on me, the smile which I remembered again irradiated his face. He was human! -- loving!

I stretched out my hands to him as I rose from my couch.

"O Seboua!" I said, the tears rising in my foolish boy's eyes as I saw this gentleness upon his face -- "Seboua, why am I here? What is it that makes them say I am different from others? Seboua, tell me, am I again to see that awful form?"

Seboua came and knelt beside me. It seemed natural in this black man to kneel down when a sense of awe overcame him.

"My son" he said, "thou art gifted from heaven with unclosed eyes. Be brave in the possession of the gift and thou shalt be a light in the midst of the darkness that is descending upon our unhappy land."

"I don't want to be," I said fretfully. I was not afraid of him, and my rebellion must out. "I don't want to do anything which makes one feel so strange. Why have I beheld this ghastly face which even now comes before my eyes and blots out from them the light of day?"

"Come with me," said Seboua, rising instead of answering my question and holding out his hand to me. "Come, and we will go among the flowers, and talk of these things when the fresh airs have cooled thy brow."

I rose, nothing loth, and hand in hand we passed through the corridors until we reached a door that admitted us to the garden.

How can I describe the sense of exhilaration with which I drank in the morning air? It was incomparably greater and keener a delight than anything in the world of nature had ever before imparted to me. Not only did I pass out of a secluded and scented atmosphere, different from any to which I had been accustomed, but also the terrified, over-excited mental state which I was in was infinitely cooled and re-assured by the renewed sense that the world was still beautiful and natural outside the temple doors.

Seboua, looking in my face, seemed by some subtle sympathy to detect my vague thoughts and interpret them to me.

"The sun still rises in all his magnificence," he said. "The flowers still open their hearts to his greeting. Open thou thine, and be content."

I did not answer him. I was young and untaught. I could not readily answer him in words, but I looked up in his face as we moved across the garden and I suppose my eyes must have spoken for me.

"My son" he said, "because in the night you have been into the darkness, there is no reason to doubt that the light still is behind the darkness. You do not fear when lying down to sleep at night that you will see the sun in the morning. You have been into deeper darkness than that of the night, and you will see a brighter sun than this."

I did not understand him, though I revolved his words in my mind. I said nothing, for the sweet air, and the sense of human sympathy, were enough for me. I seemed careless of hearing words, or understanding my experiences, now that I was out in the fresh air. I was but a boy, and the sheer delight of my reviving strength made me forget all else.

This was natural; and all that was natural seemed to me, to-day, to be abundantly full of charm. Yet no sooner had I entered the natural once more and begun to revel in my return to it, than suddenly and unawares I was taken out of it.

Whither? Alas! how can I tell? There are no adequate words in the languages of the world to describe any real thing which lies outside the circle that is called natural.

Surely I stood with my own feet upon the green grass -- surely I had not departed from the spot whereon I stood? Surely Seboua stood by me? I pressed his hand. Yes, it was there. Yet I knew by my sensations that the natural had yielded me up, and that again I was within the world of feeling -- sight -- sound which I dreaded.

I saw nothing -- I heard nothing -- yet I stood in horror, trembling as the leaves tremble before a storm. What was I about to see? What was near me! What was it that drew a cloud across my eyes?

I closed them. I dared not look. I dared not face the dimness of the realities around me.

"Open thine eyes, my son" said Seboua, "and tell me, is our lady there?"

I opened them, dreading to behold the awful face which had filled me with fear in the darkness of the night. But no -- for a moment I saw nothing -- and I sighed with relief, for I always expected to see that face uplifted close to mine, with a grin of anger upon it. But in another second my frame thrilled with delight. Seboua had brought me, without my perceiving it, close beside the lotus tank; and I saw, stooping as before, to drink the clear flowing water, the fair woman whose long golden hair half hid her face from me.

"Speak to her!" cried Seboua. "I see by thy face that she is before thee. Oh, speak to her! Not in this generation has she spoken with her priests -- speak to her, for indeed we need her help!"

Seboua had fallen on his knees by my side, as yesterday he had done. His face was full of earnestness and glow -- his eyes full of a prayer. Looking into them I sank back overcome, I could not tell by what, but it seemed as though the golden-haired woman called me to her, and as though Seboua pushed me towards her, yet in my body I was no nearer to her; but in my consciousness I appeared to rise and move towards the lily tank, until, leaning upon its ledge, I touched her garment where it fell upon the surface of the water. I looked up into her face, but I could not see it. Light radiated from it, and I could only look at it as I might look upon the sun. Yet I felt the touch of her hand upon my head, and words crept into my mind which emanated from her, though I was scarcely conscious that I heard them.

"Child with the open eyes," she said, "thy soul is pure, and upon it is laid a heavy task. But keep thou near to me who am full of light, and I will show thee the way to plant thy feet."

"Mother," said I, "what of the darkness?"

I scarce dared frame my question more plainly. It seemed that if I spoke of that terrible face it would appear in anger before me. I felt a thrill pass through me from her hands as I uttered the words. I fancied that it must be anger which was about to descend on me, but her voice passed into my consciousness as sweetly and softly as raindrops, and imparted to me the same sense of divine sending that we dwellers in a thirsty land associate with the advent of the sweet moisture.

"The darkness is not to be feared; it is to be conquered and driven back, as the soul grows stronger in the light. My son, there is darkness in that innermost sanctuary of the temple, because the worshippers therein cannot bear the light. The light of your world is excluded from it, that it may be illumined with the light of the spirit. But the blind priests, hid in their own conceit, comfort themselves with the brood of darkness. They mock my name by using it; tell them, my son that their queen holds no sway in the realms of darkness. They have no queen; they have no guide but their blind desires. This is the first message you are charged with -- did they not ask for one?"

At this moment I seemed drawn back from her. I clung to her garment hem, but my hands were powerless; as I lost my hold upon her I seemed also to lose the sense of her presence. I was conscious only of an intolerable feeling of physical irritation. My eyes had closed, helplessly, as I drew from her; I opened them with an effort. I saw before me only the lotus tank, filled with blossoms of the queen of flowers -- filled with blossoms which floated royally upon the surface of the water. The sunshine lay upon their golden hearts, and I saw in them the color of golden hair. But a voice, full of wrath, though speaking slowly and with deliberate intonation aroused me from dwelling upon the fringe of my dream.

I turned my head and beheld, to my amazement, Seboua standing between two novices; his head bowed, his hands crossed. Near to me stood the high priests Agmahd and Kamen; Agmahd was speaking to Seboua. I soon gathered that he was in disgrace on account of me, but I could not discover what he had done.

Agmahd and Kamen placed themselves on either side of me. And I understood that I was to walk between them. We advanced in silence towards the temple, and entered again its gloomy gates.

CHAPTER V.

I was led into the hall where the priests had been taking their morning meal. The room was almost deserted now; but Agmahd and Kamen remained talking, in their low subdued tones, by one of the windows, while two novices led me to a place by the table; and brought me oiled cakes, fruit, and milk. It was strange to me to be waited on by these youths, who did not speak to me, and whom I regarded with awe as being more experienced than myself in the terrible mysteries of the temple. I wondered, as I ate my cakes, why they had not spoken to me, any of the novices whom I had seen; but looking back over the brief time which I had spent in the temple, I recollected that I had never been left alone with one of them. Even now, Agmahd and Kamen remained in the room, so that, as I saw the silence of fear was upon the faces of the youths who served me. And I fancied it to be a fear, not as of a schoolmaster who uses his eyes like ordinary mortals, but as of some many-sighted and magical observer who is not to be deceived. I saw no gleam of expression on the countenance of either of the youths. They acted like automata.

The exhaustion which had again taken possession of my frame was lessened by the food, and when I had eaten I rose eagerly to look from the high window, to see if Seboua were in the garden. But Agmahd advanced, stepped between me and the window, and gazed upon me with the immovable look which made me dread him so deeply.

"Come," he said. He turned and moved away; I followed him with drooping head, and all my new energy and hope departed; why, I knew not; I could not tell why I gazed upon the embroidered hem of the white garment -- which seemed to glide so smoothly over the ground in front of me -- with a sense that I was following my doom.

My doom! Agmahd the typical priest of the temple, the real leader among the high priests. My doom.

We passed down the corridors till we entered upon the wide one which led from the gate of the temple to the holy of holies. A horror filled me at the sight of it, even with the sunlight streaming through the gateway, and making mock of its unutterable shadows. Yet so deep was my dread of Agmahd, that, left thus alone with him, I followed him in perfect obedience and silence. We passed down the corridor -- with each reluctant step of mine I drew nearer to that terrible door whence, in the darkness of the night, I had seen the hideous form emerge. I was scanning the wall with the kind of terror with which a tormented soul might gaze upon the awful instruments of spiritual inquisition. It is impossible, once looking upon some impending doom with open eyes, not to remain gazing thereon with object yet riveted attention. Such did I in my blind fear bestow upon the walls of the long corridor, which, to my fancy, as we moved down it, seemed to close upon us and to shut us from all the bright, beautiful world which I had lived in until now.

Scanning thus intently these smooth and terrible walls, I perceived, as we approached it, a little door, which stood at right angles with the door of the sanctuary. It would have escaped any observation but one unnaturally tense; for the darkness at this far end of the corridor was deep indeed, by contrast with the glowing sunlight we had left at the other.

We approached this door. As I have said, it stood at right angles with the wall of the sanctuary. It was close to the door of it, but it was in the wall of the corridor.

My steps seemed to be taken without my own volition now; certainly my will would have carried me back to the sunshine which made the world, beautiful with flowers -- which made life seem a glorious reality, and not a hideous and unimaginable dream!

Yet there it was -- the door -- and Agmahd stood, his hand upon it. He turned and looked at me.

"Have no fear," he said, in his calm, equable tones. "Our sanctuary is the centre of our home, and its near neighborhood is enough to fill us with strength."

I passed through the same experience as when first Agmahd encouraged me by his voice in the garden. I raised my eyes, with an effort, to his, that I might discover whether there was the same encouragement in his beautiful countenance. But all that I saw was the intolerable calm of those blue eyes; they were pitiless, immovable: my soul, aghast, beheld in them at that moment fully the cruelty of the beast of prey.

He turned from me and opened the door; and, passing through it, held it open that I might follow him. I followed him -- yes, though my steps seemed to recoil upon myself and lead me to the deeps.

We entered a low-roofed room, lighted by one broad window, high in the wall. It was curtained and draped with rich material; a low couch stood at one side of the room. When my glance fell on the couch I started; why, I know not; but I at once thought it to be the couch which I had slept on in the last night. I could look at nothing else, though there were many beautiful things to look at, for the room was adorned luxuriously. I only wondered, with a shrinking heart, why that couch had been removed from the room in which I had slept.

While I looked on it, lost in conjecture, I suddenly became conscious of silence -- complete silence -- and of loneliness.

I turned with a sudden alarm.

Yes! I was alone. He was gone -- the dread priest Agmahd -- he had gone without another word, and let me in this room.

What could it mean? I crossed to the door and tried it. It was fast closed and barred.

I was a prisoner. But what could it mean? I looked around the massive stone walls -- I glanced up at the high window -- I thought of the near neighborhood of the sanctuary -- and I flung myself upon the couch and hid my face.

I imagine that I must have lain there for hours. I did not dare to arise and make any disturbance. I had nothing to appeal to but the blue, pitiless eyes of the priest Agmahd. I lay upon my couch with fast-closed eyes, not daring to face the aspect of my prison and praying that the night might never come.

It was yet the early part of the day, that I felt sure of, although I knew not how long a time I had passed in the garden with Seboua. The sun was high, and streamed in at my window. I saw this as, after a long time had passed, I turned and looked around, my room with a sudden and alarmed glance. I had the idea that some one was in it -- but, unless hidden behind the curtains, no visible form was in the room.

No, I was alone. And as I gathered courage to look up to the sunlight that made my window a thing glorious for the eyes, I began to realize that it still veritably was in existence; and that, notwithstanding my recent hideous experiences, I was nothing but a boy who loved sunshine.

The attraction grew very strong, and at last fanned itself into the wish to climb up to the high window and look. The passion which caused me to desire so ardently to do this, having once thought of it, I can no more account for than I could for most of the inquisitive and headstrong purposes of a boy's brain. At all events I rose from my couch -- casting all terror of my surroundings to the winds, now that I had a purpose sufficiently childish to absorb me. The wall was perfectly smooth; but I fancied that, by standing on a table that was beneath the window, I could reach the sill with my hands, and so raise myself up to see out. I soon climbed the table, but I could barely reach the sill with upstretched arms. I jumped a little, and just catching hold of the sill managed to draw myself upwards. I suppose that part of the enterprise must have been the delight to me; for I certainly did not anticipate seeing anything but the temple gardens.

What I saw, though there was nothing perhaps very startling, sobered my enjoyment.

The gardens were not there. My window looked out upon a small square piece of ground, which was surrounded by high blank walls. I soon saw that these were evidently walls of the temple, not outer walls. The piece of ground was enclosed in the very heart of the great building, for I could see its columns and roofs rising beyond each side, and the walls were blank. Mine was the only window I could perceive any trace of.

At that moment I heard a faint sound in the room, and, quickly letting myself drop, I stood upon the table, looking round in consternation. The sound seemed to proceed, from behind a heavy curtain that half covered one wall. I stood breathless, and, even in this broad daylight and gleaming sunshine, somewhat in terror of what I might see. For I had no idea that there was any mode of entrance but that door by which I had come, so that I scarce dared to hope for a wholesome human presence!

These fears soon vanished, however, for the curtain was drawn a little back, and a black-robed novice -- whom I had not seen before -- crept from out its shelter. I wondered at his stealthy manner; but I had no fears, for he held in his hand a glorious blossom of the royal white lotus flower. I sprang from the table and advanced towards him, my eyes upon the flower. When quite close he spoke, very low and quickly.

"This," he said, "is from Seboua. Cherish it, but let none of the priests see it. Cherish it, and it will help you in hours when you will need help; and Seboua urges that you remember all the words he has said to you, and that you trust, above all, to your love for the truly beautiful and to your natural likes and dislikes. That is the message," he said, stepping back towards the curtain. "I am risking my life here to please Seboua. Be careful that you never come near this door, or show that you know it exists; it opens into the private room of the high priest Agmahd, into which none dare enter save on peril of intolerable punishment."

"And how have you come through?" I asked in great curiosity.

"They are engaged in the morning ceremonies -- all the priests -- and I succeeded in escaping unseen to come to you."

"Tell me," I cried, holding him even as he endeavored to hurry through the door, "why did not Seboua come?"

"He cannot -- he is closely watched that he may make no effort to get near you."

"But why is this?" I exclaimed in dismay and wonder.

"I cannot tell," said the novice, extracting his garment from my grasp. "Remember the words I have said."

He hastily passed through the door and closed it behind him. I found myself half smothered by the heavy curtain and, as soon as I could recover from my amazement at this sudden appearance and disappearance, I moved it aside and stepped out, the lily in my hand.

My first thought, even before I would let myself think over the words which I was to remember -- was to place my precious flower in some safe place. I held it tenderly, as though it were the breathing form of one I loved. I looked around anxiously, wondering where it would be both unseen and yet preserved.

I saw, after a few moments spent in hasty inspection that just behind the head of my couch there was a corner which the curtain fell a little away from. Here, at least, I might place it for a while; it would have room to breathe, and would not be seen unless the curtain were moved away -- and behind my couch seemed a less likely place for it to be discovered in than any other. I hastily placed it here, afraid to keep it in my hand lest the ceremonies should be over and Agmahd enter my room. So I hid it, and then looked around for some vessel of water in which I might place it, for it occurred to me that, if I did not supply it with some of that element which it so dearly loved, it would not live long to be my friend.

I found a little earthen jar of water and placed it in it, wondering the while what I should do if the priests, discovering its absence, should ask me for it. I could not tell what to do in such an emergency; but, if the flower were discovered, I could only hope that some inspiration would be given me by which I might avoid throwing further blame upon Seboua; for, though I could not understand why or how, it was very evident that he had been blamed for something in connection with me.

I went and sat on the couch, to be near my beloved flower. How I desired that I might place it in the sunshine and revel in its beauties!

In this way the day passed. No one came near me. I watched the sun pass away from my window. I watched the shadows of evening descend upon it. I was still alone. I do not think I grew more terrified. I do not remember that the coming night brought with it any agony of fear. I was filled with a deep calmness, which either the long undisturbed hours of the day had produced, or else it was wrought by the beautiful though unseen flower; for that was ever before my eyes in all its radiant and delicate beauty. I had none of the intolerable visions which I had been unable to drive from me in the former night.

It was quite dark when the door which communicated with the corridor opened, and Agmahd entered, followed by a young priest, who brought me food and a cup of some strange sweet-smelling syrup. I should not have stirred from my couch had it not been that I longed for food. I had not thought of it before, but I was indeed faint and fasting. I rose eagerly, therefore, and, when the young priest brought the food to my side, I drank first of the syrup -- which indeed he offered me first -- for my exhaustion suddenly became plain to me.

Agmahd looked on me as I drank. When I had put down the cup, I raised my eyes to his with a new defiance.

"I shall go mad," I said boldly, "if you leave me in this room alone. I have never been left alone so long in all my life."

I spoke under a sudden impulse. When I had been passing the long hours in solitude they had not seemed so terrible; but now, with a quick apprehension of the evil of this solitariness, I spoke out my feeling.

Agmahd said to the young priest --

"Set the food down and fetch hither the book that lies upon the couch in my outer room."

He departed on his errand, Agmahd said nothing to me; and I -- having said my say, and not having, as I rather expected, been annihilated for it -- took up an oiled cake from the platter, and cheerfully went on with my meal.

Five years after I could not have faced Agmahd in this way. I could not have eaten my all having just defied him. But now I was elated by the supreme ignorance and indifference of youth. I had no measuring line for the depths of the priest's intellect -- the wide embracingness of his stern cruelty. How should I have? I was ignorant. And, moreover, I had no clue to the mode of his cruelty -- the purpose, the intention of it. I was in the dark altogether. But I was well aware that my life in the temple was not what I had looked for if it was to be like this, and I already cherished boyish notions of escaping from it (even down the terrible corridor) if I were to exist after such an unhappy fashion. I little knew when I thought of this how well I was guarded.

Agmahd said no word while I ate and drank, and presently the young priest opened the door and entered, bearing in his hands a large black book. He placed it on a table which Agmahd told him to draw near to my couch. A lamp was then brought by him from a corner of the room and placed on the table. He lighted it, and this done, Agmahd spoke:

"You need not be lonely if you look within those pages."

So saying, he turned and left the room, followed by the young priest.

I opened it at once. It seems, looking back on that time, that I was to the full as inquisitive as most boys; at all events, any new object riveted my attention for the time being. I opened the black covers of the volume and gazed on the first page. It was beautifully colored, and I looked in pleasure at the colors a little while before I began to spell out the letters. They stood out from a gray background in letters of so brilliant a hue that they seemed like fire. The title was -- "The Arts and Powers of Magic."

It was nonsense to me. I was a comparatively uneducated boy, and I wondered what companionship Agmahd supposed such a book could afford me.

I turned idly over its pages. They were all unintelligible to me, by very reason even of the words used, apart from the matter. The thing was ridiculous, to have sent me this book to read. I yawned widely over it, and closing the book was about to lie down again upon my couch, when I was startled to observe that I was not alone. On the other side of the little table whereon my book and lamp were, stood a man in a black dress. He was looking earnestly upon me, but when I returned his gaze he seemed to retreat from me a little. I wondered how he could have entered so noiselessly and approached so near me without sound.

CHAPTER VI.

"Have you any wish?" said the man in a clear, but very low voice.

I looked at him in surprise. He was a novice, it seemed, by his dress; yet he spoke as though he could gratify my wish -- and that, too, without the tone of a mere servant.

"I have just taken food," I answered. "I have no wish -- but for freedom from this room."

"That," he answered quietly, "is soon gratified. Follow me."

I stared in astonishment. This novice must know my position -- must know of Agmahd's will with regard to me. Dare be thus defy him?

"No," I answered; "the high priests have imprisoned me here; if I am found escaping I shall be punished!"

"Come!" was all his answer. And as he spoke he raised one hand commandingly. As in physical pain I cried aloud; why, I could not realize. Yet my sense seemed to be that I was held as by a vice -- that some intolerable power grasped my frame and shook it. A second after I stood beside my mysterious visitor, my hand tight clasped in his. "Look not back!" he cried. "Come with me."

And I followed him. Yet, at the door I desired to turn my head to look; and by what seemed a great effort, I did so.

Little marvel that he bade me not look back! Little marvel that he strove to hurry me from the room, for when my eyes had once turned I remained spellbound, gazing -- resisting his iron grasp.

I saw myself -- or rather my unconscious form -- and then for the first time, I understood that my companion was no denizen of earth -- that I had again entered the land of shadows.

But this wonder was wholly swallowed up in a larger one -- one sufficient to make me strong against the effort of my companion to draw me from the room.

Leaning over the couch -- standing behind it and bending forward, in that delicious drooping attitude in which I had first seen her when she stooped to drink the water -- I saw the Lily Queen.

And I heard her speak. Her voice came to me like the dropping of water -- like the spray of a fountain.

"Wake, sleeper -- dream no more, nor remain within this accursed spell."

"Lady, I obey," I murmured, within myself, and instantly a mist seemed to enwrap me. I was but dimly conscious -- yet I knew that, in obedience to the wish of the beautiful queen I was endeavoring to return to my natural state. I succeeded by degrees, and opened my eyes wearily and heavily, to behold a desolate empty room. The novice had left me -- of that I was glad -- but, alas! the Lady of the Lotus had left me also. The room seemed empty indeed, and my heart was heavy as I looked around me. I felt the sweet Lady of the Flower more as a beautiful mother in my childish heart, than as a queen. I yearned for her soft presence. But it was not there. I knew only too well that she was not in the room hidden from me. I felt her absence with my soul as well as perceived it with my eyes.

I raised myself languidly enough, for, indeed, this last struggle had out-wearied me, and went to the corner behind my couch where my dear flower was hid. I drew back the curtain a little way, to look at my treasure. Alas! it was already drooping its lovely head! I sprang forward to assure myself that I had indeed given it water. Yes, its stem was deeply plunged in its lower element. Yet the flower drooped like a dead thing, and the stem bent inertly over the edge of the vessel.

"My flower," I cried, kneeling down beside it, "art thou too gone? -- am I quite alone?"

I took the languid flower-form from the vessel and placed it upon my breast, within my robe. And then wholly disconsolate for the moment, I flung myself again upon my couch and closed my eyes, endeavoring to make them dark and visionless.

How? -- who knows the way to hide visions from the inner eye, that eye which has the terrible gift of sight which no darkness can blind? I did not, then at all events.

The night had descended on the earth, when I aroused myself from my long and silent rest. It was moonlight without, and a silvery streak of light entered at the high window and streamed into my room. Within that streak of light came the hem of a white garment; a hem gold-embroidered. I knew the embroidery -- I raised my eyes slowly, for I expected to recognize Agmahd, as indeed I did. He stood just within the dim shadow; but his bearing was not easily confused with that of another man even if his face were unseen.

I lay perfectly still; yet he seemed immediately to know that I was awake.

"Rise," he said. I rose, and stood beside my couch, with wide eyes of fear fixed upon him.

"Drink that which is beside you," he said. I looked and saw a cup full of red liquid. I drank it, blindly hoping it might give me strength to bear whatever ordeal the silent hours of this night might be destined to bring upon me. "Come," he said; and I followed him to the door. I half unconsciously cast a glance up to the window, in the thought that perchance fresh air and freedom lay before me. Suddenly I felt myself blinded -- quickly I put my hand to my eyes; a soft substance was bound over them. I was silent with the silence of wonder and of fear; I felt myself supported and led onward carefully. I shuddered as I thought that it must be the arm of Agmahd which upheld me, but I submitted to the contact, knowing that I was powerless to resist it.

We moved onwards slowly; I was conscious of leaving my own room and of traversing some distance beyond it, but how far or in what direction I was unable to guess, bewildered as I was by my blindfold state.

We paused in utter silence; the arm around me was removed, and I felt the bandage taken from my eyes. They opened upon a darkness so complete that I raised my hand to assure myself that the kerchief was not still upon them. No -- they were free -- they were open -- yet they gazed upon nothing but a blank wall of deep and total darkness. My head was full of pain and dizziness -- the fumes of the strong syrup that I had drunk seemed to have filled it with confusion. I remained motionless, hoping to recover myself and realize my position.

While I waited, I suddenly became conscious of a new presence close beside me. I did not shrink from it. I seemed to know it to be beautiful, to be friendly and glorious. I was thrilled with a yearning, an indescribable sense of leaning in spirit towards the unknown presence.

Amid the silence suddenly came low, sweet speech close to mine ear.

"Tell Agmahd that he disobeys the law. One priest alone may enter the holy of holies, and no more."

I recognized the liquid water-like voice of the Lily Queen. Although I was unaware of the priest's presence I unhesitatingly obeyed my queen.

"One priest alone may enter the holy of holies," I said, "and no more. Agmahd being here the law is disobeyed."

"I demand to hear the utterance of the queen" came the reply in the solemn tones of Agmahd.

"Tell him," said that other voice which thrilled my soul and made my frame vibrate, "that had I been able to reveal myself in his presence I had not waited for you."

I repeated her words. There was no answer, but I heard a movement -- footsteps -- and a door closed softly. Immediately a soft hand touched me. I was simultaneously conscious of the touch, and of a faint light upon my chest. I felt in a second that the hand was put within my dress to draw forth the withered lily which I had hid there. But I did not attempt to hinder this, for, looking up as a light attracted my eyes, I beheld standing before me the Lily Queen. My queen as in my boyish heart I had begun to call her, I saw dimly and as enveloped in a shadowy mist, but yet plainly enough to make me rejoice in her near presence. And as I looked I saw that she held close to her bosom the withered flower which she had taken from mine. And I saw, wonderingly, that it faded yet more, grew dimmer, and wholly vanished. Yet I did not regret it, for, as it died away, she grew more bright and distinct to my sight. When the flower had wholly disappeared she stood beside me, clear and distinct, illuminated by her own radiance.

"Fear no longer," she said, "they cannot harm thee, for thou hast entered within my atmosphere. And though they have placed thee in the very dungeon of vice and falsehood, have no fear, but observe all things, and remember what thine eyes perceive."

The darkness appeared to become illumined by her confident and gracious words. I grew bold, and full of strength.

She held out her hand and touched me gently. The touch filled me with a fire that excelled any warmth I had ever experienced.

"The royal flower of Egypt dwells upon the sacred waters, which in their purity and peace fitly form its eternal resting-place. I am the spirit of the flower; I am sustained upon the waters of truth, and my life is formed of the breath of the heavens, which is love. But the degradation of my earthly resting-place, over which my wings of love yet brood, is driving from it the light of heaven which is wisdom. Not long can the spirit of the royal lotus live in darkness; the flower droops and dies if the sun be withdrawn from it. Remember these words, child, grave them upon your heart, for as your mind becomes capable of grasping them, they will enlighten you in many things."

"Tell me," I said, "when may I again visit the lilies? Will you not take me there in to-morrow's sunshine? Now it is night, and I am tired; may I not sleep at your feet, and to-morrow be with you in the garden?"

"Poor child," she said, stooping towards me so that her breath fanned me, and it was sweet like the scent of wild flowers, "how hardly have they taxed thee! Rest here in my arms, for thou art to be my seer, and the enlightener of my loved land. Strength and health must dwell upon thy brow like jewels. I will guard thee; sleep, child."

I lay down at her bidding, and though I knew that I was upon a cold, hard floor, I felt that my head rested upon an arm soft and full of magnetic soothing; and I fell into deep, dreamless, undisturbed slumber.

There was writ in Agmahd's secret volume of records but one word that night, -- "Vain."

CHAPTER VII.

A white flower was in my hand when I awoke. Its beauty filled my heart with gladness, I looked on it and was refreshed and content, as though I had slept in my mother's arms, and this was her kiss on my lips, for I held the flower, a half-blown lotus-blossom, close to my mouth. I did not wonder at first how I had obtained it, I only looked upon its beauty and was happy, for it made me know that my queen, my one friend, did indeed guard me.

Suddenly I saw some one enter the room, yet she did not so much enter it, as seem to come out of the shadow. I lay, as now I saw, on the couch in the room to which Agmahd had brought me. I was scarcely aware of how, or in what place, I had spent the dark hours of the night, but I felt that it was in his arms I had been carried back to my couch. I was glad to be there again and I was glad to see this child that approached me. She was younger than myself, and bright as the sunshine. She came near to me, and then paused; I put out my hand to her.

"Give me the flower," she said.

I hesitated, for the possession of the flower made me happy, but I could not refuse her, for she smiled, and none within the temple had smiled on me till now. I gave her my blossom.

"Ah!" she cried, "there is water on its leaves!" and she flung it away from her as if in disgust. I started from my couch in angry haste to rescue my treasure. Instantly the child snatched it up again and fled from me with a cry of laughter. I followed her at my utmost speed. I was only a boy, and like a boy I chased her, for I was angry, and determined she should not win. We sped through great rooms wherein we saw no one, the child darting through the great curtains, and I following with the swiftness of a lad of the country. But suddenly I came against what seemed to me a wall of solid stone. How was it she could have eluded me? for I was close on her footsteps. I turned back in a passion of rage that made me blind, but I was silenced and stricken into quiet, for the priest Agmahd stood before me. Had I done wrong? It could not be, for he was smiling.

"Come with me," he said; and spoke so gently that I did not fear to follow him. He opened a door, and I saw before my eyes a garden full of flowers, a square garden enclosed in hedges, thickly covered too with flowers, and this garden was full of children all running hither and thither as swiftly as possible, in the intricacies of some game I did not understand. There were so many, and they moved so swiftly, that at first I was bewildered, but suddenly I saw the child among them who had taken my flower. She wore it on her dress, and she smiled in mockery as she saw me. I plunged into the crowd immediately, and seemed, though I knew not how, at once to obey the laws of the game or dance. I scarce knew which it was, for though I moved rightly among them, I could not tell what object they had in pursuit. I followed, and chased the figure of the girl. Although I did not succeed in approaching her, so swift was she, yet I grew quickly to enjoy the motion, the excitement, the merry faces, and laughing voices. The scent of the innumerable flowers filled me with delight, and I became passionately desirous to possess myself of some of them. I forgot the lotus blossom in thinking of these others, and yet I hurried on in the maze of the dance, promising myself a great cluster of flowers when the dance ceased; at that moment I did not fear Agmahd or his displeasure, even if this garden were his. Then suddenly I heard a shout of a hundred gay children's voices.

"He has won it! He has won it!"

It was a ball, a golden ball, and light, so light, that I could throw it far, far up in the sky; yet it always return to my uplifted hands. I had found it at my feet when I heard the others shout, and immediately I knew the ball was mine. Now, I saw there was no one near me but the child, who had taken my lotus flower. It was not on her dress now, and I had forgotten it. But she was smiling, and I laughed to see her. I threw her the ball, and she threw it back to me, from one end of the garden to the other.

Suddenly a bell rang out clear and loud in the air. "Come," she said; "it is school-time, come." She caught my hand and threw the ball away. I looked longingly after it.

"That was mine," I said.

"It is no use now," she answered. "You must gain another prize."

We ran away, hand in hand, through another garden into a great room which I had not seen before. The children with whom I had played were here and a great many more. The air was heavy and sweet in this room. I was not tired, for I had but just risen from my long sleep and the morning was yet fresh, but now that I entered this room I felt weary and my head burned.

Very soon I fell asleep, hearing the children's voices round me. When I awoke it was to hear a shout like that in the garden. "He has won it! He has won it!"

I stood upon a kind of throne -- a lofty seat of marble. And I could hear my own voice in the air. I had been speaking. The children were round me, but they were clustered upon and about the marble seat. I remembered that the child who brought me here had said the teacher stood upon this throne. Why then were we, the children here? I looked, and lo, I saw that the room was full of priests! They stood in the place of the taught. They stood silent, immovable. Again I heard the children cry, "He has won it! He has won it!" I sprang from the throne in a sudden frenzy, I knew not why. As I stood upon the ground I looked and saw that the children were gone. I could not see any one of them but the child who had brought me here. She was standing on the throne, and she laughed and clapped her hands with glee. I wondered what it was that pleased her, and looking down I saw that I stood in a circle of white robed priests who had prostrated themselves until their foreheads touched the ground. What did this mean? I could not guess, and stood still in terror, when suddenly the child cried out as if in answer to my thought, "They worship you!"

My wonder at her words was not greater than another wonder which fell on me. For I understood that I alone heard her voice.

CHAPTER VIII.

I was taken back to my own room, and there the young priests brought me food. I was hungry, for I had not broken my fast, and I found the food exquisite. The young priests who brought it to me fell on one knee when they offered it; I looked wonderingly at them, for I could not guess why they should do so. Many of them came with fruits and rich syrup and delicate sweetmeats, such as I had never seen, and with flowers. Great clusters of flowers were brought and placed near me, and bushes covered with blossoms were put against the wall. I cried out with pleasure to see them, and as I cried out I saw Agmahd standing within the shadow of the curtain. His eyes were on me, cold odd smiles. Yet I did not fear him now; I was full of a new spirit of pleasure, which made me bold. I went from flower to flower, kissing the blossoms. Their scent filled all the room with its richness. I was glad and proud, for I felt as if I need no longer be afraid of this cold priest, who stood motionless as though cut in marble. This sensation of fearlessness lifted a weight of agony from my childish soul.

He turned and vanished, and as he passed under the curtain I saw the child at my side.

"See," she said, "I brought you these flowers."

"You!" I exclaimed.

"Yes, I told them you loved flowers. And these are strong and sweet; they grow in the earth. Are you tired, or shall we go out and play? Do you know that garden is our own and the ball is there? Some one took it back for you."

"Tell me," I said, "why the priests kneel to me to-day.

"Do you not know?" she said, looking at me curiously. "It is because you taught from the throne today, and spoke wise words they understood, but we could not. But we saw you had won a great prize. You will win all the prizes."

I sat down upon my couch, and held my head with my hands and looked at her in wonder.

"But how could I do that and not know it?" I demanded.

"You will be great when you do not struggle, when you do not know it you will win all the prizes. If you are quiet and happy you will be worshipped by all these priests, even the most splendid."

I was dumb with wonder for a moment, then I said --

"You are very little. How can you know all this?"

"The flowers told me," she said with a laugh. "They are your friends. But it is all true. Now come and play with me."

"Not yet," I said. And indeed I felt my head was hot and heavy, and my heart filled with wonder I could not understand her words.

"It is impossible I can have taught from the throne," I exclaimed.

"You did! and the high priests bowed their awful faces before you. For you told them how to perform some strange ceremony where you would be in the midst."

"I!"

"Yes, for you told them of what should be your dress, and how to prepare it, and what words to utter, as they placed it on you."

I watched her with passionate interest. "Can you tell me more?" I cried, when she ceased.

"You are to live among earth-fed flowers, and to dance with the children often. Oh, there were many things. But of the ceremony I cannot remember. But you will soon see, for it is to be to-night."

I started from my couch in a sudden frenzy of fear.

"Do not be afraid," she said, with a laugh. "For I am to be with you. That makes me glad, for I belong to the temple, yet have I never been admitted to one of the sacred ceremonies."

"You belong to the temple! But they cannot hear your voice!"

"Sometimes they cannot see me!" she said, laughing, "only Agmahd can always see me, for I am his. But I cannot talk to him. I like you because I can talk to you. Come, let us go out and play. The flowers in the garden are as sweet as these, and the ball is there. Come."

She took my hand and went quietly away. I let her lead me, for I was lost in thought. But outside the air was so rich and sweet, the flowers so bright, the sun so warm, that soon I forgot my thoughts in happiness.

CHAPTER IX.

It was night. I was sleepy and content, for I had been happy and amused, running hither and thither in the sweet-scented air. All the evening I had slept on my couch among the flowers that made my room fragrant, and I dreamed strange dreams in which each flower became a laughing face, and my ears were full of the sound of magic voices. I awoke suddenly and fancied I must be still dreaming, for the moonlight came into my room and fell upon the beautiful blossoms. And I thought with wonder of the simple home I had been reared in. How have I ever endured it? For now it I seemed to me that beauty was life.

I was very happy.

As I lay dreamily looking at the moonlight, the door in the corridor was suddenly opened from without. The corridor was full of light, such brilliant light that the moonlight seemed like darkness, and I was blinded. Then a number of neophytes entered my room, bringing with them some things that I could not see, because of the strong light. Then they went away and closed the door, leaving me alone in the moonlight, with two tall, white-robed, motionless forms. I knew who was with me though I dared not look -- it was Agmahd and Kamen Baka.

At first I trembled, but suddenly I saw the child glide forth from the shadow, her finger on her lips and a smile on her face.

"Do not be afraid," she said. "They are going to put on you the beautiful robe you told them to prepare."

I rose from my couch and looked at the priests. I was no longer afraid. Agmahd stood motionless, his eyes fixed on me. The other approached me, holding in his hands a white robe. It was of fine linen and covered with rich gold embroidery, which I saw formed characters I could not understood. It was more beautiful than Agmahd's robe and I had never seen anything so beautiful as that when I entered the temple.

I was pleased, and held out my hand for the robe. Kamen came close to me, and when I flung aside the one I wore, put this upon me with his own hands.

It was steeped with a subtle perfume, which I inhaled with delight. This seemed to me a royal robe!

Kamen advanced to the door and opened it. The brilliant light streamed in full upon me. Agmahd remained standing motionless, his eyes fixed on me.

The child looked upon me with admiration and clapped her hands in delight. Then she held out one hand and took mine. "Come," she said. I yielded, and together we went into the corridor, Agmahd close behind us. The scene we entered startled me, and I paused. The great corridor was full of priests, save just where I stood, close to the door of the holy of holies. Here a large space was left, and in this space stood a couch covered with silken drapery, embroidered with gold, in characters resembling those upon my dress. About the couch was a bank or hedge of sweet smelling flowers, and all around the ground was strewn with plucked blossoms. I shrank from the great crowd of motionless white-robed priests, whose eyes were fixed on me, but the beautiful colors pleased me.

"This couch is for us," said the child, and led me to it. No one else spoke or moved, and I obeyed her. We advanced, and upon the couch found our golden ball with which we had played in the garden. I looked in a sudden wonder to see if Agmahd watched us. He stood by the door of the holy of holies; his eyes were on me. Kamen stood nearer to us, and he was gazing at the closed door of the sanctuary, and his lips were moving as if he were repeating words. No one seemed angry with us, so I looked back at the child. She snatched up the ball and sprang to one end of the great couch; I could not resist her gaiety; I sprang to the other end of the couch, and laughed too. She flung me the ball; I caught it in my hands, but before I could throw it back to her, the corridor was plunged into complete profound darkness. For a moment my breath died away in the sudden agony of fear, but suddenly I found that I could see the child, and that she was laughing. I flung her the ball, and she caught it, and laughed again. I looked around, and saw that all else was black darkness. I thought of the awful figure I had seen before in the darkness, and I must have cried aloud with fear but for the child. She came to me and put her hand in mine.

"Are you afraid?" she said; "I am not. And you need not fear. They would not harm you, for they worship you!"

While she spoke, I heard music -- gay, wonderful music -- that made my heart beat fast and my feet long to dance.

A moment later and I saw the light come round the sanctuary door, and the door open. Was that awful figure coming forth? My limbs shook at the thought, but yet I did not lose all courage as before. The child's presence and the gay music kept from me the horror of solitude. The child rose, holding my hand in hers. We approached the sanctuary door. I was unwilling, yet I could not resist the guidance which led me on. We entered the door, and as we did so the music ceased. All was still again. But there was a faint light within the sanctuary which seemed to come from the far end of the chamber. The child led me towards this light. She was with me, and I was not afraid. At the end of the chamber was a small inner room, or recess, cut, as I could see, in the rock. I could see this, for there was enough light here. A woman sat on a low seat, her head bent over a great book, which she held open on her knee. My eyes were riveted to her instantly, and I could not remove them. I knew her, and the heart within me shuddered at the thought that she would raise her head, and I should see her face.

Suddenly I knew my companion the child, was gone. I did not look to see, for my eyes were held by a supreme fascination, but I felt my hand had no answering clasp. I knew her presence was gone.

I waited, standing still as one of those figures carved in the avenue of the temple.

At last she lifted her head and looked at me. My blood shivered and grew cold. It seemed to myself that I froze, for those eyes cut like steel, yet I could not resist or turn away, or even hide my eyes from that awful sight.

"You have come to me to learn. Well, I will teach you," she said, and her voice sounded low and sweet like the soft tones of a musical instrument. "You love beautiful things and flowers. You will be a great artist if you live for beauty alone, but you must be more than that." She held out her hand to me, and, against my will, I lifted mine, and gave it her but she barely touched it; at the touch my hand was suddenly full of roses, and all the place was filled with their scent. She laughed, and the sound was musical; I suppose my face pleased her.

"Come now," she said, "and stand nearer me, for you no longer fear me." With my eyes upon the roses, I approached her; they held my sight, and I did not fear her when I did not see her face.

She put her arm round me and drew me close to her side. Suddenly I saw that the dark robe she wore was no garment of linen or cloth -- it was alive -- it was a drapery of coiling snake, who clung about her and made folds that had seemed to me like soft hanging draperies when I stood a little away from her. Now terror overcame me; I tried to scream but could not, I tried to fly from her but could not. She laughed again but this time her laugh was harsh. But while I looked all was changed, and her robe was dark -- dark still but not alive. I stood breathless, wondering in cold with fear -- her arm was still about me! She raised her other hand and placed it on my forehead. Then fear left me altogether; I seemed happy and quiet. My eyes were shut, although I saw; I was conscious, yet I did not desire to move. She rose, and lifting me in her arms, placed me on the low stone seat where she had herself been sitting. My head fell back against the wall of rock behind me. I was dumb and still, but I could see.

She rose up to her full height and stretched her arms aloft above her head, and again I saw the serpents. They were vigorous and full of life. They were not only her dress but they were about her head. I could not tell if they were her hair or if they were in it. She clasped her hands high above her head, and the terrible creatures hung wreathing from her arms. But I was not afraid. Fear seemed to have left me forever.

Suddenly I became aware that there was another presence in the sanctuary. Agmahd was there, standing at the door of the inner cavern.

I looked in wonder at his face, it was so still; the eyes were unseeing. Then I knew suddenly that they were in very fact unseeing; that this figure, this light, I myself, were all invisible to him.

She turned to me, or leaned towards me, so that I saw her face, and her eyes were on mine; otherwise she did not move. Those eyes that cut like steel no longer filled me with terror, but they held me with a grasp as of some iron instrument. While I watched her, suddenly I saw the serpents change and vanish; they became long sinuous folds of some soft gray gleaming garment, and their hands and terrible eyes changed into starry groups of roses. And a rich strong scent of roses filled the sanctuary. Then I saw Agmahd smile.

"My Queen is here," he said.

"Your Queen is here," I said, and did not know I had spoken till I heard my own voice. "She waits to know your desire."

"Tell me," he said, " what is her robe?" I answered, "It shines and gleams, and on her shoulders are roses."

"I do not desire pleasure," he said; "my soul is sick of it. But I demand power."

Until now her eyes fixed on mine had told me what to speak; but now I heard her voice again.

"In the temple?"

And I repeated her words, unconscious that I did so till I caught the echo of my voice.

"No," answered Agmahd contemptuously. "I must go outside these walls, and mix with men and work my will among them. I demand the power to do this. It was promised to me; that promise has not been fulfilled."

"Because you lacked the courage and the strength to compel its fulfillment."

"I lack those no longer," answered Agmahd, and for the first time I saw his face flame with passion.

"Then utter the fatal words," she said.

Agmahd's face changed. He stood still for some moments, and his face grew colder and more stony than any carven form.

"I renounce my humanity," he said at last, uttering the words slowly, so that they appeared to pause and rest upon the air.

"It is well," she said. "But you cannot stand alone. You must bring me others ready like yourself to brave all and know all. I must have twelve sworn servants. Get me these, and you shall have your desire."

"Are they to be my equals?" demanded Agmahd.

"In desire and in courage, yes; in power, no; because each will have a different desire; thus will their service be acceptable to me."

Agmahd paused a moment. Then he said, "I obey my Queen. But I must be aided in so difficult a task. How shall I tempt them?"

At these words she flung out her arms, opening and shutting her hands with a strange gesture, which I could not understand. Her eyes gleamed like hot coals, and then grew cold and dull.

"I will direct you," she answered. "Be faithful to my orders and you need not fear. Only obey me and you shall succeed. You have every element within this temple. There are ten priests ready to our hand. They are full of hunger. I will satisfy them. You I will satisfy when your courage and steadfastness is proved -- not until then for you demand much more than these others."

"And who shall be the one to complete the number?" asked Agmahd.

She turned her eyes again upon me.

"This child," she answered. "He is mine -- my chosen and favorite servant. I will teach him: and through him I will teach you."

CHAPTER X.

"Tell Kamen Baka, that I know his heart's desire, and that he shall have it, but that he must first pronounce the fatal words."

Agmahd bowed his head and turned away. He silently left the sanctuary.

I was again alone with her. She approached me and fastened her terrible eyes on mine.

While I gazed at her she vanished from before me, and in her place was a golden light which gradually shaped itself into a form more beautiful than any I had ever seen.

It was a tree full of foliage that hung soft like hair rather than leaves, and on each branch was a multitude of flowers growing in thick clusters, and among the flowers were a number of birds all golden and gay with brilliant colors, and they darted hither and thither among the glowing blossoms, till my eyes grew dazzled, and I cried aloud, "Oh give me one of these little birds for my own that it may come to me and nestle as it does in those flowers."

"You shall have a hundred of them, and they will so love you they will kiss your mouth and take food from your lips. By-and-by you shall have a garden in which a tree like this shall grow, and all the birds of the air will love you. But first you must do my bidding. Speak to Kamen and bid him enter the sanctuary."

"Enter," I said, "the priest Kamen Baka shall enter."

He came and stood within the doorway of the inner cavern. The tree had vanished, and I saw before me the dark figure with its shining flowing robes and cruel eyes; they were fixed on the priest.

"Tell him," she said slowly, "that his heart's hunger shall be satisfied. He desires love -- he shall have it. The priests of the temple have turned cold faces towards him, and he feels that their hearts are as stone. He wants to see them on their knees around him, adoring him, willing slaves. He shall have it; for he shall take upon him this once, which until now has been mine. He shall gratify their heart's lust, and in return they will put him alone upon a pedestal above all but myself. Is the bribe great enough?"

She said these words in a tone of intense contempt, and I could read in her terrible face that she despised him for the narrow limit of his ambition. But the sting left the words as I repeated them.

Kamen bowed his head, and a strange glow of exultation came upon his face.

"It is," he said.

"Then pronounce the fatal words!"

Kamen Baka fell upon his knees and Rung his hands high above his head. The look in his face changed to one of agony.

"From henceforward, though all men love me, I love no man!"

The dark figure swept towards him and touched his head with her hand. "You are mine," she said, and turned away, a smile that was dark and cold like a northern frost upon her face. She gave me the idea of a teacher and a guide with Kamen; to Agmahd she had rather spoken as a queen might to her chief favorite, one whom she values and fears at once; one who has strength.

"Now, child, there is work to do," she said, approaching me. "This book has written in it the hearts of the priests who shall be my servants. Thou art weary and must rest, for I will not that they injure thee. Thou must grow to a strong man worthy of my favor. But carry the book with thee in thy arms; and as soon as thou shalt wake in the early morn Kamen shall come to thee, and thou shalt read to him the first page of this volume. When he has succeeded in accomplishing the first task, then he shall again come to thee at early morn and thou shalt read to him the second; and in this way the book will be finished. Tell him this; and bid him not despair at any time, because of difficulties. With each difficulty surmounted his power will increase, and when all is done he will stand supreme."

I repeated these words to Kamen. He was standing now at the doorway, his hands clasped in front of him, and his head drooped low, so that I could not see his face. But as I ceased, he raised his head and said, "I obey."

His face wore still the strange gleam which I had seen on it before.

"Bid him go," she said, "and he is to send Agmahd hither."

When I repeated this, he quietly withdrew; and I could see by his movements that the place to his eyes was all darkness.

A moment later and Agmahd stood in the doorway. She approached him and laid her hand upon his forehead. Immediately I saw a crown there; and Agmahd smiled.

"It shall be yours," she said. "Say this to Agmahd; it is the greatest crown but one upon the earth; and that greater one he would not wear. Now bid him carry thee in his arms and lay thee on thy couch. But thou clasp tight the book."

While I was repeating her words, she came to me and touched my forehead. A deep delicious languor came upon me, and I thought the words faded on my lips. But I could not say them again; all had vanished. I was asleep.

CHAPTER XI.

When I awoke it was broad daylight; and I felt that I had slept a long deep sleep. My room was like a garden it was so full of flowers. My eyes wandered around them in pleasure, but presently lighted on an object which kept them fixed. It was a kneeling figure in the midst of the room; a priest whose head was bowed low; but I knew it was Kamen Baka. I moved, and at the slight sound I made he raised his head and looked towards me. In moving, I found that the book lay beside me open. My eyes became fastened to the page. I saw words that shone, and unconsciously I read them aloud. I ceased at last, because no more was writ in plain language, but all was hieroglyphics.

Kamen Baka started to his feet. I looked at him, and saw his face was all alight with what seemed like wild exultation.

"He shall kiss my feet to day," he cried out. Then observing my wondering gaze, he said, "Have you read all?"

"All that I can understand," I answered. "The rest is in strange characters that I do not know."

He turned instantly and left my chamber. I looked back at the page of the book which I had read to see what were the words which had so strangely excited him. They were now no longer intelligible to me -- they too were writ in hieroglyphics -- and I gazed at them in despair, for now I found I could remember no word of what I had read. I grew weary with puzzling over this strange thing, and at last I fell asleep again my head upon the open pages of the mystic book. I did not rouse from the deep dreamless sleep in which I was, until a sound startled me. Two young priests were in my room; they carried cakes and milk, and fell upon their knees to offer me the food. I was afraid, or I should have laughed to see them thus kneeling to me, a boy of the country. When I had eaten they left me, but I was not long alone. The curtain lifted, and at the sight of one who entered, I sprang to my feet and laughed with pleasure. It was Seboua, the gardener.

"How is it you have come to me?" I asked. "I thought indeed I was never to see you again."

"Agmahd sent me here," he said.

"Agmahd!" I cried in amazement. I approached him and pressed his arm between my hands.

"Oh yes, I am real," he answered. "They cannot make a phantom of me. Do not doubt when you see me it is I myself."

He spoke angrily and roughly, and for a moment I was afraid, but not for long. The strange smile came on his ugly face.

"You are to come with me into the garden" he said, and held out his dark large hand. I put mine in it, and together we left my room and went quickly away through the large empty chambers and long passages of the temple till we reached that narrow iron gateway through which I had first seen Seboua's face. As then so now, the garden shone beyond, a vision of greenness and light and color.

"Oh! I am glad to come back here," I said.

"You came first to work; you were to be the drudge for me," said Seboua, proudly. "Now all's changed. You are to play, not work, and I am to treat you like a little prince. Well! have they spoiled thee yet, I wonder, child? Would'st like to bathe?"

"But where," I said, "in what waters? I would love to plunge in and swim in some water that was cool and deep."

"Thou canst swim? and thou lovest the water? Well, come with me and I will show thee deep water that will be cool indeed. Come thou with me!"

He walked on and I had to hurry to keep pace with him. He muttered to himself as he went, but I could not understand his words. Indeed, I did not listen for I was thinking of how glorious the plunge into cool water would be on this warm languid morning.

We came to a place where there was a wide, deep pool, into which water came dropping, dropping, in a quick swift shower from some place above.

"There is water for thee," said Seboua, "and no flowers are there for thee to hurt."

I stood on the brink in the warm sunlight and flung my white robe from me. Then with one instant of pause to look around and think how sweet the sun was, I plunged into the water. Ah! indeed, it was cold! My breath was almost gone with the sudden chill, but I struck out and began to swim, and soon began to glory in the sense of keen refreshment. I felt strong and eager, here in the sweet fresh waters. No longer languid as amid the fragrant odors of the temple, or the rich scents of the flowers in my chamber. I was so happy, I wanted to stay a long while here in the water mid the sun; so presently I ceased swimming and let myself float idly, and, closed my eyes that the sunlight should not blind me.

Suddenly I felt something so strange, I grew breathless, yet it was so gentle it did not terrify me. It was a kiss upon my mouth. I opened my eyes. There, beside me, lying upon the surface of the water, was my own Queen, the Lily Queen, the Lady of the Lotus. I uttered a cry of joy. Immediately all pleasure which I had had since last I saw her vanished from my mind. She was my Queen, my beautiful friend; when she was there I had none other in all the world.

"Child, thou art come to me again" she said, "but soon thou wilt leave me; and how can I aid thee if thou forgettest me utterly?"

I made no answer, for I was ashamed. I could hardly believe that I had indeed forgotten and yet I knew that it was true.

"The waters thou liest in now," she said, "come from that place where my flowers, the lotus blossoms, dwell in their glory. Thou wouldst die wert thou to lie thus in the water where they dwell. But this that drops from them has but little of their life in it, and has given up its own to them. When thou must plunge into the water of the lotus tank, then thou wilt be strong as the eagle and eager as the young life of the newborn. My child, be thou strong; listen not to the flattery which confuses thee; listen only to the truth I keep in the sunlight, dear child, and let not the phantoms delude thee; for there is the life of lives awaiting thee, the pure flower of knowledge and love is ready for thee to pluck. Wouldst thou be a tool, a mere instrument in the hands of those who desire only for themselves? No! acquire knowledge and grow strong; then shalt thou be a giver of sunshine to the world. Come, my child, give me thine hand; rise in confidence, for this water will support thee; rise and kneel upon it and drink of the sunshine; rise and kneel upon it, and address thyself to the light of all life, that it may illumine thee."

I rose, holding her hand. I knelt beside her. I rose again and with her stood upon the water -- and then I knew no more.

"Wouldst thou be a tool, a mere instrument in the hands of those who desire only for themselves? No! acquire knowledge and grow strong; then shalt thou be a giver of sunshine to the world."

These words seemed whispered in my ear as I awoke; I repeated them over and over, and remembered every separate word rightly. But they were vague and unmeaning to me; I had fancied I understood them when first I heard them, but now they sounded to me as the good words of the preacher sound to the dancers at the festivals.

* * * * * * *

I was a child when these words were breathed into my ear -- a lad, helpless because ignorant and full of youth. Through the years of my growth, the cry to my soul from the Lily Queen rang dimly and without meaning in the obscure regions of my brain. They were to me as the song of the priest to the babe that hears but its music. Yet I never forgot them. My life was given up to the men who held me in bondage, in spirit and in body; fetters lay heavy on my unawakened soul. While my body yielded dully to the guidance of its masters, I was a slave, yet knew that freedom existed beneath the free sky! But, though I obeyed blindly, and gave all my strength and powers to the base uses of the desecrated temple, in my heart I held fast the memory of the beautiful queen and in my mind her words were written in fire that would not die. Yet as I grew to man's stature, my soul sickened within me. These words which lived like a star in my soul cast a strange light upon my wretched life. And as my mind developed I recognized this, and a heavy weariness, as of death or despair, shut away from me all the beauty of the world. From a gay child, a happy creature of sunshine, I grew into a sad youth, whose eyes were large and heavy with tears, and whose sick heart held hidden within it many secrets, but half understood, of shame and sin and sorrow. Sometimes, when I wandered through the garden I gazed into the still water of the lily tank and prayed to see again the vision. But it came not I had lost the innocence of childhood, and had not yet won the strength of the man.

PART II.
CHAPTER I.

I was in the garden of the temple, lying beneath a wide tree that cast deep shade upon the grass. I had been very weary, for all the night before I had been in the sanctuary, speaking the messages of the dark spirit to her priests. I slept a little in the warm air and awoke strangely full of sadness. I felt that my youth had gone, yet I had never enjoyed its fire.

On each side of me was a young priest. One was fanning me with a broad leaf that he must have plucked from the tree above. The other, leaning on one hand upon the grass, regarded me earnestly. His eyes were large and dark and pleasant, like the eyes of a kindly animal. I had often admired his beauty, and I was glad to see him at my side.

"You have been too much within doors. See now," he said, when he saw my eyes open wearily, and gaze into his face. "They shall not kill thee with the ceremonies of the temple, even if thou art the only one that can give them life. Wilt come into the town with us, and taste something different from the air of the temple?"

"But we cannot," I said.

"Cannot," said Malen contemptuously. "Do you suppose we are prisoners here?"

"But even if we can find a way out the people will know us. The priests do not go among the people."

"The people will not know us," said Malen with a merry laugh. "Agmahd has given us liberty. Agmahd has given us power. Come, if thou wilt -- we are going."

The two rose and held out their hands to help me to rise; but I was no longer weak. I sprang to my feet, and arranged my white garment. "Are we to wear these robes?" I asked.

"Yes, yes, but none will know us. We shall appear as beggars, or as princes; what we will; Agmahd has given us power. Come!"

I was as delighted as they at this prospect of adventure. We ran across the garden till we came to a narrow gate in the wall. Malen touched it, and easily pushed it open. We were outside the temple.

My companions, laughing and talking as we went, ran across the plain to the city. I ran too, and listened; but I understood little of what they said. Evidently they knew the city, which to me was only a name. True, I had walked through it with my mother, a barefoot country lad. But now, it seemed, I was to enter houses, and mix with great and rich people. I felt afraid at the thought.

We hurried on until we entered one of the busiest streets. It was crowded with gay people in beautiful dresses, and all the shops seemed to sell only jewelry. Then we turned through a great gateway, into a courtyard, and from that passed into a marble hall where a great fountain played, and large flowering shrubs threw out a strong scent.

A wide marble stairway went out of this hall, and we immediately commenced to climb it. And when we reached the top Malen opened a door, and we entered a room all hung with golden tapestry, and where were a number of people whose dresses and jewels dazzled me. They were seated round a table drinking wine and eating sweetmeats. The air was full of talk and laughter, and heavy with perfume. Three very lovely women rose and welcomed us, each taking one of us by the hand, and giving us a place beside her. In a moment we seemed to be of the party, and to mingle our laughter with theirs, as though we had sat out all the feast. I know not whether it was the scented wine I drank or the magic touch of the beautiful hand that often touched mine, as it lay upon the embroidered table-cover -- but my head grew light and strange, and I talked of things I did not know anything about till now, and laughed at sayings that an hour before would have seemed dull to me, because of my want of understanding.

She who sat next me pressed her hand in mine. I turned to look at her; she was leaning towards me; her face was brilliant with youth and beauty. Her rich dress had made me feel a child beside her, but now I saw that she was young, younger than myself, yet she was of such rich form and radiant loveliness that though a child in years she was a woman in charm. As I gazed into her tender eyes, it seemed to me that I knew her well, that her charm was familiar, and the stronger for its familiarity. She spoke many words that at first I hardly understood, indeed scarcely heard. But gradually, as I listened, I grew to understand. She told me of her longing for me in my absence, of her love for me, and of her weariness of all others on the earth. "The room seemed dark and silent till you came," she said. "The banquet had no mirth in it. The others laughed, but their laughter sounded as sobs in my ears -- the sobs of those in torment. Is it for me, who am so young and strong and full of love, to be so sad? No -- no, it is not for me. Ah, lover, husband, leave me not again alone. Stay by my side, and my passion will make thee strong to fulfill thy destiny."

I rose from my seat suddenly, holding her hand clasped tight in mine.

"It is true," I cried in a loud voice. "I have done ill to neglect that which is the glory of life. I confess it, that thy beauty, which indeed is mine, had been blotted from my mind. But now I see thee with mine eyes I wonder I could ever have seen beauty in aught else in heaven or earth."

Suddenly, while I spoke, there was a movement among the startled guests. With wonderful rapidity, they left the table and were at once gone from the room. Only the two young priests remained. Their eyes were fixed on me. They seemed grave, serious, disturbed. They rose slowly. "You will not return to the temple?" said Malen. My answer was a gesture of impatience. "Do you forget," he demanded, "that we were but to look at the follies of the city, that we might know of what clay men are made? You know that the initiated priests must retain their purity. What of you, the seer of the temple? Even I, who am but a novice, dare not yield the fierce longing for liberty that fills my soul. Ah, to be free! to be a child of the city, to know the meaning of life! But I dare not. Else am I less than nothing, I should have no place in the temple, no place in the world. How then will it be with thee, the seer? How are we to answer to Agmahd for thee?"

I made no answer. But she who sat beside me rose and advanced towards him. She took a jewel from her neck, and put it in his hand.

"Give him this," she said, "and he will ask no more."

CHAPTER II.

From this hour there is a time of which I cannot give so careful an account as of the other days of my life. It is blurred and veiled by the similarity of the emotions through which I passed. Indeed, they merged together and became one and the same. I drank deep of pleasure each day; each hour it seemed to me that my beautiful companion grew more beautiful, so that I gazed upon her face in wonder. She led me through the rooms of our palace, and I could not stay to see their splendor, because always beyond were chambers yet more splendid. With her I wandered through the gardens, where the fragrant flowers grew in a profusion each as I had never seen in any other place. Beyond the gardens were meadows; in the short, sweet grass grew many wild flowers, and lilies blossomed in the stream that ran through the fields. Here the city maidens came at evening, some to fetch water, some to bathe in the stream and sit afterwards upon its bank, and talk and laugh and sing until the night was half spent. Their gleaming forms and sweet voices made the evenings doubly beautiful, and I would linger among them under the stars, and would often have stayed until the dawn the playmate of them all, but only whispering words of love to those who were most beautiful. And then, as they, singing in low voices, left me, she my own most beautiful went with me back to the palace, wherein we lived amid the city, yet apart from it. For we were happy as were none else within that city.

I cannot tell how long passed thus. Only I know that one day I lay within my own chamber, and she the most beautiful sang sweet low songs while her head lay upon my arm, when in a moment the song was hushed upon her lips and she lay pale and still. I heard, in the silence, a slow, soft footfall on the stairs. The door was opened, and Agmahd the high priest stood motionless within it.

He gazed at me one moment with his terrible eyes, that were cold as though they were jewels; there was a smile upon his face, but that smile struck me with fear, and I trembled.

"Come," he said.

I arose unhesitatingly. I knew that I must obey. I looked not back until I heard a swift movement and a sob; then I turned. But she, the most beautiful, was gone. Had she fled from before this unexpected appearance in our chamber? I could not stay to see, or go to comfort her. I knew that I must follow Agmahd; I felt as I had never felt before, that he was my master. As I came to the doorway, I saw across the threshold a snake that reared its head at my approach. I sprang back with a cry of horror.

Agmahd smiled. "Do not fear," he said. "This is a favorite of thy queen and will do her chosen servant no harm. Come!"

At his command I felt compelled to follow; I dared not disobey. I passed the snake with averted eyes, and as I reached the stairway I heard its hiss of anger.

Agmahd went through the gardens to the meadows beyond. It was evening, and already the stars were gleaming in the sky and the eyes of the maidens shone as they sat in groups by the side of the stream. But they did not sing as was their habit. In the midst of the stream was a boat, and in it two oarsmen. I recognized the young priests who had come with me to the city. Their eyes were downcast, and they did not raise them even at my approach. I understood as I passed by the girls that they had recognized old acquaintances and merry companions in those two young priests, and were amazed and full of wonder to see them in this dress, and of such changed demeanor.

Agmahd entered the boat; I followed him; and then we rowed silently towards the temple.

I had never seen the entrance to the temple from the water. I had heard when I was in the city with my mother that this entrance used to be often used, but now it was reserved only for festivals, so that I was much amazed to enter by this way. I was more amazed to find all the sacred precinct full of boats decorated with flowers and occupied, by white-robed priests, who sat with their eyes downcast. But I soon saw that today was a festival.

This temple! It seemed a hundred years since I had dwelled within it. Agmahd himself looked strange and unfamiliar to me. Was I indeed grown much older? I could not tell, for I found no mirror in which to see my face, and I found no friend to ask. Only this I knew, that compared with the youth who ran from the garden of the temple, eager for adventure, I was now a man. And I knew my manhood had, come to me not in glory, but in shame. I was a slave. A deep gloom settled on my soul as we entered the temple. The boat was drawn up to some wide white marble steps, which were within the walls of the temple and beneath its roof. I had never known the great river was so near. When we had reached the top of the steps, Agmahd opened a door, and lo! we were immediately at the entrance of the holy of holies. Only a few faint torches, held by silent priests, lit the great corridor. It was but dusk outside, on the river; here it was like deep night. At a sign from Agmahd the torches were extinguished. But all light was not gone! for round the door of the sanctuary gleamed that strange light which once had so terrified me. It did not terrify me now. I knew what I had to do; and, unhesitatingly and without fear, I did it. I advanced, opened the door, and entered.

Within stood the dark figure, whose robes gleamed and whose eyes were cold and terrible. She smiled and put out her hand and laid it upon mine. I shuddered at the touch, it was so cold.

"Tell Agmahd," she said, "that I am coming. That I will be beside you in the boat. That he is to stand in the midst with us, and my other servants to surround us. And that then if all is done as I order, I will work a wonder before all the priests and before the people. And this I will do because I am well pleased with my servants, and because I desire them to have power and wealth."

I said her words again, and when I had ceased Agmahd's voice came out of the darkness.

"The Queen is welcomed! The Queen shall be obeyed."

A moment later and the torches were again lit. I saw that they were ten in number, carried by ten priests, who all wore white robes deeply embroidered in gold, as was that of Agmahd. Among them was Hamen Baka. His face looked strange to me. It was as the face of an ecstatic.

Agmahd opened the door which admitted us to the river steps. A different boat was moored here now. It was large, with a wide desk surrounded by vases, in which burned something strongly fragrant. Within these vases a circle was drawn in crimson and mingled with that a figure which I could not understand. At the sides of the boat, below this raised deck, sat the rowers -- white-robed priests. All were still and mute, waiting with downcast eyes. The boat was hung with thick garlands of flowers, massed together till they seemed like great ropes. A lamp was burning at each end.

We entered the boat. Agmahd went first and stood in the midst of the circle. I took my place at his side. Between us, clearly visible to my eyes, was the figure. She shed a light like that which illumined the sanctuary, only less brilliant. But I saw that none perceived her presence but myself.

The ten priests entered the boat also, and placed themselves within the crimson circle, thus completely enclosing us. Then the boat slowly swung from the steps. I saw that a number of boats were before and behind us, all hung with flowers and lamps, all filled with white-robed priests. Silently the procession shot out upon the bosom of the sacred river and advanced towards the city.

When we were at last outside the temple, I heard a deep murmur rise and fill the air. It was so long and deep, it made me tremble with wonder but it disturbed none else, and soon I saw its meaning. As my eyes grew accustomed to the starlight, I saw that all the fields on each side of the river were full of a surging, swaying, mass of forms. A vast multitude of people crowded at the water's edge, and filled the fields as far as I could see. This was a great festival, and I had not known it. I wondered a while; but soon I remembered that I had, indeed, heard it spoken of, but I had been so saturated with the immediate pleasures about me that I had not heeded. Perhaps, had I remained in the city till now, I should have mingled in the crowd; but now I was isolated from the crowd, and, as it seemed to me, from all that was human. I stood silent and immovable as Agmahd himself. Yet, my soul was torn with a despair I could not understand, and crushed by a horror of the unknown which was yet to come.

CHAPTER III.

As the boats glided down the river, suddenly the deep silence was broken by a burst of song. It came from the priests who rowed. From every boat the hymn rushed forth in a volume of sound, and I could see by the great movement, visible even in the dimness, that the people fell upon their knees. But they were silent; they adored and listened while the priests' voices rang out upon the air.

When the song ceased, there was a silence that was not broken for some minutes. The people remained motionless, kneeling, silent. But on a sudden they flung themselves prostrate upon the ground, and I would hear the sigh, the long breath of awe that came from the multitude: for the priests had burst out anew, with a cry of melodious triumph, and the words they uttered in so loud and strong a voice were these --

"The goddess is with us! She is in our midst! Fall down O people, and worship!"

At this moment the figure which stood between me and the priest Agmahd turned and smiled into my face.

"Now my chosen servant," she said, "I must ask your service. I have paid you beforehand that you might not hesitate. But do not fear. You shall be paid again and that doubly. Give me your hands. Place your lips upon my forehead, and fear not, move not, utter no cry, whatsoever faintness, whatsoever tremor come upon thee. Thy life will become mine. I shall draw it from thee: but I shall return it. Is it not precious? Do not fear."

I obeyed her without hesitation yet with dread unimaginable. But I could not resist her will I knew myself her slave. Her cold hands clasped mine, and instantly it seemed that they were no longer soft, but had become rivets of steel, which held me fast and were inexorable. Impelled by my sense of helplessness, I dared the glitter of these terrible eyes, and drew close to her. I longed for death to release me, but I could hope for no other help. I placed my lips upon her forehead. The vapor from the lamps and vessels had filled my brain with a strange sleepiness, and I was dull and heavy. But now, as my lips touched her forehead, which searched them, I knew not whether with cold or heat, a frenzied sense of joy, of lightness, of almost insane delight filled me. I knew myself no longer; I was swayed and dominated by a surging sea of emotions which were not my own. They swept through me, and their rush appeared to wash away my individuality utterly, and, as it then seemed, for ever. Yet I was not unconscious; my consciousness grew momently more intense and awake. Then in one strange second, I forgot the lost individuality -- I knew that I was living in the brain, in the heart, in the essence of that being who had so utterly dominated me. A wild cry, instantly hushed, rang out from the people. They saw their goddess. And I, looking down saw at my feet the seemingly dead form of a young priest, robed in white garments, gold-embroidered. I paused for one instant, in my joy of power to wonder, Was he dead?

CHAPTER IV.

I could see the great multitude which was on each side clearly; a light fell upon them which they did not perceive. It was not the starlight by which they saw, but a brilliance that came not from the heavens but from my eyes.

I saw their hearts -- I saw not their bodies but themselves. I recognized my servants, and my soul lifted itself as I perceived that nearly all of this multitude were ready to serve me. Mine was a worthy army; they would obey, not from duty but desire.

I saw in each heart what was its hunger, and I knew that I could feed it. One long moment I remained visible; then I left my chosen servants. I bade them draw near to the shore; for now that I was no longer intent upon making myself seen by these dull eyes of men, I could speak to and touch those whom I chose. The strong life of the young priest was enough to feed the lamp of physical power for some time if I did not use it too swiftly.

I stepped upon the shore, and moved among the people, speaking into the ear of each the secret of his heart -- more, I told him how to obtain that which he only thought of silently. No man or woman was without some longing which shame would have held them forever from uttering even to a confessor. But I saw it, and made it no longer a thing of shame, and showed how small an effort of will, how slight a knowledge was needed for the first step in self-gratification. All through the throng I went, hither and thither, and as I passed I left a maddened and impassioned crowd behind me. At length the intoxication which my presence produced could no longer be held in check. With one voice the people burst out into a wild song that thrilled my blood, and made it burn within me. Have I not heard this song under other skies, sung in the voices and languages of all peoples? Have I not heard it from peoples who are long since extinct and forgotten? Shall I not hear it from peoples whose dwelling-places are not yet created? It is my song! It gives me life! Uttered silently in one heart, it is the cry of the unspoken passion the hidden madness of self. When it comes from the throat of the multitude, shame is gone and concealment at an end. Then it is the frenzied utterance of the organ, the outcry of the devotees of pleasure.

My work was done. I had lit a great fire which raged on like the fire in the forest. I turned back to the sacred boat where it awaited me. Motionless they stood there, waiting my return those my chosen servants, the high priests of the temple. Ah, my mighty ones in passion! Kings in lust! Monarchs in desire!

And the young priest -- was he still there? Still looking like one dead? Yes, he lay motionless, pallid, in the midst of the circle formed by the high priests, lying at the feet of Agmahd, who stood here alone.

As this thought came to me, I seemed suddenly to withdraw myself in some mysterious way from the sea of passion in which I had been submerged. I knew myself again -- that I was not the goddess, but had been only absorbed by her, sucked up into her embracing personality. Now I was again separated from her. But I did not return to that pale shape which so lifelessly lay upon the deck of the sacred boat. I was in the temple; I was in darkness; yet I knew that I was in the holy of holies.

A light came in the darkness. I looked, and, lo! the inner cave was full of light: and within it stood the Lady of the Lotus.

I was at the door of the inner cave, close to her, within the glance of her eyes. I tried to escape -- I tried to turn -- I could not. I trembled as I had never trembled before even with horror or dread.

For she stood silently, her eyes upon me. And I saw that they were full of a great anger. And she who had been to me a tender friend, gentle as a kind mother, now stood in her majesty before me, and I knew that I had angered a god the most to be dreaded of all that are known to men.

"Was it for this, O Sensa! beloved of the gods! that thou wert born? Was it for this that thine eyes were opened and thy senses made clear to perceive? Thou knowest it was not; yet those seeing eyes and those swift senses have at last served their master, and shown thee who and what it is thou hast been serving. Wilt thou serve her always? Now that thou art a man, choose! Art thou fallen so low that thou wilt be a slave forever? Go, then! I have come to cleanse my sanctuary. I will endure no longer. It shall be silent, and the people shall not know that any god exist, rather than that they shall be lied to by false lips, and tempted by the darkness. Go! None shall enter here again. I close the door! The sanctuary is dumb, and knows no voice. I sit here alone and silent; yea, through the ages I will dwell here without speech, and the people shall say I am dead. Be it so! In the ages to come my children will rise again and the darkness shall break. Oh! Thou hast chosen! Fall! Thy estate is lost. Leave me to my silence!"

She raised her hand with a gesture that bade me leave her. It was so imperative, so royal, that I could not disobey. I turned, I drooped my head, I went with sad steps to the outer door of the sanctuary. Yet I could not open it; I could not pass out; I could advance no further. My heart turned sick within me and held me back. I fell on my knees and cried out in a voice of agony, "Mother! Queen and Mother!"

A moment passed in an awful silence, I waited, I knew not for what. My soul was hungry and desperate. An awful memory came to me in the darkness and silence. I saw in the past not only pleasure, but deeds. I saw that I had done these blindly, accepting the stupefaction of my soul as men accept the dulness of wine. And I had done the work given me to do in a stupor, thinking not of it, but of the rewards, of each pleasure that was to come. I had been the mouthpiece, the oracle of her, that black soul, whom now I had seen and whom now I knew. The past grew so terrible, so present, so fierce in its denunciation that again I cried out in the darkness, "Mother! Save me!"

A touch came on my hand and on my face. I heard a voice in my ear and in my heart, "Thou art saved. Be strong." And the light came upon my eyes, but I could not see, for a rain of tears washed from them the frightful visions they had seen.

CHAPTER V.

I was no longer in the sanctuary. I felt the air on my face. I opened my eyes and saw the sky above me, and the shining stars in its depth. I was lying prostrate, and I felt strangely weary. Yet I was roused by the sound of a thousand voices, whose cries and songs struck on my ears. What could this be?

I raised myself. I was in the midst of the circle of priests, of the ten high-priests. Agmahd stood beside me; he was watching me. My eyes fixed on his face, and I could not look away. Pitiless, heartless, soulless! Had I feared him? This image, this unhuman being? I feared him no longer. I looked round at the priests who surrounded me. I read their faces; they were absorbed, self-conscious. Each and all were bitten and eaten by one deep desire, one hunger for gratification which he cherished like a serpent, next his heart. I could no longer fear these men. I had seen the light. I was strong.

I rose to my feet. I looked round at the multitudes who crowded the banks of the river, beneath the clear sky. I understood then the strange voices I had heard. The people were mad; some with wine, some with love, some with absolute frenzy. Numbers of small boats had crowded the water; the people had come in these to make offerings to the goddess whom they adored, and whom to-night they had seen and heard, and felt. The sacred boat on which I stood was weighted and heaped with the offerings the people had flung into it, standing up in their low vessels, their rafts, by the side of ours. Gold and silver, jewels, and vessels of gold set with shining stones. Agmahd looked at these things, and I saw the smile on his lips. These riches might feed the temple, but for himself it was very different jewels he desired and worked for. My soul spoke suddenly unawares. I could look on and be silent no longer. I spoke in a loud voice, and commanded the people to hear me, and immediately there was a stillness which grew till it spread over the multitude.

"Listen to me, you that are worshippers here, of the goddess. What goddess is it you worship? Can you not tell by the words she whispers into your hearts? Look within and if she has seared you with the fierce heat of passion know she is no true god! For there is no truth save in wisdom. Listen and I will speak to you words that have been uttered in the sanctuary, and breathed by the spirit of light, our Queen Mother. Know that in virtue, in true thoughts, in true deeds, only can you find peace. Is this dark organ a fit surrounding for the goddess of truth? Are you her worshippers, who are drunk with wine and passion here beneath the open sky? You with wild words of impiety and frenzied songs on your lips, and thoughts of shame at your hearts, ready to spring boldly into deeds? No! down on your knees, and lift your hands to heaven and ask that beneficent spirit, our queen of wisdom, who broods over you with wide wings of love, to forgive your shamelessness, to help you in a new effort. Hear me. I will pray to her, for I see her in her splendor. Speak to her the words I utter, and she shall surely listen for she loves you even though you offend -- "

A burst of melody, a number of strong voices singing, drowned my voice. The priests had burst out into song with the rich music of a hymn. The people, swayed by my voice and words, had in masses fallen upon their knees. Now, intoxicated by the music, they sang the hymn with fervor, and the volume of sound rose majestically into the sky. A strong sweet scent entered my nostrils. I turned from it with dislike, but already it had done its work. I felt my brain swoon.

"He is in an ecstasy," said Kamen Baka.

"He is mad," I heard uttered in another voice -- a voice so cold, so enraged, I hardly recognized it. Yet I knew it was Agmahd who spoke.

I strove to answer him, for I was inspired in all I did by a new and strange courage, and I knew nothing of fear. But already the stupefying vapor had done its work. I was dumb, as in sleep; my head grew heavy. In a few seconds I was asleep.

CHAPTER VI.

When I awoke I was in my old chamber in the temple; the one in which my first boyish terrors came to me.

I was very tired; so tired that the first sensation I experienced was that of intolerable weariness, which numbed all my body. I lay still a little while, thinking only of my discomfort.

Then suddenly the events of yesterday came into my memory. It was like the rising of the sun. I had found her again, my Queen Mother, and she had taken me back to her protection.

I rose, forgetting my pain and weariness. It was just dawn and through the high window the faint gray light came softly into my room. It was brilliant with rich material and rich embroidery; full of strange and beautiful things which made it seem like a chamber for a prince. But for its peculiar shape and the high window, it could hardly have been recognized as the room which in my childhood had been made a garden of flowers for my pleasure.

The air within seemed to me heavy and dull; I longed to be outside, in the air, sweet with the newness of morning; for I felt that I too needed to be new-made and strong with the strength of youth. And here the perfumed atmosphere, the heavy draperies and weight of luxury, oppressed me.

I lifted the curtain and crossed the great room which was next mine. It was empty and silent; so was the wide corridor. I went softly on through the long corridors, till I reached that in which the gate opened to the garden. Through the iron grating I could see the gleam of the grass as I approached it. Ah, that beautiful garden! Oh, to bathe in that sweet water of the lily tank!

But the iron door was fast locked; I could but look through all the grass and sky and flowers, and drink the sweet air in through the narrow openings. Suddenly I saw Seboua approaching down one of the garden walks. He came straight to the iron door within which I stood.

"Seboua!" I cried.

"Ah, thou art here," he said, speaking in his rough tones. "The man and the child are alike. But no longer may Seboua be thy friend. I have failed, and I may not try again. I angered both my masters when you were a child; I could not hold you fast for either. Be it so; you must now stand alone."

"Can you not open the gate?" was all my answer.

"No," he said; "and I doubt if it will ever be opened for thee again. What matters it? Art thou not the favorite priest of the temple, the darling, the cherished one?"

"No," I answered, "I am that no longer. They already say I am mad. They will say it again to-day."

Seboua looked at me earnestly. "They will kill you!" he said in a low voice full of tenderness and pity.

"They cannot," I answered, smiling. "My Queen will protect me. I must live till I have spoken all she wishes. Then I care not."

Seboua raised his hand from where it had remained hidden in the folds of his black dress. He held in it a bud of the lotus flower that lay in a green leaf which seemed its bed.

"Take it," he said. "It is for thee; it speaks a language that thou wilt understand. Take it, and may good go with thee. I that am dumb, save in common speech, yet am worthy to be a messenger. That makes me glad. But thou mayst rejoice, for thou canst hear and speak, learn and teach."

Immediately he was gone; while he had been speaking he had pushed the flower to me through one of the narrow openings of the grating. I drew it towards me carefully. I held it now in my hands; I was content. I needed nothing else.

I went back to my room and sat down holding the flower in my hand. It was the same thing over again as when I had, long ago, a mere child, sat in this same chamber, holding a lily and gazing into its centre. I had a friend, a guide; a union with that unseen Mother of Grace. But now I knew the value of what I held; then I did not. Was it possible that it would be again taken from me so easily? Surely no.

For I could understand its language now. Then it spoke to me of nothing save its own beauty; now it opened my eyes, and I saw; it unsealed my ears, and I heard.

A circle was round me; such as had surrounded me when I had taught, unknowingly, in the temple. These were priests, white-robed, as those had been who knelt and worshipped me. But these did not kneel; they stood and gazed down upon me with profound eyes of pity and love. Some were old men stately and strong; some were young and slender, with faces of fresh light. I looked round in awe, and trembled with hope and joy.

I knew, without any words to tell me, what brotherhood this was. These were my predecessors, the priests of the sanctuary, the seers, the chosen servants of the Lily Queen. I saw that they had succeeded each to each, keeping sacredly the guardianship of the holy of holies since first it was shaped out of the great rock, against which the temple rested.

"Art ready to learn?" said one to me -- one whose breath seemed to me to be drawn from long-forgotten ages.

"I am ready," I said; and knelt upon the ground in the centre of that strange, holy circle. My body fell, yet my spirit seemed to soar. Though I knelt, I knew I was held up in soul by those who surrounded me. Henceforth they were my bretheren.

"Sit thou there," he said, pointing to my couch, "and I will talk with thee."

I rose, and turning to go to the couch, saw that I was alone with this one who spoke to me. The others had left us. He came and sat beside me, and began to speak. He poured into my heart the wisdom of the dead ages; wisdom which lives forever, and is young when the race of its early disciples is no longer even a memory. My heart grew green with the freshness of this ancient knowledge and truth.

Throughout that day he sat beside me and taught. At night he touched my forehead with his hands and left me. As I lay down to sleep, I recollected that I had seen none but my teacher since yesterday, nor had I tasted food. Yet I was not weary with learning, nor was I faint. I laid my flower beside me, and slept quietly.

When I awoke I started up, fancying some one touched my flower. But I was alone, and my flower was safe. A table stood near the heavy curtain which separated my room from the next; on this table stood food; milk and cakes. All yesterday I had not eaten: I was glad now of the food. I put my flower within my dress, and went to the table. I drank the milk and ate the cakes; and then with new strength in me, I turned to go to my couch, and there meditate earnestly on what I had learned yesterday, for I knew that these were golden seeds which must bear fruits of glory.

But I stood still and my heart sank within me; for again I was surrounded by the beautiful circle. He who had taught me yesterday, looked at me and smiled, but he did not speak. Another approached me, took my hand and led me to the couch, and I was alone with him.

Alone, yet not alone, and never to be any longer alone, for he took my heart and soul, and showed them to me in their nakedness, unsoftened by any fancied sanctity. He took my past, and showed it to me in its simple, dark, unbeautiful poverty; that past which might have been so rich. Until now, it seemed to me I had been living in unconsciousness. Now, I was guided through my own life again and bidden regard it with clear vision. The chambers I passed through were dark and dreary; some of them were full of horrors. For now I saw that I had been won by the magic which I myself had interpreted to Kamen Baka. Like the others, I had existed for desire and its satisfaction. And steeped in the joys of pleasure, of beauty, I had been as one intoxicated, and I knew not all that I did. Remembering my past, I saw the meaning of Seboua's words, which at the time I hardly understood. I had indeed been the darling of the temple, for when my body was steeped in pleasure, and silenced in the dim sleep of satiety, my lips and voice had become docile to the will of that dark mistress. Through my physical powers she made known her wishes, and obtained the service of those slaves who had bartered their all for the sake of gratification. By her fierce and terrible insight into the dark caverns of men's souls, she saw their needs, and with my speech she showed them how to obtain that which they longed for.

As I sat there, dumb and amazed at the visions which passed through my awakened memory, I saw myself first, a mere child, lulled from terror and alarm by pleasure. I saw myself within the temple, in its inner sanctuary, a creature helpless, a tool, a mere instrument played upon mercilessly. I saw myself later, a youth fresh and beautiful, lying unconscious on the deck of the sacred boat, rising in the frenzy of unconsciousness, and uttering strange words. I saw myself later, grown pale and faint, yet always the willing instrument, although the soul was beginning to stir and weary the body with its struggle; and now I saw that the soul had awakened, had touched its mother, the queen of light, and could never again be silenced.

The night came, and my teacher left me. None else had come to my chamber; no food had been brought to me since the early morning. I was faint with the terrible sights which I had seen in this short day. I determined to go in search of the food I needed. I lifted the heavy curtain that covered the archway, which led into the great room beyond. A door was there -- a massive door -- such as might close the portal of a dungeon. Then I understood I was a prisoner, and now that I had recovered from my weakness and excitement, I was to have no food. Agmahd had seen that my spirit had awakened; he had determined to kill it within me, and preserve the mere broken body for his purpose.

I lay down upon my couch, and fell asleep with the drooping lily-bud upon my lips.

When I awoke, one stood beside me whom I knew to be my new teacher. I had met his smile when I had seen the beautiful circle around me. I sprang up gladly; from him I looked, for encouragement. He came and sat beside me, and took my hand in his.

And then I knew that his smile was the light of a great peace. He had died in this chamber -- died for the truth. He called me brother, and suddenly I became aware that the roses of my life had blown and fallen and passed away forever. I had to live for the truth in the light of the pure spirit, and no suffering must make me afraid, and from the moment that his hand touched mine, I knew that no suffering could make me afraid. Until now, pain had always blinded me with terror, but now I knew that I could meet and grasp it with strong hands unterrified. I sank to sleep that night in an ecstasy; I knew not whether I waked or dreamed; but I knew that this my brother, whose physical life had been torn from him in the long ages past, had poured the strength of his fiery soul into mine, and that I could never lose it again.

CHAPTER VII.

On the morrow when my eyes opened my bed was surrounded by the beautiful circle. They regarded me with grave looks; I saw no smile on any face; but the infinite tenderness which I felt from them gave me strength. I rose and knelt beside my couch, for I saw that some great moment was approaching.

The youngest and the brightest of them all left the circle and approached me. He knelt beside me and clasped my hands, holding within them the faded lotus blossom which lay upon my pillow.

I looked up -- the others were gone. I regarded my companion. He was silent; his eyes were fixed on me. How young he was and beautiful! Earth had left no soil on his spirit. I knew that its stain must be on mine until in the course of ages I had washed it clean again. I felt a fear of this my companion, he was so white and spotless.

As we remained thus in silence a soft voice fell on my ear.

"Look not up yet," whispered he who knelt at my side.

"Twin stars of the evening, thou the last of the long line of seers who have made the wisdom of the Temple and crowned the greatness of Egypt with glory! The night is at hand, and the darkness must fall and hide the earth from the beauty of the heavens above it. Yet the truth shall be left with my people, the ignorant children of earth. And it is for you to leave behind you a burning light, a record for all time which men shall look at and wonder at in ages hence. The record of your lives, and of the truth which inspired you, shall go to other races, in other parts of the dim earth, to a people who have only heard of the light, who have never seen it. Be strong, for your work is great. Thou, my child of the snowy soul, thou hadst not strength to battle alone with the growing darkness; but now, give of thy faith and purity to this one, whose wings are smirched with stains of the earth, but who has gathered from that dark contact strength for the coming battle. Fight thou to the last for thy Queen Mother. Speak to my people, and tell them of the great truths; tell them that the soul lives and is blessed, unless they drown it in degradation; tell them there is freedom and peace for all who will free themselves from desires; tell them to look to me and find rest in my love; tell them there is the lotus-bloom in every human soul, and that it will open wide to the light unless they poison its roots; tell them to live in innocence and seek after truth, and I will come and walk in their midst, and show them the way into that place of peace where all is beauty and all are content. Tell them I love my children and would come and dwell in their homes and bring that content which is more than any prosperity, even unto these their hearths of the earth. Tell them this in a voice like a trumpet-call, which cannot be misunderstood. Save those who will hear, and make my temple once more a dwelling for the Spirit of Truth. The temple must fall, but it shall not fall in iniquity. Egypt must decay; but it shall not decay in ignorance. It shall hear a voice it cannot forget; and the words which that voice utters shall be the hidden heirloom of ages, and shall again be spoken under another sky, and herald the dawn which must break through the long blackness. Thou, my youngest, thou who art both strong and weak, prepare! The struggle is at hand; do not flinch. One duty is thine; to teach the people. Do not fear that wisdom shall fail thy tongue. I, who am Wisdom, will speak in thy voice. I, who am Wisdom, will be at thy side. Look up, my child, and gather strength."

I raised my eyes, and as I did so felt the tightened grasp of the hand of my companion who knelt at my side. I understood that he desired to give me courage to face the blinding glory which was before my eyes.

She stood before us, and I saw her as the flower sees the sun which feeds it. I saw her without disguise or veil. The fair woman who had soothed my boyish tears was lost in the god, the glory of whose presence filled my soul with a burning that seemed to me like death. Yet I lived; I saw; I understood.

CHAPTER VIII.

The beautiful young priest rose and stood beside me, while I still gazed upon the glory.

"Hear me, my brother," he said. "There are three truths which are absolute, and which cannot be lost, but yet may remain silent for lack of speech.

"The soul of man is immortal, and its future is the future of a thing whose growth and splendor has no limit.

"The principle which gives life dwells in us, and without us, is undying and eternally beneficent, is not heard or seen or smelt, but is perceived by the man who desires perception.

"Each man is his own absolute lawgiver, the dispenser of glory or gloom to himself; the decreer of his life, his reward, his punishment.

"These truths, which are as great as is life itself, are as simple as the simplest mind of man. Feed the hungry with them. Farewell. It is sundown. They will come for you; be thou ready."

He was gone. But the glory did not fade from before my eyes. I saw the truth. I saw the light. I remained, holding the vision with my passionate regard.

Some one touched me. I was awakened and stirred immediately by a sudden startling sense that the hour of battle had come. I rose and looked round. Agmahd stood beside me. He looked very serious; his face was less cold than was usual; there was a fire in his eyes such as I had never seen there before.

"Sensa," he said in a low voice, very clear, that seemed like a knife, "art thou prepared? To-night is the last night of the Great Festival. I need your service. When last you were with us you were mad; your brain was frenzied with the follies of your own conceit. I demand your obedience now, as you have hitherto given it, and to-night you are needed, for a great miracle has to be worked. You must be passive, else you will suffer. The Ten have determined that, unless you are obedient as hitherto, you must die. You are too well versed in all we know to live, unless you are one of us. Your choice lies plain before you. Make it quickly."

"It is made," I answered.

He looked at me very earnestly. I read his thought, and saw that he had expected to find me sad with solitude, sick with the long fast, and broken in spirit. Instead, I stood erect, unexhausted, filled with fearlessness; I felt that the light was in my soul, that the great army of the glorious ones stool behind me.

"I have no fear of death," I answered; "and I will no longer be the tool of men who are killing the royal religion of Egypt, the great and only religion of truth, for the benefit of their own ambitions and desires. I have seen and understood your miracles and the teachings which you give to the people; I will aid you no longer I have said."

Agmahd stood silent, regarding me. His face grew whiter and more rigid, as though cut in marble. I remembered his words that night in the inner sanctuary, when he said, "I renounce my humanity." I saw it was so, that the renunciation was complete. I could look for no mercy; I had to deal not with man but with a shape animated by a dominant and absolutely selfish will.

After a moment's pause he spoke, very calmly --

"Be it so. The Ten shall hear your words and answer them; you have a right to be present at their deliberations; you are yourself as high in the temple as I myself. It will be a trial of strength against strength, of will against will. I warn you that you will suffer."

He turned away and left me, moving with that slow and stately step which had so fascinated me when a child.

I sat down upon my couch and waited. I was not afraid; but I could not think or reflect. I was conscious that a moment was at hand which would need all my strength; and I remained without motion and without thought, reserving all the force I possessed.

A star rose in front of me, a gleaming star, which seemed to me shaped like the full-blown lotus flower. Excited and dazzled, I rose and sprang towards it. It moved from me -- I would not lose it, but followed eagerly. It passed through the doorway of my room into the corridor; I found that the door opened at my touch. I did not stay to wonder why it was unlocked, but followed the star and its light, which momently grew clearer, and its shape grew more defined; I saw the petals of the royal white flower, and from its yellow centre streamed the light that led me.

Swiftly and eagerly I went down the wide dim corridor. The great door of the temple was open and the star passed through it into the outer air. I too went out of the temple door, and found myself in the avenue of strange statues. Suddenly I became aware that there was a presence at the outer gate which called me. I fled down the long avenue with feet that knew not whither they led me; yet I knew that I must go. The great gates were locked; but, so close to them that I felt as though I were in the midst of it, was a great crowd, a mass of people. They were awaiting the great ceremony, the final glory of the festival, which to-night was to take place at the portals of the temple itself. I looked up and saw the Queen Mother standing beside me. She had, in her hand a flaming torch, and I knew that its light had formed the star which guided me hither. She it was, then, the light of life, who had led me. She smiled and was, in an instant, gone; I was alone with my knowledge; and the people, crowded together and plunged in ignorance, waited at the gates to be taught of the priests.

I remembered the words of my predecessor, my brother, who had given me the three truths for the people.

I lifted up my voice and spoke; my words carried me on as though they were waves, and my emotion grieve into a great sea upon which I was lifted; and as I looked into the eager eyes and rapt wondering faces before me, I knew that the people also were being swept along on that swift tide. My heart swelled with the delight of speech, of giving utterance to the great truths which had become my own.

At last I began to tell them how I had caught fire from the torch of holiness, and was resolved to enter upon a true life of devotion to wisdom, and to discard all the luxury which surrounded the priestly life, and to put aside forever all desires but those which belong to the soul. I cried aloud, praying all those who felt the light kindle within them, to enter upon a similar path, even in the midst of their life in the city or on the mountains. I told them that it was unnecessary because men bought and sold in the streets, that they should utterly forget and drown the divine essence within them. I bade them burn out by the light of the spirit the grosser desires of the flesh which held them back from the true doctrine, and sent them in throngs as devotees to the shrine of the Queen of Desire.

I paused suddenly with a heavy sense of weariness and exhaustion. I became aware that some one stood on each side of me; an instant later, I saw that I was surrounded. The ten high priests had formed a circle around me. Kamen Baka stood facing me, and fixed his eyes on mine.

I cried out aloud, standing there in the midst of this circle --

"O, people of Egypt, remember my words! Never again may you hear the messenger of the mother of our life, the mother of the God of Truth. She has spoken. Go to your homes and write her words on tablets, and grave them on stones, that people yet unborn may read them and repeat them to your children that they shall know of the wisdom. Go, and stay not to witness the sacrilege of the temple which is to-night to be committed. The priests of the goddess desecrate her temple with madness and lust and rich filling of all desires. Listen not to their words, but go to your homes and ask of your own hearts their lesson."

My strength was gone. I could utter no word more. With drooped head and weary limbs, I obeyed the menacing circle which surrounded me, and turned my steps towards the temple.

In silence we moved up the avenue, and entered the doorway. Within it we paused. Kamen Baka turned and looked back down the avenue.

"The people murmur," he said.

Again we moved on down the great corridor. Agmahd came out of a doorway, and stood before us.

"Is it so?" he said in a strange voice. He knew what had happened by the group he regarded.

"What shall be done?" said Kamen Baka. "He betrays the secrets of the temple, and excites the people against us."

"He will be a great loss," said Agmahd, "but he has become too dangerous. He must die. Speak I well, brethren?"

A faint murmur passed round me from lip to lip. Every voice was with Agmahd.

"The people murmur at the gate," repeated Kamen Baka.

"Go to them," said Agmahd, "tell them this is a night of sacrifice, and the goddess will herself speak with her own voice."

Kamen Baka left the circle, and Agmahd immediately took his place. I stood motionless, silent. I dimly understood that my fate was sealed, but I neither knew nor desired to ask in what way I was to die. I knew myself to be utterly helpless in the hands of the high priests. There was no appeal from their authority, and the crowd of inferior priests obeyed them as slaves. I, one alone, was helpless amid this crowd, and under this absolute authority. I did not fear death, and I thought it due to the Queen Mother that her servant should go to her with all gladness. It was my last testimony on earth to her love.

CHAPTER IX.

I was taken into my own chamber, and there left alone. I lay down upon my couch and fell asleep, for I was very weary, and I was not afraid, it seemed to me that under my head was the tender arm of the Lady of the Lotus.

But my sleep was short. I was plunged in a deep unconsciousness, that was too sweet for any dream to enter, when suddenly I was roused by a vivid sense of being no longer alone. I awoke to find myself in darkness and silence, but I recognized the sensation. I knew I was surrounded by a great crowd. I waited motionless with watchful eyes for the light, wondering what presences it would reveal to me.

Then I became aware of something I had never felt before. I was not unconscious, yet I was helpless as though without sense or knowledge. I was not motionless from indifference or peacefulness. I desired to rise and demand that light should be brought, but I could neither move nor utter any sound. Some fierce will was battling with mine, so strong that I was all but utterly mastered, yet I struggled and would not yield. I was determined not to be a blind slave, overpowered in the darkness by an unseen adversary.

It became terrible, this fight for supremacy. It became so fierce that at last I knew it was a fight for my life. The power that weighed me down desired to kill. What was it, who was it, that endeavored to draw my breath from out my body?

At last -- I cannot tell how long this intense silent warfare was waged -- at last the light came flashing round me on every side, as torch was lighted from torch. I saw dimly, for my sight was faint. I saw that I was in the great corridor before the door of the sanctuary, lying upon the couch where I had played with the strange phantom-child who first taught me pleasure. I lay upon it outstretched as I had lain on my own couch in sleep. As when it had been used in the ceremonial before, so now it was covered with roses -- large, rich, voluptuous, crimson and blood-red roses; thousands lay upon and about the couch, and their strong perfume overpowered my faint senses. I was clothed strangely in a thin white linen robe, whereon were embroideries, such as until now I had never seen hieroglyphs worked in thick, dark, red silk. At my side was a stream of red blood, which flowed from the couch into a beautiful vessel that stood upon the ground amid a heap of roses. I looked at this a while in idle curiosity, until on a sudden the knowledge came to me that this was my life's blood flowing away.

I raised my eyes, and saw that I was surrounded by the Ten. Their gaze was all fixed on me, their countenances were implacable. I knew then what that terrible will was with which I had done battle. It was their united resolution. Was it possible that I alone could struggle against this band? I knew not, yet I was not cast down. By one great effort I raised myself on the couch. I was already weak from want of blood, but they could no longer keep me silent. I rose to my feet, and stood upon the couch, and looked past them to the crowd of priests beyond, and further still to the throng of people, who waited close-packed at the entrance of the great corridor, to see the promised miracle.

I stood one instant, and thought I had power to speak, but I fell back helpless in my weakness. Yet a deep, profound, vivid happiness filled my soul, and suddenly I heard a murmur which rose and grew stronger.

"It is the young priest that taught at the gate! He is good, he shall not die! Let us save him!"

The people had seen my face and knew me. A great rush was made in the sudden enthusiasm, and the crowd of priests was pressed towards the couch, so that the Ten were unable to remain around it. And as the wave of struggle came up towards the holy of holies, many of the priests rushed into the vacant space between the couch and the door. And as they passed by in the confusion and surprise, I saw that the vessel which held my life was overturned and the red blood was spilled at the door of the sanctuary. The door opened; Agmahd stood within it; he looked majestic in his impenetrable calm. He gazed upon the surging crowd before him. At his cold gaze the priests grew calmer and gathered strength to withstand a little longer the onrush of the crowd. The Ten drew together again and with difficulty reached my couch and again formed a barrier about it.

But they were too late. Already some of the people had reached my side. I smiled dimly into their kindly rough faces. Tears fell upon my face and penetrated my heart; and then suddenly one caught my hand and clasped and kissed it, and wetted it with hot tears. Surely that touch thrilled my blood as did none other! Then I heard a voice cry: "It is my son -- it is my son that is dead. He is killed. Who will give me back my son?

It was my mother who knelt at my side. I strained my fading sight and saw her. She was worn and weary, yet her face was good. And as I looked I saw behind her, overshadowing her, the Lady of the Lotus, standing there in the midst of the people! And a gentle smile was on her mouth.

My mother rose, and I saw a strange dignity in her face.

"They have killed his body," she said, "but they have not killed his soul. That is strong, for I saw it in his eyes as this moment they closed in death."

CHAPTER X.

And on my dim ears fell the sound of a great sigh that came from the heart of the people. And then I knew that my body did not die in vain.

But my soul lived. It was not only strong, it was indestructible. It had worked out its time of misery in that pale form; it had escaped from the imprisonment which so long had held it fast. But only to reawaken in another, a strong, a beautiful and pure temple.

As the great surging crowd, driven to fury by the resistance of the priests, pressed on menacingly, some victims to its rage fell around me. Close to my lifeless form lay Agmahd, trampled to death by the enraged people, and at my very side against the couch on which I lay, Malen died, his breath pressed out from his beautiful form. As I hovered there in the strange consciousness of soul, I perceived these tainted spirits, dark with the lust and ambition which the Queen of Desire had kindled within them, forced into that circle of necessity from which there is no escape. Agmahd's soul fled with a fierce rush, like the dark passage of a bird of the night, and Malen that young priest, who had led me to the city, followed him swiftly. He, who obedient to the rules of his order had preserved the purity of the body, was black within with ungratified and ceaseless desire, but his body lay a broken flower, fair as a lily when first it opens its bloom on the surface of the clear water.

I felt that my Queen Mother held me fast in her tender grasp, that I might not escape from the scene of horror.

"Return to your work," she said; "it is yet unfinished. This is the new robe that you will wear, which will be your covering while you teach my people. This body is sinless, unstained and beautiful, although the soul that inhabited it is lost. But thou art my own. To come to me is to live through eternity in truth and knowledge. This is thy new garment."

I found that I was yet strong, not only in the spirit, but in physical life. New vigor came to me, my weariness was forgotten. I rose from the place, where but a minute since I had lain prostrate and lifeless. I rose, and standing hidden under the eyes of my Queen looked in horror at the scene around me.

"Go, Malen go in safety," she said. "Thou art to live in the hearts of the people, thou wilt be to them an image and symbol of the glory. Thou wilt be again a martyr to my cause, one who will forever be remembered with love by the dusky children of Chemi. Yet, though thou diest in my service, thou shalt teach for ages to come among the ruins of this temple; and though thou diest for me a hundred deaths, yet shalt thou live to teach my truths from the adytum of the new fane that shall arise in the distance of time."

I hurried away, and passed unnoticed through the surging, furious crowd. The statues in the avenue were thrown down; the temple gates were broken and destroyed.

My soul was sad and yearned for peace. I looked with longing eyes to the quiet country where my peasant mother dwelled; but she believed her son was dead. She would not know me in this new shape. I turned towards the city, now deserted by the maddened people.

A wild shout from a thousand throats tore the air. I paused, and looking back, saw that the unchecked vengeance of a generation betrayed by its teachers, had indeed fallen upon the glorious old temple. Already it was desecrated, and its sinful inmates sacrificed. Soon it would be a ruin.

I wandered through the empty streets of the city, and knew that here where I had drunk of pleasure, I must taste the joy of the worker. Here my voice must be heard unceasingly. The truth, long driven from the degraded temple, must find its home in the heart of the people, in the streets of the city. Long time must pass before my sin should fall from me, and leave me stainless, pure, prepared for the perfect life towards which I labor.

Since then, I live, change form, and live again; yet know myself through the long ages as they pass.

Egypt is dead, but her spirit lives, and the knowledge that was hers is still cherished in those souls who have remained true to the grand and mysterious past. They know that out of the profound blindness and inarticulateness of an age of unbelief shall arise the first signs of the splendor of the future. That which is to come is grander, more majestically mysterious than the past. For as the whole life of humanity rises upward, by slow and imperceptible progress, its teachers drink their life from purer founts, and take their message from the soul of existence. The cry has sounded through the world. The truths are uttered in words. Waken dark souls of the earth, who live with eyes upon the ground, raise those dim eyes and let perception enter. Life has in it more than the imagination of man can conceive. Seize boldly upon its mystery, and demand, in the obscure places of your own soul, light with which to illumine those dim recesses of individuality to which you have been blinded through a thousand existences.

Though a land of dusky forms, Egypt stands as a white flower among other races of the earth, and the hieroglyph readers of the old heretic writings, the professors, and the thinkers of the day will be unable to stain the petals of that grand lily blossom of our planet. They do not see the stem of the lily, and the sunlight shining down through the petals. They can see nothing of the real blossom, neither can they disfigure it by modern gardening, because it is out of their reach. It grows above the stature of man and its bulb drinks deep from the river of life.

It flowers in a world of growth to which man can only attain in his absolute moments of inspiration when he is indeed more than man. Therefore, though its lofty stem lifts itself from our world, it is not to be beheld or adequately described, save by one who is in truth so much above the stature of man that he can look down into the face of the flower, wherever it blossoms, whether in the East or the dark West. He will there read the secrets of the controlling forces of the physical plane, and will see, written within it, the science of mystic strength. He will learn how to expound spiritual truths and to enter into the highest self, and he can learn also how to own in life for of that higher self, and yet to retain life upon this planet so long as it shall last, if need be; to retain life in the vigor of manhood, till his entire work is completed, and he has taught the three truths to all who look for light.

THE END

BOOK SIX.
ILLUSIONS

PREFACE.

The following essay is an effort towards the freeing of our consciousness from the limitation in which it habitually dwells, and which exists only by means of certain illusions that are common to all men. To encounter illusions which are universal and which are practically unanimously accepted, is a task of great difficulty; it has, therefore, seemed both excusable and necessary to relate, as illustrations to the essay, various experiences. These experiences have come to a psychic sometimes in dream-consciousness and sometimes in trance-consciousness; they have been given under the guidance of a teacher or Master, evidently to make dear the illusions under which man labours. In the case of such guidance as this it is easy to turn the pages of the records of the past and therein again experience events which have occurred long since, and by this means obtain enlightenment. Man is so engrossed in that which is happening, when it happens, that he is unable to realize the methods by which events are brought about, and the relations existing between the visible and the invisible. If he could do so at the time it would be possible for him at any moment of acute experience to attain knowledge and freedom from illusion; but it is not possible because his whole being is absorbed either in pain or pleasure, and in desire. In the schools of the psychic world the history of each incarnation is used for reference, and as each spirit begins to acquire knowledge it is shown pages in its own past which illustrate and confirm that knowledge. The reading of such pages is the same to the spirit as the re-enacting of the events; and the forgetfulness of the present is similar to that which is experienced by a novel reader in reading an absorbing picture of life, with the added interest of feeling that you are yourself one of the actors in the drama. When the page is finished and the book of records closed the sensation of returning from the past to the present occurs, and the disciple is only then aware that he has been reading, not living. This overwhelming interest in the revelation of the long past is one of the experiences which await us across the threshold, and those who look for oblivion beyond physical death will be amazed to find not only intense activity and consciousness in the immediate moment, but in all the volume of the past which will be re-enacted in due course with full freshness of sensation.

That while we are dwelling in bodies upon the earth we are dwelling also in the midst of illusion is a very familiar idea to all students of occultism. Many believe that death is not only the doorway .to an increased intensity of life, but also to a state of greater reality. But these may find that when the body is laid aside the spirit is still within the dominion of desire, and this being so, illusion still surrounds it and holds it in a blinding and baffling atmosphere. It seems often as necessary for the spirit to have facts, which it is perfectly capable of perceiving for itself, pointed out to it, as it is for a child to be led and guided and shown the truth as to everyday physical life.

Guides and teachers come to those who are passing away from this life into other lives, and help them to escape from the illusion which makes the way so difficult. We need not fear for those who are freed from the physical state; from out of that which is to us now invisible come the .sure and certain friends to help them. When we can recover our memory of the periods between our incarnations one of the deepest feelings that will come to us will be gratitude to those who helped us in these times of perplexity. Always the spirits of men have had this unfailing aid, so that illusion has never been allowed to baffle those who desired to pass beyond it.

But now the whole race is reaching a point when it must put off childish things and become a man. It is no longer seemly that it should dwell in ignorance, only a few of its advanced members knowing the truth about the simplest facts of its condition. The order is given that by degrees much shall be explained in such a way that all who read shall understand. The things which require explanation are, many of them, of so very simple a nature that the best way of making them clear seems to be that of the relation of experiences. The bare statement of a fact, a condition, common to all men, but not observed by them, carries but little conviction with it, unless it is illustrated by some recital of events which reveal its truth. It is for this reason that certain experiences are included in this essay.

Some of the experiences are those of a psychic who has been able to bring across the threshold a memory of something just then seen, or something which has just then occurred, and which illustrates or explains the subject. There are many psychics in the world now who are able to retain more or less of the memory of their experiences on the other side of the threshold; it is to be hoped that some will think fit to record their own experiences and give them to the public. It is time for man to begin to know himself and not to remain in the dark, a seed hidden in the earth.

M. C. August 7, 1905.

THE FIVE ILLUSIONS.

Illusion 1. — That man is imprisoned in the body.
Illusion 2. — That the Unborn are unknown.
Illusion 3. — That there is any secret in the mind or memory of man.
Illusion 4. — That the earth exists apart from man.
Illusion 5. — That Nature is indifferent to Man.

ILLUSION I. That Man is Imprisoned in the Body.

It is an illusion that the spirit of a man is within his body all the time. It is only within it for certain periods of time. When within it consciousness, knowledge, perception, apprehension, are limited by its senses and its brain capacity. These literally form a cage in which the spirit is confined, and such confinement would be absolutely insupportable even to the most materialistic of human souls, were it maintained consecutively. But this cage is an instrument, and the spirit enters it to use it, as a hand is thrust into a glove. Moments of deep thought, amounting to unconsciousness, occur throughout the whole of life, from childhood to old age, and in these moments the spirit stands out from the body. Usually it remains beside it, but if the abstraction is deep and lasts some time it will go some distance if called by any interest. 'Sometimes it will do so in order to speak to another embodied spirit when outstanding, and communications are thus exchanged of a nature not to be reached by either spirit when within the limitation of the human body, and not to be expressed in human language. But this is only possible to those who understand the conditions of embodiment, and cannot be attempted by the persons who believe themselves to be encased in bodies from the time of the birth of those bodies to their death. The materialist believes that his body is himself; the religious man and the spiritualist frequently believe that they cannot be separated from their bodies while life lasts except during sleep or trance.

The truth is that this earth is the scene of a drama of which we only perceive scattered portions, and in which the greater number of the actors are invisible to us while we are inside our bodies. But in the moments of abstraction, of deep thought, of reverie, the spirit frees itself and uses its psychic senses. It is then among those who are invisible to its physical eyes, and if not entirely absorbed in the affairs of its physical body, is aware of their presence and can be as one of themselves. It is then that the spirit of man, during his physical life, grows and expands and develops, so that when released from the physical body he has outgrown it and casts it aside like a worn-out garment.

It is necessary to understand in what sense man is now a spirit and can claim the position and power of a spiritual being while living in the physical body. To this end some experiences are_ given which shed a light on certain states. The first of these, given in a vision, is a recollection of a past episode between two incarnations.

An Experience.

I was walking about in a large, fine old house, late in the evening. The corridors were very shadowy and, in some places, quite dark, but there were lights in the rooms, where people were talking a great deal. There was a sense of trouble and agitation everywhere, and I myself was in a very confused and distressed state of mind. I hardly knew what had happened; it seemed as if so many events had occurred, one coming rapidly after another, that I was left by them simply in a state of confusion. I wandered down a long corridor, pushing open the doors of the rooms and looking in; no one seemed to notice me and I felt very lonely and unhappy. And yet I knew that I was the mistress of the house, who should have commanded more attention than anyone else in it. I could not understand why I was so disregarded, and searched my confused memory in vain for the reason. My husband was in one of the rooms, sitting in the midst of a group of persons and talking very loudly and positively. His voice grated on my ears; it was harsh and sometimes very sneering. The sneers were often directed at me. I heard him say more than once " Lady Ann's wishes! What do they matter? I can't attend to those now — there is more important business to be done than attending to her wishes!"

I left the room when he sneered like this. That was my way. His sneers were very painful to me, and I had never been able to bear them. I went on down the corridor, my heart beating fast and aching sorely. What should I do? I knew my husband intended to carry out plans of his own which I entirely disapproved of, some of which would vitally affect the future of my boy, my one child — his heir, and my idol. I must find sufficient courage to encounter him, to state my views and to insist on their being respected. I was dreadfully timid, and overwhelmed by a feeling of loneliness. I could not go in among all those people who paid no attention to me. I would wait till I could "be alone with him. So I went away from the room he was in, down the shadowy corridor, and saw my little dog coming running to meet me. He had been my consolation in the early days of my loveless marriage, my one companion before my boy came. He was always a little friend and comforter to me. I stretched out my hands to him and he rushed to me with delight, jumping upon me and fawning on me. But suddenly he turned and fled, darting down the long corridor like lightning, and disappearing round the corner without a single glance back at me.

Then I knew! I stood still, amazed at the discovery I had made. I had been very ill, and had lain in delirium for some days. I thought I had recovered! Instead of that I must be dead, for evidently I was a ghost.

Now I understood what my husband had been saying about disregarding my wishes. There were many things which I had prevented him from doing which now lie would do without any interference. Of course, he would sneer at those who reminded him of my wishes.

Now that I really understood what had happened and what I was, strength and intelligence began to : in me and I lost all fear. It was a relief to know that I was free, that I was myself, a being in my own right, no longer under the dominance of the man who had made my life so dreary. That was the first feeling, followed by a sense of power, and freedom, and exultation. I went on down the corridor, moving lightly and easily, realizing for the first time that I no longer suffered, that my head did not ache, that my mouth was not parched and dry, that my limbs were not heavy and tired. My youth had come back to me and pain and sickness were gone. I turned the corner round which my dog had disappeared, and came to the servants' quarters. Here there were loud voices, and heated discussions were going on. I passed the door of the steward's room, which was closed; I heard the steward say in a raised angry voice, " I have to go — the master has given me notice to go! — it's a shame — but there's no help for it — "

"Hush!" said someone in a quivering voice. " I hear Lady Ann's silk dress in the corridor!" Instantly there was silence. I went on, trying hard to make no noise. But I could not manage it. I myself heard the sweep of my dress on the stone floor. It seemed strange, for I saw no silk dress, when I looked down. All that I saw were floating white draperies about me, soft and soundless. ^

"The steward to go! — all these changes to be made directly! — no one to guide my boy's life or protect his interests!"

I went swiftly back down the long corridors, past all the doors, caring not who heard my dress, or who was plunged into fear and silence by the sound; I reached the great oak staircase and hastened up to my boy's room. He should be asleep — it was growing late.

He sat in a chair by the window, stupefied with grief, paralysed by it. He was utterly alone, with no one to turn to, no one to comfort or help him. He knew not that I was there — he neither saw nor felt me. What could I do? I could not leave him like this. I must go to him. I must find some way of returning to the earth life I had left, and of being with him, to help him through the difficulties I saw before him and the bad influences that surrounded him. Oh, my son! This boy of fourteen was the one love of my life, for him I experienced the only passion of feeling my heart had ever known. I must and would return to him. The sense of power was growing in me; I felt capable of performing miracles in order to accomplish what I ^desired. But to be with him now, intangible, invisible, unfelt, was more than I could endure. I turned away and left the room.

It opened on to a large, wide corridor, carpeted and hung with family portraits. There was no light but that of the moon, which came in through a high window at the end. I saw that someone stood there, looking at me, evidently intending to speak to me. The figure was that of a tall man in a white dress, with an intensely black beard cut in the Egyptian shape, penetrating and most brilliant eyes, and wearing on his head some fine white linen in folds, coming to a point and with a blazing jewel in the centre. This was a very extraordinary figure to see in the thoroughly English surroundings. But he seemed as familiar to me as the surroundings themselves. I went towards him unhesitatingly.

"I see your desire," he said. " You want to return to earth to be with your twin soul, the one you love, who has come to you in this life as your son."

"Can you help me?" I demanded eagerly. " Will you? I must return to him. I cannot leave him."

"Passion is as strong in you as it was when you were born into ancient Egypt," he said, looking at me very coldly; " you fell from your place then because you would not be parted from the one you loved. Do you remember how he came to you then as your child, and died while still a baby and you would not accept the decree, but tried to follow him and killed yourself? Do you remember how you wandered in darkness, an earth-bound soul? And how I came to you when I left the earth life, and pitying you, enabled you to incarnate again in a human body?"

"I remember — indeed I remember," I said, and tears came to my aid. " How greatly have you pitied and helped me in the past. Will you not pity and help me now?"

"How many times have you been born and re-born since then!" he said, " and I, not once."

"Hut you are a master in life and freed from passion," I said. 1 am but a poor human soul."

"My love is greater than yours," he answered, " as my knowledge and power are greater. The one I love is at the foot of the Great White Throne, in deep peace; 1 know that is so, and that I must find my way there by tortuous paths, helping, climbing myself and helping others to climb. Therefore am I here. But I am told to help you on — not back, out of the earth darkness — not into it."

"I must go back," I said, with overwhelming power and passion, such as I had never been capable of while in my body. " I will not leave him."

"You could help him much more if you entered into a spiritual state than by remaining on the earth."

"I cannot do it. I cannot and will not go away from him," I said fiercely.

"Then it is the shortest way for you to reincarnate," he said; " you must be re-born as a child at once, and then you will again meet him during the life he is to spend on earth. You must understand that it is only by my help that it is possible for you to do this and to return to earth immediately. There is an opportunity at hand, and you shall take it if you choose."

"Yes!" I said, " yes, and I will thank you for ever."

He smiled a little at this — a strange, subtle smile, with no sneer in it at all, and yet a great deal of scorn. But it was tempered by a sweetness that overmastered all else in him, and therefore I could bear it.

"This is but a small debt of gratitude," he said, " compared to some that you owe me in the long past. Think nothing of this. If you will have it so you must have it so, though I would greatly wish it might be otherwise. Come, I will guide you. The first thing is that you choose whether you will be born as man or woman this time."

I was surprised — I faltered and hesitated. Perhaps as his friend and fellow-man I might be nearer his heart than as a woman. My recent experiences had mad§ me feel that women have but little power in the world and little chance of winning real regard from the men they care for.

"It is difficult for you to decide," he said, " I see that it is. You shall put the matter to the test. It is easy for you, if I show you how to do it, to enter into the bodies of the persons who are awake in this house, and then you will be able to tell whether you like the man's or the woman's body best."

I stood still, wrapped in thought on this subject, brought so suddenly before me. I found the idea strange.

"I did not know I could choose," I said. " Surely I have not been able to choose before?"

"Yes," he answered, " you have always chosen, as all do; but without thought. You chose just what you wished for at the moment, and that needs no reflection. You have had more experience now and you know that your choice is of importance to yourself and to another whom you care for more than yourself."

"I will be a man," I said, " then I can be his friend. A woman is never a man's friend."

"You speak out of the experience of your latest incarnation," he observed. "Wait until you have recovered more memories of the past; and it would be well, perhaps, to wait also for more experiences. In the meantime do not decide too hastily. Come and put the matter to the test, as I have suggested. Come down into the library, where your husband and his friends are sitting. They are just preparing to separate; but we have still time. Come."

He led the way and I followed him down the oak staircase, and along the corridor, to the lighted room into which I had already been more than once. We went straight in and stood in the midst of the group. The men had all risen and were speaking some last words. One was the family lawyer. He, I knew, would fetch his horse out of the stable himself, and ride home to his house in the neighbouring town. It was his custom to do this when he came, which he often did. He was very intimate with my husband, and I feared and distrusted him. He was nearest to us as we entered the room, and the Egyptian paused by him.

"Now," he said, " watch this man's spirit attentively. You will see that constantly, m moments of deep self-absorption, it stands out from his body, which remains at its command, like an automaton. The next time you see this you yourself step into his body, for the fraction of time for which he vacates it."

I obeyed. The man was standing near the door, ready to go out. He had said good night. His soul was absorbed in the effort to probe my husband's secret thoughts and intentions, and as he pondered deeply on this he stood outside his body, beside it and I saw the two figures plainly, with equal distinctness. I stepped into the body, as one might step into a carriage — but 1 could only remain there for a second — the pain of it was intolerable — and the spirit stepped back and pushed me out. The lawyer said " good night " again, and went quickly out of the room.

"What an awful cage for an immortal spirit to dwell in!" I exclaimed. " How coarse and hard and fierce and unbearable! Oh, never, never could I endure such an imprisonment."

"Look at the others, 1 ' said the Egyptian. " You will see the same thing occurs constantly. You are mistaken in supposing you are imprisoned in a body. You only enter it to use it, as you would enter a machine. It is literally only an instrument, but men do not understand this, because while they are inside it they are limited by its senses and power of apprehension, and they know nothing of the life they live apart from it. And that is going on the whole time. See, your husband is standing there in deep thought — he is apparently listening to what is being said to him, but he will not remember anything about it, because his spirit is standing outside his body."

I looked and saw that it was so. The two figures stood side by side.

"Speak to his spirit," said the Egyptian.

I shrank from doing this, but dared not disobey. When I approached him I entered again into the thought and intention which had made me desire so much to speak to him before I discovered that I was now a spirit.

"Robert," I said, " can I talk to you alone. There are some things I want so much to say to you."

The two figures abruptly became one. He looked round, with a dazed, half-frightened look.

"Heavens!" he said to himself, under his breath. " I felt as if Ann was here, I could swear I heard her speak."

"Watch for the next opportunity," said the Egyptian, " and step into his body."

"No! no!" I cried. " No, that I cannot and will not do! Let me go upstairs and see if my boy is awake. Let me try his — but not this one."

He made no objection. This time I led the way, hurrying along the corridor and up the stairs. I heard the sweep of my dress as I went, and I felt that my husband heard it, and that it filled him with horror and dismay. I was careless as to this, but I did not want to frighten my boy. I tried my utmost to repress the sound when I went into his room. But I could not. It arose from some law of being which I did not understand. Had I been in my body I could surely have held the skirt of my dress tight and close so that even if it rustled, at least it would not make that sweeping sound. But I could not do this, for I could not perceive or feel that which made the sound. I saw that my boy had tried to rest, had tried to sleep, and in vain. He had left his bed and was standing at the open window looking out. It was very warm, and the moon shone brightly on a lake that lay at a little distance from the house. I saw at once, without having to be told to look, that his spirit stood outside his body. Both were regarding the lake very earnestly. Both turned at the sound of my dress.

"Quick!" said the Egyptian, "Enter his body now."

I did so, without pause or hesitation, and stood within it, gladly, lovingly, longingly. It was my child's body, the shape 1 had borne, that I had nursed and reared, and always loved.

I experienced two fearful shocks during the second that I stood within. The first came from the brain; the deep pre-occupation which made the spirit stand out so long was the result of an intense desire to die and come to me. The physical eyes looked longingly at that bright moonlit lake, as a way of passing on to where I was. And the spiritual eyes looked chilly and unintelligently upon the same thing. The whole being was unenlightened and sunk in despondency. My poor, poor boy! Then, before the shock of realizing the mental and spiritual state had passed away from me, came the consciousness of the physical body. The developing manhood, the overwhelming longing for physical life and physical exercise and physical power and supremacy struck upon me like a great wave of pain. It pressed upon my spiritual body everywhere, from every nerve centre. I was thankful when the second of time had passed during which his spirit stood outside, and when it pressed back into its place and pushed me out.

"Oh, no! no!" I cried to the watching figure which stood beside me. " Never will I enter a man's body again. I must return to him, but I will return as a woman."

"Be it so," answered the Egyptian. " Your opportunity is at hand. Come with me, and I will show you where it is."

"Have I to go away from here?" I asked in dismay. " Surely I am not to leave the boy in this dreadful state of mind?"

The Egyptian paused and looked at .my son who had gone up to the window and was leaning out.

"He is falling into deep thought again," he said, " very soon the spirit will stand out. Go then and speak to it, touch it, give it the feeling that you are close to it."

I watched, and waited. Soon I saw the boy lean his head upon his hand and fall into a deep reverie.

, The spirit withdrew from the physical body and stood beside it. I went close to the spiritual shape and touched it — timidly — and with a strange sense of something like fear. For this was not the shape which I had borne, which I had nursed, and reared and loved. It stood taller than the boy, taller than myself. When 1 touched its hand it turned towards me and looked down upon me with a grave, sad scrutiny.

"Beloved," I whispered, " I am returning to the earth. Do not leave it! Wait for me! We shall meet again. Will you wait for me?"

"I will wait," came the answer, in tones of ineffable love and sweetness.

The boy moved slightly, drooping a little — sleep was overpowering the physical frame. Instantly the spirit was within it and lost to my sight. I saw again one figure only — my son — worn out — utterly exhausted. He wearily turned from the window and went towards his bed. There he lay down and very soon the opiate of sleep came upon the tired brain.

"Come!" said the voice of the Egyptian.

I found myself held, impelled, guided, and was obliged to yield to the guidance. We were immediately outside the house, passing swiftly through the warm air of the still summer night.

ILLUSION II. That the Unborn are Unknown.

When a new-born child opens its eyes upon this world there is often what seems like a strange familiarity in its gaze, to those who are watching it. The mother will say that these new eyes remind her of some other eyes now closed for ever; the father will see a family likeness in the unformed features which is no likeness, since none is yet possible. It is the recognition of the spirit which looks out upon them that gives them this confused sense of a likeness. Most often all have come together from a far past and have been together through a long interval between the incarnations; and then the familiarity is intense and very bewildering to the unaided physical consciousness. Sometimes a soul from another sphere of life has arrived in the new-born child, and the development of its character will, in that case, be a source of great surprise and wonder to the parents. But when this is so the acquaintanceship is begun further back in the history of its arrival than is generally supposed, even by students of occultism, because only a few as yet are aware of the fact that the spirit of man is outside his body almost as much as it is in it, and that during the outstanding he is conscious of the spirits near him. Those who have lately passed away can speak to the spirits of those they have left, face to face in these moments of outstanding, and so can the spirits of those about to arrive. The soul which comes from another sphere of life is drawn by the attraction of its desire for re-birth into the neighbourhood of its parents long before the actual birth takes place. The ideas conveyed by the words accident and chance exist only for the materialist. The student of psychology sees law and order more and more plainly every day, and sees that each incident is evolved and that nothing can be accidental. Of whatever order the spirit is which enters a new body it enters by the well-known road, and obeys the laws governing human birth. If it is seeking fresh experiences, in a race and a country hitherto unfamiliar to it, it is gradually drawn there, long before its birth and dwelling among the incarnated spirits becomes acquainted with them during their outstanding moments.

Otherwise the human life would be too strange to be useful in the short space of one incarnation. Vital differences of thought and feeling have, of course, to be fought out during that space, but there must be a certain familiarity established before this or the climax would not arrive at the required time. The young man who takes a separate course from his father and shows good reason for so doing, has known before his birth that this would be necessary. The spirits have become acquainted as equals, and have weighed and measured each other. Often in such instances the father is aware that his child is of another order, and will offer to his creed of life a steadily growing opposition, from that child's infancy. Sometimes the order is higher, sometimes lower. But if it is entirely different the fundamental opposition will be felt from the first. It does not come as a shock or a surprise. It makes itself known as a familiar fact.

The formation of family ties involves a protracted and difficult exercise of powers possessed by the spirits of men. Before each incarnation the spirit has to discover what conditions will best suit its needs, and will best aid its growth and then to search these out. In the search for these it is drawn by the mystic threads of affinity and attraction. That family life should be a state of mutual helpfulness made possible by natural affection, is the scheme on which it is based. When deep hatred or cold dislike exist among blood relations the law of Karma has been imposed upon the original scheme, and repulsion has compelled souls to come together instead of separating, in order that they shall make straight that which they have rendered crooked in a former incarnation together. When we see the inborn hatred, or dislike, die out in time, then we may know that these two have become ready for a better state, in which mutual toleration has become possible. When we see one of the two deliberately put aside the painful feeling caused by the other, and not allow it to interfere with the affairs of life, we may recognise one who is ready to take a great step forward, and who will either be born next time into a family bound together by pure love, or be free to take a long rest from re-birth. It is the laying down of personal desire and passion which is a chief agent in giving such freedom. The second part of the experience related in the last chapter illustrates how personal desire, which seems like love to the soul which feels it, draws that soul back to the earth. This soul, having in past incarnations learned the help of an advanced teacher, is given the chance of immediate re-birth in order to live out this personal desire, instead of becoming an earth-bound soul, a haunting ghost. Her relations with her parents show in what way the unborn become known.

The Second Part of the Experience.

When I went out into the soft air of that longpast summer night, guided and led by the Egyptian spirit, I suddenly sank away, and left him. I returned into the normal consciousness of this present incarnation, and at first my only feeling was that of great exhaustion and fatigue. The vividness of the recollection overpowered the consciousness of the present, and for some time I believed that this was a new experience into which I had been suddenly taken, and that I was now going into a new incarnation, but by degrees I understood, and I realized that I had been sent back into my present body in order to understand. The object of the memory of this experience between the incarnations being so clearly recalled to me has that I might be able to remove from my material mind the illusions that man is imprisoned in his body, and that the unborn are unknown. When I had thoroughly grasped the fact, a new one to me, that man is continually freeing himself from his body, as had been shown to me, I was again called completely out of mine and found myself close beside the Egyptian spirit. He had brought me into another large country house, but a much more beautiful one than that in which I had lived. This was a splendid old English mansion, and I recognised art and the spirit of art on every side. I knew the house; it was one I had visited; but I had not appreciated its beauty then as I could now, when I recognised the spiritual power and meaning of the architecture and carvings. The brooding spirit of love overhung the whole house; no discord had ever entered here — it had always been a house of love. I felt that it was now more deeply that than ever before. The Egyptian led me up the stately stairway to a great room. It was unfamiliar to me, I had never been into it before. He led the way, drawing me in through the beautifully carved door. I saw a splendid room flooded with moonlight which streamed in through a great window. The window was wide open and two persons stood beside it looking out. We went across the room and stood close beside them. A very fair young woman, in a soft white gown, leaned her white arms upon the window sill,

"This is more beautiful than anything we have seen abroad," she said, in a low voice, almost like a whisper. She seemed awed at the beauty that lay before her.

"And this is home," said the man who stood beside her. " All that you see is mine and yours."

She gave a long, low sigh as of ecstacy, and I saw her spirit pass from her body and float away a little in the moonlight, as she leaned forward in absorbed contemplation.

"Enter her body quickly," said the Egyptian.

I did so, and through her eyes the scene was all strange to me and very wonderful. I looked upon a great garden, a wide green lawn, and a rosery at the side of it. The roses were trained upon arches and all the arches were covered with masses and clusters and wreaths of flowers, and the scent of them came to me so rich and strong in the still summer night that I almost fainted with the sense of the sweetness and the joy of it. And beyond the garden was a wide park — and then great woods — and a gleam of water shining in the moonlight in the far distance. And all this was his — and mine — I was his wife, his bride; my brain burned with the wonder of it. My heart throbbed with the joy of it.

I stood back by the Egyptian, pushed out by the spirit of this lovely woman — she returned to look with love at her husband. She was a complete stranger to me, both spirit and body. I had never known her before.

"This is your opportunity," said the Egyptian. " She will be your mother. You must speak to her spirit when next it comes out of her body. But now look at this man, who is your father. You know him."

Yes, I knew him well. He had long been one of my friends. I did not know of his marriage because I had been lying ill when he met and married this woman, who had suddenly taken possession of his heart. I seemed to remember vaguely some talk of it in the first days of my illness. And now he had brought her home.

As we stood watching them he turned towards her, and the depth of his love acted like a drug upon him so that his spirit withdrew completely from his body, and drew much nearer to hers than it ever could while within the body. They mingled like two flames. His body stood upright, immoveable, his eyes fixed on her. I passed into it and became aware of the thoughts which had been in his brain. He wanted a son, an heir, to inherit this great estate and lovely house. It was only natural. I recognised, as I paused within his mental sphere, that it was both natural and right. But again I felt the intolerable pressure and the fierceness of the man's physical body; and I stepped back, again crying out to my guide and teacher that I must be born again as a woman.

"Be it so," he said. " You must stay here now with these two, and dwell with them, and you must talk to them when they are in the spiritual state. Your choice will clash with your father's wish. The decision will depend on which of you has the strongest will power. I leave you to this task. Farewell."

He was gone — I had not said farewell, for I was going to entreat him to stay — but when I looked round to speak he was gone. I soon forgot that I had no longer a guide at hand — I was drawn by the irresistible power of the forces which had been set in motion. I returned to the two to whom I now belonged, and passed continually within their bodies when they left them, becoming aware of all their thoughts and feelings. I entered into their love idyl as though it were my own. The love and passion beat upon my heart, rousing its deepest feelings and memories. The heavy fragrance from the rosery in that garden spoke of love, and for ever the scent of roses speaks to me of love.

At last I learned how to speak to them, spirit to spirit. I accomplished this first when both were asleep, before their spirits went too far away. For a long while we talked there, and they accepted me as the one sent to them. But my choice of a woman's shape brought a faint cloud upon their happiness. I would not, could not yield in this; and my will power proved to be the strongest. I was full of power and the determination to accomplish what I desired. It seemed to me a trifling thing that this man should be without an heir. When he had his love and perfect happiness to make life beautiful for him what could such a detail matter? I was starving, without love — without happiness. It might seem that this being so I could have yielded on such a point as in what shape I was to have the opportunity of seeking them. But to me that did not seem to be so. I felt that it was I, I myself, who would suffer if compelled to enter upon a physical life in a body entirely unsuitable to me; whereas of my friend and father I only demanded a surrender of ambition, something which would not affect him hourly and momently as the mode of incarnation would affect me.

So it ended by my will being the conquering one. A change resulted from this — my father seemed to draw a little away from me when our spirits met; while my beautiful mother clung the closer. I began to love her very much, and the feeling grew so intense as time went on that it became almost painful. To her I know it was truly so — it became a delicious agony for her to think of me with her physical brain or to clasp me close with her spiritual arms.

When I opened my new physical eyes and looked round the beautiful room in which I and my mother lay, I recognised that room in which I had first seen her, when the moonlight streamed in and the air was heavy with the scent of roses. And I recognised her and saw that she was more lovely than ever. And when we both fell into a deep sleep of happiness we were together as equals, as close and dear friends in the spirit.

My father came and stood beside us, his face transfigured by love. His spirit stood out from his body while he looked upon us, and our spirits came close to his and spoke. But he did not hear us distinctly, for he was much absorbed in the affairs of the material world just then. He longed for the time when my mother would be well enough for him to talk to her and consult her; and deep down in his heart, unexpressed and kept very quiet, was still the great wish that I had been born a boy. His desire had been overmastered, but it was still there.

ILLUSION III. That there is any Secret in the Mind or Memory of Man.

It is only in the moments of complete embodiment that men have the idea of secrecy. It is one of the ideas which belong exclusively to the state of physical limitation. Outside the human brain and its narrowness the notion is inconceivable.

Many persons are aware of this as a broad statement, and believe it to mean that while a secret can be retained so long as the physical life lasts, it must be surrendered on the other side of the grave; and some determine therefore, to keep their secrets the more safely so long as the power to do so is theirs. Herein is the illusion. There is no such power. If the spirit was imprisoned in the body there would be, and the one illusion is based upon the other. No materialist is able to imprison himself in matter, though his belief in such imprisonment be never so profound. His spirit passes in and out of its physical instrument according to the universal law. The materialist is unaware of this, in the same way that all men are unaware of laws which govern both spiritual and physical life. We unconsciously maintain our equilibrium upon the earth, and we unconsciously maintain our position in the spiritual sphere to which we belong. Matter is opaque to the physical vision, and a secret can be hidden within the brain of a man as a body can be hidden within the ground. But spirit is translucent and luminous, dwelling in light and visibility, and the spiritual being possesses sight which penetrates through all opaqueness; or, rather, to express it more correctly from the spiritual point of view, for which opaqueness does not exist. The veil of matter is an illusion; thus it is that even materialists who keep the secrets of their lives close hidden find themselves in dream consciousness to be discussing them quite openly with their acquaintances, sometimes with friends, and sometimes with the enemies from whom they . would most wish to hide all facts concerning themselves. This occurrence in dream life is one of the things which gives men the idea that dreams are the opposite of reality, and the sheer topsy-turveydom of an exhausted or excited brain. The truth is that the brain has recorded something of what has happened while the spirit was free from its physical limitations in sleep. But during the waking hours the same condition exists, only it is perpetually checked and kept from manifestation by the action of the physical brain. Two men will sit in diplomatic conversation, each possessed of facts which must be kept secret from the other, and this secrecy will be apparently preserved fully. But later on, when something has been revealed, one of these men will say, " I always thought so. I felt it that day when I was talking to him, and all the time that he denied it so absolutely I felt sure he was not telling the truth." Such feelings and convictions are often expressed, and sometimes the convictions are so strong that they are acted upon. Then the man who has so acted is credited with great acumen, or with intuition, or even with the power of thought-reading. The idea of thoughtreading is a clumsy one — there is no need to read thoughts. When the spirits of men stand out from their bodies, they naturally interchange thought. Such interchange is a part of the common condition of the spiritual being, which knows nothing of separation or secrecy, darkness oi° opaqueness, time or space, death or decay, or of any of the illusions which belong to man's material mental state and exist only within its limitations. The facts of which each spirit is aware are the property also of the others, when outstanding and communicating, and those facts are vital things, such as the motives for action and the direction in which each spirit is going, whether towards good or ill, love or hatred. These spiritual facts, affecting the spiritual life of each being, are attached to the details of material life, and the thought about these details is visible and superficial and instantaneously interchanged.

"I was certain he never meant what he said," one human being will say of another; from the spiritual standpoint it would be correct to say?

"His spirit told mine that he did not mean what he said to me in the physical state."

The complicated web of human living is in truth a game, and all the men and women only players; their spirits are behind the bodily instruments, and use them in much the same way that players . at cards use the cards. The great men, the men who lead and rule, know this well, though they might not be able to put it into words. They use the language of the eye in preference to that of the tongue, because it is less material and confusing. The spirit looks out through a physical window, it is true, but it is the actual spirit which looks out. It is hampered and limited by the narrowness of the physical vision which is entirely baffled by the physical illusion of opaqueness, but it speaks directly to another spirit when the communication is from eye to eye. And the spirit reveals itself of necessity through these narrow windows when it looks forth from them. No liar and no person who is hiding secrets has a straightforward glance, as everyone knows; and that is for the very simple reason that they do not wish to reveal themselves.

The memory of man is a great storehouse, filled to overflowing with the wonderful experiences of incarnated life, of life between the incarnations and of the thoughts and feelings brought both from above and below — from that depth of material life to which passion and desire take us, and from the Great White Throne before which we do obeisance in our high moments of inspiration and adoration. Nothing is lost or forgotten, or passed by. The inexorable record is made under all conditions, and persists as ceaselessly as does our consciousness of existence. It is the working of a spiritual law which cannot be evaded or altered. With every breath a man draws he unconsciously writes down an indelible record of his action and thought during the second of time. He cannot exist, as man or as spirit, without making this record. These records, both of the immediate past and the far past, are continually spread out for the survey of the angels and powers which guide and help the race; their glances pass over them as the glances of generals pass over maps of countries and of battlefields, to see what has been done and what can be done.

When these records are opened for the enlightenment of the man himself the experience is a very severe one, until he is so advanced as to be superior to suffering. Because in recalling the past he literally lives it over again in all its keenness, and often he is aware that his actions of the past time were wrong and inexcusable, according to his present knowledge, yet he is carried away by the force of recollection into all the fever of the passions which misled him. He feels the temptation again, but he pities himself in ignorantly succumbing to it, as the angels and guiding powers pitied him at the time. And not only is the record of his error indelibly written in the spiritual sphere to which he belongs, but the mark of it is upon his own nature and character. He may superimpose other marks, but he cannot eradicate this one. Acts disintegrate with the passage of time, as forms do, but the mark made by them upon the spiritual nature has helped to shape it and must, therefore, of necessity remain. At the end of the incarnations, when the spirit is freed from embodiment and all material conditions, it stands forth finally in the shape which has been gradually evolved by the acts # and thoughts done during embodiment and in material conditions. Not any one of these is eliminated or omitted; by the very nature of man's spiritual life each tiling done and every thought which has inspired action has its .share in the formation of the spiritual shape. Those thoughts and actions which are definitely non-spiritual hamper the growth of the spirit and lessen its power, so that a human being who is strong upon this plane will find himself a child, a helpless infant, in the spirit. This fact destroys the possibility of a man's life being really a secret one. There # are men and women who wear masks throughout their whole physical lives, and who believe all their evil deeds are hidden. This is an illusion. There may be no physical proof, or mental knowledge, of the actions of these persons, but the spirits of other men and women know them for what they are. They are seen, in the spiritual state, (which they are in during the continual moments of outstanding from the body as completely as when the body is dead), to be helpless infants becoming more helpless as they persist in materiality of life. It is because the spirits of other men and women perceive the spiritual helplessness of evil men that they are often regarded with indifference, or at all events, without fear, in spite of their apparent possession of power. For the spirit of man knows the truth, and cannot be deceived; to a spirit no secrets exist. This illustrates the supreme fact that good is stronger than evil. What we know as evil is materiality, and can only exist in a material condition. The man who has been a monster of cruelty and wickedness and who has, perhaps, had power over human life, has created no spiritual shape and has no power in the spirit. He is like a plant which has chosen to remain under the ground instead of growing up out of it into the air and sunshine. His infant shape, the spiritual seedling sown in the earth-world, is still all that he has outside matter. The victims of a tyrant in the earth-world may very naturally regard him with pity and contempt, if they are growing spirits and he is a mere embryo. Evil is the negation of spirit and the absence of spiritual life; therefore, it will all pass away with the material illusion to which it belongs and of which it is a part. Therefore is it so necessary that all souls shall be given enough time and help to enable them to grow into spiritual beings and enter upon real life when the race is freed and matter has disappeared. Therefore is it that the growing spirit, the one who has entered upon the open road, is fearless and strong under all circumstances, however adverse. Physical conditions are adverse because adversity is essential for growth; and outside physical conditions no harm can befall him. If he is injured by an evil enemy that enemy can only act within the earth-world. If the evil man has obtained power to create an evil shape which will exist after his physical death and work evil to successive generations, as is sometimes the case, that evil shape can only affect the material brain of those it injures, can only destroy their physical • bodies, and can never itself pass beyond the boundary of the earth-world. It is essentially a material thing. And it can only affect those whose own tendency is earthward. When the spiritual sun shines upon it, black magic, with all other evil, disappears like the morning mists before the physical sun. Black magic consists solely in obtaining increased physical power, and in securing the help of beings who live within the earth world, but who are invisible to man's physical vision. Some of these beings are malignant and opposed to the spiritual growth of man. But many more are willing and glad to help him on in his progress, and all who are growing are sure of their aid, and obtain it constantly without making any of the efforts necessary for the evil soul which requires the aid of evil powers. The invisible hordes of non-human beings, who are associated in the affairs of the earth world, are thus associated for his benefit, the whole effort being made that he may grow; therefore, it is evident that in their ranks good is stronger than evil, and that it must be so.

As an illustration of how a merely worldly life affects the spirit of a man the following experience is given.

An Experience.

In dream-consciousness I was shown the passing of a relation, a man who had led an entirely worldly life. He had not done evil, but neither had he done good, being aware only of the physical existence. His mother had come to the earth world to help him pass out from it, and it was she who showed me his passing. With the help of some of the friendly beings who are invisible to man's physical sight, she had carried him up into the ethereal world. I saw that his body lay upon the bed on which he had died, and was not yet put into its coffin; and his spirit, wearing all the appearance of the man as he had been upon earth, was gazing in amazement and with delight upon a scene of great activity. A procession was passing down a wide road, amid the most beautiful surroundings, and many were seated in gardens and balconies by the roadside looking at it as it passed. Among these was the spirit of this man newly come from earth; he looked incongruous in the crowd of bright and lovely shapes, wearing exquisite draperies and jewels. But he was entirely happy, pleased beyond words to find that he was in a place so full of life and activity. His feeling, as he looked, was " I never thought it would be like this!"

His mother said to me, " When this is over I shall take him away into a safe place, and then he will have to begin to move about without my help."

Some time later she came to me and said, " Would you like to see how he is getting on? Will you come with me?" I went with her and found him in a wild woodland place trying to walk about. I understood that his mother was constantly near him and guarded him from harm. He had lost the appearance of the man I had known upon earth. He was a young boy, full of desire of life and movement. His whole consciousness was filled with a sense of great perplexity because he found himself unable to use his limbs. He was without power. He could only walk a few steps, he could not lift his arms, when he sank to the ground he had the greatest difficulty in lifting himself up again. He had entirely neglected the development of the spiritual life during the incarnation which was just over, and consequently he was without any strength or power. His mother told me that some of his previous incarnations had been less earthly in character, and that during them he had grown this shape, which was full of promise though powerless. He did not suffer, except from perplexity and disappointment. His efforts to move were continual; he knew that he was in a place and condition in which life was most desirable; yet it was impossible for him to enter into that life. He paced a few yards up and down, with difficulty, looking the while longingly at the exquisite landscape which stretched on every side, and at the gleaming spires and roofs of a distant city. But his life was limited by his powers. He was guarded, and watched by the spirit that loved him; but more than this she could not do without infringing the immutable laws.

"What will happen to him next? 55 I asked her.

"He will remain like this," she said, " sometimes falling into unconsciousness here. Then he will revisit the earth, and be among his children and his friends, although invisible to their physical senses. The desire to return to earth life will awake and grow until at last he will be strong enough to seek for the opportunity for rebirth. His next incarnation will, alas, be an obscure and unfortunate one; he has not the power to secure anything else. I can only hope adversity may teach him what he has not learned from success and prosperity."

This experience shows very clearly how impossible it is for the memory of man to hold any secret of his past or to hide any fact of his earth life from the knowledge of others. In the period between the incarnations the spirit is seen in the shape and state produced by those facts, and on reincarnating the conditions and circumstances of his incarnation are all ordered by them. It is the past which makes the present, and the present which makes the future.

The following experience gives some idea of what effects are produced upon the spirit of man by evil deeds, and how the marks of these deeds are easily seen and recognised.

An Experience.

The vision I am about to relate came to me at night, but I was not asleep, for I had not the time to fall asleep naturally. The instant that I put out the light I became aware of a presence beside me, and saw a face close to mine. It was an Oriental face, thin, eager, with the most piercing, commanding eyes looking into mine. A slender hand beckoned to me, and 1 rose instantly and went forth from my body into another state of consciousness.

Immediately I was horrified by a dreadful spectacle. I found myself by a roadside, and all around were beautiful things I wished to look at, but I could not because of the awful thing which came into view and which I was compelled* to look at steadfastly, though I longed to turn away or close my eyes. A vehicle passed by, coming along the road by which I stood. It Wets drawn by a stumbling horse which continually fell and rose again and went stumbling on. The man who was driving it seemed in great distress — in greater distress than was the horse itself — and yet I saw in a flash of horror that one of the horse's legs was quite short, cut off, a bleeding stump "most shocking to see. How it could run at all was the amazing thing.

My guide's voice said to me very emphatically —

"We are the things we make." He then stood beside me, and as the strange, jolting, halting vehicle passed out of sight, lie explained the meaning of it. I found it so difficult to retain this in such a way as to bring it into my physical consciousness that I clung to him and he returned with me. As I awoke from the trance in which I had lain I found him standing beside me, and he endeavoured to place some of what he had told me in my physical brain.

He said that the man who drove the vehicle I had seen and who was trying to get from one place to another with such inadequate help, had been a vivisector, and that by his misuse of animal life he had created this bad servant which he had to use. He could have no better horse than this because of his deeds in earth life — this I understood, but what seemed so strange to me was that it appeared that the vivisector was the horse, as well as the man. It was a limitation of power which was a limitation in himself. The maimed animal was not the soul of any animal he had tortured on earth. My guide told me that those who love animals and would give them freedom find, on other planes of consciousness, free animals who are their glad and willing friends and servants, ready to use powers for them — birds which are messengers, horses and great eagles able to carry the spirit through space from sphere to sphere.

To the vivisector only maimed and inadequate help of this order is possible; and he is hampered and limited by this until he has outlived his evil deeds and they have disintegrated. And he can never hide from any other spirit that he is the evil thing he is because it is apparent whenever his spirit has need of the help of the friendly beings which encompass the spirits of men.

ILLUSION IV. That the Earth exists apart from Man.

When the subject of this chapter was given to me I heard a voice speaking as I awoke from a deep sleep. And it said

"Any space, of any size, is limited and small, directly you begin to walk up and down in it. But a knife edge is wide enough to progress upon."

I wondered what kind of space could be referred to, and immediately the answer came. " I speak now of the earth. The soul of the race has called the earth into existence, as the individual man gets a house built to live in. It was necessary for human experience that there should be a material centre. But the man who gets a house built for himself knows he will only live in it for a time; that others will follow him, and that in due course the house will become old and eventually crumble away. So it is with the earth. Limit yourself to it and it becomes a prison. But that prison must of itself, in the nature of things, cease to be. Man must learn to walk from it, not up and down in it, before that day comes."

Much more was said to me, which I must put into my own words, for I cannot recollect exactly those which were used. It was shown to me that the kind of house which a man requires to live in suits himself, as a man, and no other being. Other animals may live in it, but they only use some portions of its construction. Man alone appreciates the special arrangement which is known to him as a dwelling place. And the two chief purposes served by such a dwelling place, are, first the keeping of the human body at the desired state of equilibrium between heat and cold and, secondly, the supplying it with specially prepared food. This secondary purpose is a mere matter of supplying an engine with suitable fuel; the engine is only constructed to last for a certain length of time, and when that time comes to an end the need of fuel evidently ceases. This, of course, occurs at death, and the need is non-existent between the incarnations; but the spirit is often during the periods between the incarnations fully within the sphere of desire and under the influence of the pairs of opposites, The sensations of heat and cold are the most material form taken by the pairs of opposites, and necessitate a material dwelling place for each man, in which he may keep each of these enemies at bay in turn. Good and evil, love and hate, attack the spirit of man as cold and heat attack his body; and when the spirit of the race submitted itself to the- fierce ordeal of encountering the pairs of opposites, it became necessary for a dwelling place to be formed in which the great struggle might take place under protection and with help on all sides.

The illusion is not that the earth exists, but that it exists apart from man and his need of it. Were the whole race capable of lifting itself suddenly in an instant of time, above the sphere of desire, the earth would crumble to pieces and vanish away. The forces and beings which are engaged in serving the desire of man by keeping it together for him would be released from their task and immediately all that which is visible to our physical sight would change its character permanently. The solidity and hardness of matter which appear to the physical man among the most absolutely certain factors that present themselves to his consciousness, are complete illusions produced by the influence of invisible beings on the brain of the man himself. The qualities of solidity, hardness and straightness are less easily apprehended by a psychic who is accustomed to consciously leave his body, than by the man who believes himself to be imprisoned.

Once, on returning from a long absence from the body I stood beside it perplexed because the bed on which it lay did not appear to me to be there. And I heard a voice say, " Wait — and I will make the iron and wood hard for you." And then I became aware of solidity and firmness, even before entering my body; and I knew that the change effected was not in the iron and wood, but in me. I had been so far from the material sphere that the illusions which belong to it and which must be accepted while the spirit is acting within a physical body, had faded away from me. It was necessary that I should resume them before I entered the physical body or else I should not be able to act like a sane human being when within it. All the sane actions of a spirit in the body are based upon these illusions and the consistent acceptance of them.

Practice in obtaining temporary release from these illusions, while the body is in a state of deep quiescence, or trance, is a mode of rapid development known to all occultists. The link with the body, and the control over it, must be preserved intact throughout the trance, otherwise the value of the experience is lost. It is common for all persons, whether conscious psychics or not, to pass far beyond the sphere of illusions during the sleep of the body. But very rarely is any knowledge of this brought back into the physical brain, the veil of oblivion falling between the consciousnesses as the spirit passes from the one to the other. The falling of this veil can be seen and felt by the spirit which is acquiring knowledge; it resembles the quick closing of a door. The sensation of passing from the one full life to the other full life and of the one being absolutely shut off from the other in a fraction of an instant of time, is one of the most wonderful experiences in the early stages of development. But the great wonder is when the falling of the veil can be arrested ever so little, and the spirit can look back across the threshold and bring even a faint memory of that which it is leaving into the consciousness to which it is entering. Illusions then begin to lose their power over the spirit even while in the body, and become its tools. From the moment when the man has glanced across the threshold and retained the memory oi* so doing he loses all fear of the pairs of opposites, that fear which lies like a pall upon the race. The words life and death as used by men in ordinary life, have no longer any meaning for him, because he has caught sight for himself of that which is beyond the threshold of physical consciousness. As he gains power the other illusions pass away from him, and he recognises them to be as much a part of the purely physical state as life and death, heat and cold. When he becomes fit to pass away into states of spiritual being and in returning to arrest the fall of the veil long enough to bring back a clear memory of what he has seen and experienced, he is able to force upon his physical brain a recognition of the fact that the evil in a man destroys his psychic powers and limits his capacity for growth, so that it drives him back into the material life where the good in him has again its opportunity to become strong. In the same way he becomes aware that hatred has no place in the spiritual spheres, and that the man who has hated finds himself without the power of emotion in any spiritual sphere he may enter, and therefore sinks back to physical surroundings in order to feel once more. When he compels his physical brain to accept this from his spiritual self, the advanced psychic can regard the material world with equanimity. For he perceives that hatred is only a temporary emotion, arising out of the temporary condition of evil. Rebirth perpetually gives to all men the opportunity of growth, if they have become so deeply imbedded in material conditions that the spiritual seedling cannot spring up during the lifetime in which evil and hatred have crushed it down. These conditions cannot create, and have nothing to do with life. So soon as the spirit begins to live, and grow and expand, the man casts them from him naturally. That evil and hatred have any permanent power is an absolute illusion. They have to be ceaselessly encountered and fought against in the physical life because they cake over the spirit till it becomes convinced that it is literally imprisoned, and remains within the material state as a creature embedded in a rock would remain in the same place, without any attempt to free itself. And this profound illusion must be dispelled because it is that which is hindering the progress • of the race and keeps the spirit of mankind from attaining its due growth and approaching its complete freedom. Each one who commences the work of attaining his own freedom is helping the whole race by so doing. And it is inevitable and of necessity that he will help others towards freedom; to give help is a natural action of the growing and developing spirit. The black magic born of selfishness, which leads a man to look for power for himself and to hide it from others is only possible within the earth sphere. And the giant weed of spiritual ambition can grow only within the state ruled by desire. All that is evil will be outgrown, as a man outgrows childish things. The terrible dangers which beset the path cause delay and suffering; but freedom is the heritage of man's spirit and eventually he must enter into it. When once his physical brain has recognised that the earth and its powers and pleasures exist purely as an illusion in that brain, he will without pause or hesitation cease to walk up and down within such an imaginary limitation and will enter upon the open road of progress. This will lead him over the threshold of physical consciousness, and over successive thresholds, till he is able to pass beyond the rule of desire. Then he will become a helper of the race, dispassionate, all-loving.

ILLUSION V. That Nature is indifferent to Man.

That nature is indifferent to man is an illusion which could not have come into being without the other illusion that the earth exists apart from man. The spirit knows that nature is not indifferent; in moments of great agony or great exaltation it realizes the spirit of nature as a companion, and this companion has the power of speech and the power to help. The creative impulse throbs ceaselessly within the heart of our beautiful green mother, who carries us like helpless infants on her bosom so long as we are her children, and she gives to us out of her amazing abundance that we may breathe, and bathe, and eat, and drink, and be supported in the ways without number that we require and demand of her. She fits the gifts to the requirements unerringly. She is a careful giver, choosing that which is needed out of her vast storehouses, and giving to the one who needs. The waste of nature, which is constantly brought up as a reproach against her, is entirely physical and superficial; or, rather, it is apparent only and not real. The millions of seeds and of seedlings that come to nothing from a physical point of view are not failures or wasted. Physically the matter constituting them is merely rearranged, spiritually the impetus which drew them over the threshold of matter has reversed and drawn them back again. It is no loss to them, because they are not beings engaged upon a pilgrimage, to whom every step taken should be one of progress, and to whom every step backward is a hindrance of that progress. The beautiful green mother is man's friend, a sphere of gracious non-human entities who encompass and uphold him during his pilgrimage. The infinite variety of form and beauty contained in that which we call Nature is the expression of its spiritual loveliness, so far as that can be apprehended by man through his physical senses; and these forms would never appear as solid or as capable of destruction but for the illusions in man's brain. Once freed from these illusions and the spirit of man recognises that while to him a birth or a death is of vital importance, to the nature spirits they ire nothing but a part of the play of life. As a soap bubble to the child that flings it on the air, so is a material incarnation to one of nature's seedlings. Nature is engaged in making a hearth and home for man so long as he needs it, and she passes in and out of the sphere of illusion without ^being affected by it and without any sense of the meaning put by man into the words birth and death.

Psychics who have learned to go far into spiritual life and to bring back memories across the threshold of physical consciousness, tell us of wonderfully beautiful forms of nature which they have seen. It is evident from the testimony of those who have explored in this manner that the nature spirits surround and uphold the spirits of men in the spiritual spheres. Where the spirits of men are seen as translucent forms having powers and possibilities unintelligible to men still embodied, translucent forms of flowers and trees are seen, with beauty in them which cannot be expressed in human language. It is seen there, also, that there is attraction and communication between the spirits of men and the spirits of nature, in a manner unknown to us now. In the ethereal world it is perceived that the flowers which form garlands in places of worship do so because they desire to do so, as the souls which come there to worship do so because they desire to do so. In the purely spiritual states this is even more plainly seen to be the law of life, love governing all things. In the earth life man takes, and holds; when his spirit advances into spiritual states it finds that there can be no taking and holding. All that surrounds the spirit and glorifies its life comes willingly, of its own volition, in the action of love.

A great crisis in the life of a man, which frees him temporarily from his physical body, will sometimes make him aware that nature is his friend and companion. Men go to the fields and woods for the silent society they find there, and return to their work and struggle among other men strengthened and calmed by it. But in times of spiritual agony the silence is sometimes broken by a seeming miracle. One who has suffered greatly has told of an incident which was a turning , point in the life; when lying at the foot of a tree in the last hopeless despair of grief the silence of nature became speech — the spirit of the tree bent over the prostrate form and touched it, saying, in a voice of intense pity, " Poor human being!" The touch and the voice roused the human spirit from its blind torpor of pain. Rising slowly, in amazement and wonder, the man leaned against the tree, and found strength and healing in its pitiful and beautiful companionship; and so took up his pilgrimage again.

FINIS.

BOOK SEVEN.
THE STORY OF SENSA

A MYSTERY PLAY IN THREE ACTS
ADAPTED FROM THE IDYLL OF THE WHITE LOTUS

This Drama is a story which has been told in all Ages, and among every people. It is the tragedy of the Soul.

Attracted by Desire, the Ruling Element in the lower nature of Man, the Soul stoops to sin; brought to itself by suffering, it turns for help to the redeeming Spirit within, and in the final sacrifice, achieves apotheosis and sheds a blessing on mankind.

DRAMATIS PERSONAE (and *Symbolism*)

AN EGYPTIAN PEASANT WOMAN: *Isis or Mother Nature.*

SENSA (Her Son): *The Human Soul entering into possession of its temple, the Body, at adolescence.*

THE LADY OF THE LOTUS: *The Spiritual Principle in Sensa.*

THE DARK GODDESS: *The Sensual Principle in Sensa.*

SEBOUA (A Gardener): *Intuition.*

AGMAHD (A High Priest of the Temple): *Ambition.*

KAMEN-BAKA (A High Priest of the Temple): *Desire.*

"THE TEN": *The Five Senses in their two aspects; active and receptive.*

"THE FOUR" Priests of the Temple: *Psychic Senses and their spiritual counterparts.*

THE OLD PRIEST: *Intellect without Vision.*

HESEP-TI (A Nobleman) and THE PEOPLE: *Represent demands from the Outer World.*

A DREAM WOMAN: *The Artistic Principle in Sensa.*

NEOPHYTES and OTHER PRIESTS: *Instruments of Action.*

ACT I

Scene i - The Adolescent

PERIOD *Ancient Egypt.*

TIME *Dawn.*

PLACE *A broad green plain outside a massive Temple on the banks of the Nile. The river can be seen winding away in the distance. The Morning Hymn to Ra at the Rising of the Sun, is just dying away within the Temple.*

[*Enter an Egyptian peasant woman, and Sensa, a young Egyptian fellah.*]

Sensa What a glorious sunrise! I am longing to go into the city streets and hear the noise, and be among the crowds. It is a feast day, Mother. I hear the cries of the men already, selling sweets and flowers and holy water. Let us go there, Mother.

Mother No, Sensa, that cannot be! You have been at my side since your baby feet first learned to run, but that is all over now, for here is the gate of the Temple which you are to enter.

Sensa At last!

Mother Yes, at last -- and we must part.

Sensa Do not go, Mother. Do not leave me yet. Let me spend the day in the city with you, first.

Mother No, Sensa, no. It is not now that you can enter the city and look upon its pleasures. You are still a child, a pupil, and have to enter upon your noviciate.

Sensa Oh, I have always longed for the haunts of men! I do so want to know all things.

Mother And so you shall, Sensa, but now you have to enter upon your destiny, through the gate of that Temple.

Sensa But, Mother, I need not enter the Temple till the day is ended. I long for the hours of the feast day in the city.

Mother You have first to become a man, and if you desire to enter the city then, you will be a part of it. Now you would be but a child, lost and helpless. For I could not guide you as I have done hitherto. The moment has come. The hour has struck which parts us. You have to enter upon the great ordeal of manhood, and I must go back to my other children who will follow you to this gate, ever pressing into life and longing for manhood.

Sensa Go? You are going, Mother! You will not leave me alone in this strange place? I am only a boy -- I am not able to go on alone.

Mother You will not be alone, for you will at once find yourself with others on the great pilgrimage through life to immortality.

Sensa Dare I enter this mysterious gate! What strong walls -- what a fast-closed door! Mother, I am afraid!

[*Draws back from the Temple and clings to her.*]

Mother Have no fear. Shake it from you! Be bold!

[*Puts off his clinging hands, and makes him stand alone.*]

For so soon as you have become a man, you will be in possession of powers such as belong to neither angel or demon. When man is afraid, it is because he is ignorant and does not realize himself. Be you a learner, my son, and discover your own great gifts. For great they are indeed. And greatest of all is the power to control your own destiny! Through this gate, and by the joy and pain which the soul finds within it, alone can you attain to immortality. Go! Pass bravely in. Experience all things which sensation can give you. Taste to the full all the mystery and joy of life, and having tasted them, pass beyond them -- free!

Sensa The joy of life?

Mother [*Passionately*] The unutterable, inexpressible joy of human life. Take it, glory in it, and free yourself from it.

Sensa Your words rouse me from my dreams! Yes, Mother, it is true!

[*Approaches the closed gate as he speaks.*]

The joy of life! I feel it rising within me with the strength of a great serpent uncoiling itself.

As he approaches the gate, it slowly opens, and a black-robed Novice looks out. Seeing Sensa, he opens the gate wide. Sensa hastens forward as if to enter at once, but is stayed by the sight of Agmahd within. He retreats a little towards his Mother.

Mother! Who is that? That splendid priest! How tall and stately he is, and how calm! He might be a beautiful statue. How slowly he walks -- like some great being far removed from men. His dress is all white, embroidered with gold, and his beard that lies upon it, might be cut in gold.

Mother [*Also looking in*] That is Agmahd, the High Priest of the Temple. He is very great and ambitious, and would rule all Egypt.

Sensa How common and mean my dress is! Oh, to wear a robe like his!

[*Sensa goes forward towards the gate.*]

Mother Would you wear the robe of the High Priest? Does Ambition already call you?

Sensa Yes, Yes! I want to be like him -- great and strong! Above all others! To rule Egypt! He is fitted to rule not only Egypt, but the whole world. See how he keeps his eyes upon the ground. Thought holds him. Mother, [*Turns back a little*] I dread the raising of those drooping lids!

Mother You need not fear his gaze. You can conquer him.

Sensa [*Incredulously*] I?

Mother Yes. If you are a true learner, you can control all things.

[*To the Waiting Novice.*]

Admit the youth. It is his time to enter.

Sensa Mother!

Mother [*With an imperious gesture*] Go!

Sensa Yes, I obey!

[*He crosses the threshold. As he steps within the Temple, the Mother drops a dim grey veil before her face. Sensa turns. Holds out his arms.*]

Mother!

[*She does not move.*]

Let me see your face once more before I go!

Mother [*Firmly*] It is too late. Go. Look not back. Farewell.

[*The great gate of the Temple closes.*]

Sensa, you have at last fully entered into the world of mortals. But no mortal has yet removed the veil that shades my divinity from human eyes. Thou terrible Temple! Place of suffering, place of joy, place of experience and sensation, how it draws my children from me, from me, the Mother and the lover of the souls of men. I bring all mortals hither, but I do not suffer them to look back from that inexorable gate which, once closed, Destiny alone can open! Oblivion of his mysterious past has now fallen on the soul of Sensa; he will know only that he is man!

CURTAIN

Scene ii - The Novice

A large and beautiful room in the Interior of the Temple, with pillars. It is circular in shape, and very dim. The walls and pillars are covered with hieroglyphs.

A row of 5 pillars extends across R. The pillars begin at wall up back R. of Center, and extend down R. the last being against wall just above Orchestra Pit. Between these 5 pillars are hung 4 curtains. The pillars, beginning with the lowest down R. are indigo, green, red, violet, blue, symbolical of the Five Senses. The curtains symbolize the four principal elements, and, beginning down R. are green, red, violet, blue.

Behind the curtains is the Sanctuary of The Dark Goddess of the Temple. In the Center at Back, 3 steps lead up to a closed door. Opposite the Sanctuary is an Exit leading out through pillars. Above the Sanctuary, R. is a couch. Below the center door L., sits The Old Priest and two Neophytes, bending over the papyri on their knees. Sensa is standing with his hand on the wall, reading from the hieroglyphs. He is dressed in the black robe of the Novice. The Neophyte's robes are white, stitched with black. The Old Priest's robe is white, embroidered with blue. The High Priest, Kamen-baka, stands just below the Sanctuary, R. His robe is white, delicately embroidered with golden characters. He is tall and stately, with dignified but kindly look. His beard is light brown.

Five young Priests and five young Priestesses, softly twanging musical instruments, stand grouped about the Sanctuary. Their robes are of different colors, with vari-colored embroidery. They are known throughout the Play as "The Ten."

Two young Priests and two young Priestesses stand, two on either side of the steps, Center. Their robes are yellow and blue.

Incense issues from the Sanctuary.

Priests [*Chanting*]

[*On Stage*] Queen Mother!

[*Within Sanctuary*] Queen Mother!

[*On Stage*] Great Goddess of the Temple!

[*Within*] Great Goddess of the Temple!

[*On Stage*] Hear us!

[*Within*] Hear us!

[*This alternating refrain is chanted three times.*]

Priests [*On Stage, speaking*] We demand a spell! We demand a word of power. We demand a spell!

The re-iterated chanting continues inside the Sanctuary. Sensa, with his hand upon the wall, and finger indicating one of the hieroglyphs, turns and gazes with large, fascinated eyes at the Sanctuary, deeply inhaling the incense, and listening while the chanting proceeds. As the chanting pauses, the Old Priest glances up.

Old Priest [*In a dull, level voice of reprimand*] Sensa! Have you found the sign you were bidden to look for?

[*Sensa does not hear. Louder.*]

Sensa!

Sensa [*Starts slightly*] My lord?

[*Continues to gaze dreamily.*]

Old Priest Why do you gaze, as one charmed, at the Sanctuary?

Sensa I know not. The Incense. [*Inhales deeply*] How strange and subtle it is! It draws me, yet it sickens me. And the chanting -- it thrills me with a strange, new ecstasy!

Old Priest Return to your task. You have much to learn. The service of the Sanctuary is not for you. You have this work to do.

An uproar of many voices can be heard in the distance. Every one listens apprehensively. The Old Priest shakes violently, becoming greatly agitated.

Sensa It is the people! Are they coming again to attack the Temple?

Old Priest Yes! Yes! They come to demand the Spell to cure the blindness of the Lord Hesep-ti. The Spell for which we search. It must be here. Do not lose your place, or the work of the whole morning will be lost.

The curtains of the Sanctuary are slowly drawn aside, and Agmahd appears. He looks utterly downcast. The Priests rise. Sensa looks on.

Agmahd I have placed the jewels of the lady of Hesep-ti at the feet of the Goddess. But all is dark. All is silent. No word. No sign. We have no Seer in the Temple. No one who can speak to her or see her.

Kamen-baka It is because we have no Seer that we have fallen into the power of the seven destroying spirits.

The Ten [*Intoning*] Seven are they. Seven are they. In the abyss of the deep -- seven are they. Law and order know they not. Prayer and supplication hear they not. Evil are they. Baleful are they.

Sensa turns to his task. All is still, save for the soft chanting within the Sanctuary. Sensa again becomes distracted.

Sensa [*Passionately*] Oh, I cannot stay here always, poring over these signs. This is not life! These dim letters mean nothing to me. There can be no spell of power in these pictures of a dead past.

Old Priest Patience, child; you have much to learn. Each one of those signs that you look upon contains a meaning which you will understand when you have read the whole, and another meaning which I shall understand, and yet another mysterious inner meaning which only the High Priest himself can unravel. Resume your task.

Sensa turns again to the writing on the wall. The chanting law ceased. A deep silence reigns. Only the musical sound of running water can be heard, coming from behind the door, Center.

Sensa [*Starts*] What is that sound of water? Water, falling?

[*Turns listening towards the door. "The Ten" change their positions and look apprehensively from Sensa to the door.*]

How beautiful it is! It is behind that door. All the time I have been here, I have never seen behind that closed door. Why is it always closed?

Old Priest It is only the Garden where the flowers grow that we use for the days of feasting.

Sensa A garden where the flowers grow! Why, the sun must shine there! Is it in the Temple?

Old Priest [*Indifferently*] Yes. Oh, yes, it is in the Temple -- but, see -- you have lost the place.

Enter Neophyte. Kamen-baka comes out of the Sanctuary.

Neophyte The household of Hesep-ti! And people from the city are at the Gate! They clamor for a spell. A spell to remove the blindness of the Lord Hesep-ti.

Old Priest [*Tremblingly*] We cannot find it.

Kamen-baka It is useless to ask the Goddess for it. All is dark within the Sanctuary. Go! tell the people they must be patient. [*Exit Neophyte*] If no word of power is given to the High Priest in the Sanctuary, we are lost! The Temple will be destroyed!

[*The Priests fall on their knees, horror-stricken.*]

Sensa [*Exultantly*] And I shall be free from these hateful tasks!

[*The chanting within Sanctuary is softly resumed.*]

Priests Queen Mother! Save the Temple. If the Temple falls, we are lost!

Agmahd re-enters the Sanctuary. The Old Priest crosses tremblingly to Sensa.

Old Priest Child, do not rebel. Have you kept the place?

Sensa [*Indicating*] It is here.

[*The Old Priest peers closely at signs then returns to his place, shaking his head.*]

Old Priest There is no mention of the spell of power.

Shouting and the noise of a tumult become more distinct, drawing nearer, and the sound of running feet is heard in the Corridor.

[*Enter two Neophytes, Agmahd comes out of the Sanctuary.*]

1st Neophyte The Lord Hesep-ti himself is at the Gate. He demands admission.

2nd Neophyte He asks, is there no life in the Temple? He says, 'Are we all dead, that he gets no answer.'

Agmahd He must be admitted. Open the gate.

[*Exeunt Neophytes.*]

Kamen-baka [*To Agmahd*] What shall we say to him? If we can not appease him, we shall starve. The kitchens are waiting now for cattle from his fields.

Agmahd We must make him promises.

Kamen-baka Can we make him believe us? We cannot risk losing the jewels of the Lady Hesep-ti. They are priceless. What must we do?

[*Priests groan at each sentence.*]

Agmahd Promises. Promises. We must promise that if not now, it shall be done later, even if we have to descend into the uttermost depths to obtain the spell.

[*The Priests draw back to the sides.*]

Enter Hesep-ti, a Nobleman in the prime of life, but crushed by his affliction. He is totally blind, and is supported by two Neophytes. His manner, though feeble, is regal.

Hesep-ti [*Anxiously*] Is the High Priest here?

Agmahd [*Steps forward*] I am, my lord.

Hesep-ti [*With a gesture of salutation*] Life! Health! Strength!

Agmahd [*Raising his hand*] Peace to the Lord Hesep-ti. Peace. Peace. Will you not sit, my lord?

Hesep-ti [*Trembling*] I cannot sit. I am aflame with rage. I, Hesep-ti, Chief of the Signet Bearers of the great king, the king of the world, the King of Egypt, I -- I -- [*He is speechless: then breaks out.*]

That offering! My wife's jewels! Those precious stones I gave her! I must have them back.

The Ten Back! Back! [*Sullenly*] He cannot have them back! No! No! We need them.

[*Agmahd silences them with a gesture. They draw back, but look ugly.*]

Agmahd Be calm, most noble Hesep-ti. The Casket is safe at the feet of the Goddess who is ready to befriend you. Has other evil befallen you besides the curse of blindness? Surely the offering is true; surely the lady of Hesep-ti is greatly devoted, to make so rich an offering.

Hesep-ti Devoted! She, that has taken advantage of the evil spell which has fallen upon me, to betray me in my very presence! While she was actually with me, she gave gifts into the hand of her hire-woman for a young soldier and bade her fetch him; and he came into my presence and looked on her and she on him, with favor -- I, not knowing, because I could not see!

[*He becomes speechless from rage.*]

Agmahd What is it you ask of me?

Hesep-ti That my enemy shall taste death to the full, in torture and shame. I demand that he lie in chains in the Underworld and have fetters fastened upon him. Do this, and I will give you untold gold. Do this, and I will have driven into your yards great herds of cattle.

Agmahd Your demand is just. Your enemy shall be destroyed.

Hesep-ti Swear it. Swear it on this Amulet of the Pillow which is to be placed beneath my head when I am dead.

[*Holds out Amulet.*]

Agmahd [*Placing hand on Amulet*] I swear it. Your sight shall be restored, and your enemy trampled under foot. Go in confidence. All shall be done as you desire.

Hesep-ti [*With strength*] From the country of Magan, rare stones I shall cause to be brought. Gold dust from the mountains of Gharghum. In the Interior of this Temple, a Sanctuary of cedarwood I shall cause to be built, to the Goddess. At the feet of the Sun God seven times seven shall I prostrate myself!

Agmahd 'Tis well. Go then in peace.

Hesep-ti [*Trembling and bowed*] Lead me back to my own place -- where I, Hesep-ti, Chief of the Signet Bearers to the King, my Lord, will sit and wait for my sight to be restored, and my enemy destroyed.

[*Exit, accompanied by two Neophytes. Agmahd paces up and down. "The Ten" strike sad, dirge-like chords, and there is a general air of dejection.*]

The Ten [*Intoning*] Oh, Great Goddess, pronounce Thy blessing upon our works. Command our prosperity.

Agmahd What is to be done? I have promised. I have promised a spell. And I have no spell. I have no power to speak with the Goddess. [*Turns angrily to Old Priest*] You --

Old Priest [*Turns tremblingly*] My lord?

Agmahd You! -- and you students of the Ancient Writings --

[*They rise and bow humbly.*]

Have you not been searching? Can you not find the spell that I need?

[*They look hopelessly at the Old Priest.*]

Old Priest The characters are difficult, my lord, and my eyesight is faded: -- I --

Agmahd [Sternly] And these? These students who have worked with you so long: -- are they not capable of searching for the spell?

Old Priest My lord, they, too, are losing the strong sight needed to read these difficult characters. They --

Agmahd Then have we no student fitted to do our work?

Old Priest This Novice, my lord [*Indicating Sensa*] is young, and his eyesight is strong. He --

Agmahd Bid him search, then. Keep him close here until he has found what I need.

Sensa [Starts] Keep me close here! What! Closer than I have been kept? I shall go mad!

[*Agmahd gives him a cold stare and Exits.*]

Old Priest How dare you speak before the High Priest thus? You are greatly honored. But be not over-proud. It is your youth which has marked you out for this honor.

Sensa [Starting up] My youth! I want my youth for myself! I do not want to spend it in the study of these crabbed signs. I want to use it for beauty and joy and life -- not to waste it within these dead walls!

Old Priest Child, you will make your lot the harder. The High Priest can command you. Stand you here and continue your task. We will leave you in quiet to accomplish it.

He pushes Sensa back into his place and lifts from his own stool the faded manuscripts, and Exits, followed by the Neophytes. Sensa, left with "The Ten," leans his head upon his arms against the wall. "The Ten" are by the pillars in front of the Sanctuary.

Two of The Ten [Chant rhythmically] Oh, light of the Sun! Oh, light of Moon!. Oh, glory of the fields and the flowers!

[*Sensa half turns to them.*

Two Others [Chant in rising cadence] The voice of the birds! The music of the dance! The cries from the city!

[*Sensa takes a step towards them.*

Two Others [Ecstatically] Oh, the ripe fruit from the wall! And the honey of the bees! Oh, the sweetness of the honey!

The Ten [In unison] Oh, the joy and the pride of the earth, and the life of the earth!

Sensa [*Moving dreamily towards them*] Yes! Yes! It is sweet! How sweet!

Pause and a little silence. The sound of the running water is again heard. Sensa stops. The Four Priests by the door of the Garden chant softly but clearly with uplifted expression.

The Four Priests Do you not hear the waters of Life and Truth? They flow! They flow!

Sensa Yes! Yes, I hear! 'Tis the mystic sound! Oh, how it enters into my soul!

["*The Ten*" *begin to chant.*]

Hush! [*Lifts his hand*] I must find this musical voiced water. [*At the steps*] It eases my longing. I must drink of that water!

[*He mounts the steps and knocks. "The Ten" come forward with menacing gestures.*]

The Ten Go not that way! Go not that way! We cannot follow you there. Go not! Go not!

[*They murmur angrily.*]

The Four Priests step forward and stand between "The Ten" and Sensa, who knocks again. "The Ten" threaten and snarl. Sensa knocks a third time, and steps back.

Sensa Oh, open to me, thou Mystery Gate!

The Gate opens, and a great shaft of light streams into the dim room. "The Ten" recede before it, and withdraw behind the curtains of the Sanctuary. The Four resume their places on either side of the gate.

The Two on The Right Come out of the darkness. Make the entrance on Light. Tell me my name -- what am I? Tell me my name.

Sensa [*Gazing at them*] Surely you are that which is True!

The Two on The Right [*Strike a strong chord*] It is well!

The Two on The Left Come out of the Darkness! Make the entrance on Light! Tell me my name -- what am I? Tell me my name.

Sensa [*Gazing at them*] Surely you are that which is Just!

The Two on The Left [*Strike a chord*] It is well!

All Together Enter through the hidden Lintel. Enter!

The Gate opens. Sensa steps back enraptured. A most exquisite Garden is revealed, full of light and color, glancing birds, and a great Lotus tank, fed by a rill of running water from a fountain. The Garden is full of exquisite blossoms and delicate young, pale-green foliage of Spring. The

Lotus tank is in the center of the Garden. The Lotuses are in bloom, one large blossom stands high above the green leaves.

Sensa stands speechless for some seconds and then Seboua appears.

Seboua What do you seek?

Sensa The mystery that is hidden here. How beautiful it is! Light and air! And the flowers -- how sweet they smell!

Seboua Ah, you perceive their fragrance. The dull Priests care nothing for it. This garden is wasted upon them, poor fools.

Sensa Do they not come here?

Seboua Never. All they desire from this garden is fruit for their table, and the gratification of their appetites.

[*Turns fiercely to Sensa.*]

Are you like them? Do you desire to learn only the mystery of the growth of sin and deceit?

Sensa What is sin? What is deceit?

Seboua What? You are ignorant of the meaning of those words?

Sensa Must I, then, learn these things?

Seboua Not if you stay here with the spirits of the flowers.

Sensa Have they spirits?

Seboua How else could they be beautiful?

[*Sensa looks at him in amazement.*]

Nay, ponder my words, and by and bye, you will understand them. Sit here while I water my plants.

Seboua takes Sensa by the hand and leads him towards the tank. Then he takes a water jar and fills it at the rill of running water.

[*Clasps his hands and leans toward the water.*]

Sensa Oh, how delicate-voiced is that water!

Seboua Yes. It flows only to feed the Queen of Flowers.

[*Looks at the Lotus. Then all round the Garden and back at the Lotus.*]

Sensa Thou art indeed the Queen of Flowers. And is there a spirit in this flower, too?

Seboua Yes. But no mortal eyes have seen her since I have been in this garden. That flower is her home -- and it is from her that all Wisdom comes.

Sensa Perhaps I may see her!

Seboua What? A youth like you, -- when the High Priest himself cannot see her!

Sensa Why not? I am not so young. I have become a man since I entered the Temple. I do so long to know the truth of things.

Seboua The Priests are ignorant, because none in this Temple can see or hear our Lady of the Lotus.

Sensa But do they watch for her here, beside her home?

Seboua No. They are killing the cattle of Hesep-ti for the table -- or counting the coins of the offerings at the Gate.

[*Goes on watering the plants.*]

They have not time to wait and watch for her.

Sensa [*Earnestly*] Oh, I will see her! I must see her! I shall demand to see her! I tell you, Gardener, I shall watch and wait here for ever, until I do see her!

Seboua You are a strange youth! But I cannot linger here with you. I have my work to do.

[*Exits with empty water jar.*]

Sensa moves about and examines the flowers. Returns Center. Raises his arm.

Sensa I tremble before Thee.

[*Crosses his arms on his breast.*]

Oh, glorious Flower with thy soft, gold-dusted heart, open! Open that heart that I may see the Truth! Give me of thy Wisdom! I demand that the spirit within thee shall speak to the Spirit within me!

As he stands gazing in ecstasy, a fair and glorious woman appears. Sensa, amazed, strives to move. After a moment's pause, he holds out his arms, makes a step or two forward as though to go to her, but his strength failing him, he falls forward unconscious, his arms outstretched towards her.

The Lady of The Lotus [*Rises. Stands over Sensa in a pitying attitude.*]

Poor little human being. Little child of Time! Unconscious of Eternity, not knowing of your own great future, and all that I have for you in the day when you shall pass out of this imprisonment. Grow strong in the crucible of human life and experience. Prepare for the splendid Immortality to which I shall lead you. I, the Spirit of the Sacred Flower of Egypt, will give you the wisdom you ask when you are able to take it, but your strength has failed you. Alas! Farewell.

She vanishes. The leaves and branches rustle and sway and there is a murmur, as of a slight breeze. Seboua appears, and seeing Sensa lying prostrate on the ground, hurries towards him, lifts his head, and bathes his face with water from the jar he carries.

Seboua Was the heat too much for you? You look a strong lad to faint for the heat, and that, too, in this cool place!

Sensa [*Reviving, murmurs*] Where is she?

[*He attempts to rise on his elbow and points towards the Lotus bed.*] Where is she?

[*Enter Agmahd and Kamen-baka.*]

Seboua [*Excitedly*] What? What have you seen, boy? Quickly! Speak!

Sensa I have seen the Queen. The Queen of the Garden. The Lady of the Lotus. She is most fair, and her hair is like gold, that runs upon her shoulders.

Seboua It was not your fancy? You did not dream it?

[*Raising Sensa, he moves to the gate with him.*]

Come -- Come with me!

Sensa [*Standing on the top step*] She was real! She was more real than you. I stood and gazed upon the flower -- and as I gazed, it seemed to change in form to expand and rise towards me -- and, lo, drinking at the stream -- stooping to take its drops upon her lips, I saw a woman with fair skin, and hair like dust of gold. I tried to go to her, but my strength failed me, and I fell.

Seboua [*Falls on his knees before Sensa*] You have seen her. You have seen her! All Hail! For you are destined to be a Teacher amongst us -- a help to the people! You are a Seer!

[*Seboua turns, sees the two High Priests who have witnessed this scene.*]

Agmahd My lords! My lords! This novice! This novice! He has seen! He has heard! He is a Seer. He is the one we have waited for. We are saved.

CURTAIN

ACT II

Scene i - Hypnotized

The Interior of the Temple, as in Act One. Agmahd is standing by the Curtains of the Sanctuary. Priests chant Hymn to Ra at the Setting of the Sun.

Enter Kamen-baka from L.

Kamen-baka They are bringing him! Is he to pass into the Sanctuary at once, without preparation?

Agmahd At once. There must be no delay.

Kamen-baka Is it wise? Is it safe?

Agmahd We must take the risk!

Kamen-baka But he may die! The experiment may kill him, and he would be lost to us!

Agmahd No. He is young and ignorant. "The Ten" will lead him on and sustain him.

[*Enter a Neophyte hurriedly. To Neophyte.*]

Is he ready?

Neophyte [*Agitated and fearful*] My lord, we have done all that you directed. He has slept, and we watched him as he slept. He has eaten: -- when he woke, we brought him food. We bathed him in the perfumed bath and we put upon him the Seer's robe.

Agmahd Then wherefore this delay?

Neophyte My lord, he is terrified. A sudden fear has fallen upon him.

Kamen-baka Fear? What has alarmed him?

Neophyte Not I, my lord. We have none of us spoken to him of what he is to do.

Kamen-baka But if he is afraid, can you not quiet him?

[*Enter 2nd Neophyte.*]

2nd Neophyte All is well, my lord. He is now coming. They are almost here.

The intoning of Priests draws nearer and about a dozen Priests in white, enter slowly in double file and place themselves above the Sanctuary. They are followed by four young Neophytes carrying vases of incense, who go to their places above the Sanctuary. Then a group of five of "The Ten," dressed in their violet-red robes, then Sensa, alone, in a pure white linen robe. He is followed by the other five of "The Ten."

Following are four more Incense Bearers who place themselves below the Sanctuary. Following are other Priests and Novices who fill the stage, L.

Kamen-baka [*To Sensa*] This is the chair of the Seer. Sit here.

Sensa hesitates. Looks round with an expression of uncertainty. Then takes his place, silent and alarmed.

Sensa Sit here? And what am I to do?

Agmahd [*Sternly*] Watch.

Agmahd and Kamen-baka move slowly down and draw aside the curtains, for the first time revealing the Opening to the Sanctuary, a square black hole leading into a dark corridor. They return to their places. Sensa has followed their movements fearfully.

And tell us what you see.

Sensa [*Trembling voice*] What should I see?

Agmahd Fear not. Watch.

Sensa turns his fearful eyes to the Sanctuary. All eyes are fixed on the Sanctuary, except Agmahd's. He watches Sensa. Sensa gazes with clasped hands deep into the dark opening. Gradually his hands relax on to the arms of the chair. He sinks back, chin on breast, eyes straight ahead. The light on the stage has become dimmer. There is absolute stillness. Presently Sensa lifts his head slowly as if seeing something within the corridor. He raises his whole body and leans forward gazing intently, breathing heavily. Suddenly he starts up with a strangled cry. There is a general suppressed cry of satisfaction from the Priests. Agmahd speaks calmly.

Agmahd What is it that you see?

[*Sensa shudders.*]

Tell us.

Sensa [*Pointing*] Do you not see the light? The light from the little doorway? There -- there, at the end of the corridor?

Other Priests [*Murmuring and moving*] No! No! There is no light. We cannot see a light. We cannot see . . .

Sensa Surely you see that the door has opened a little way, and a veiled figure stands there?

[*He looks round on them.*]

A Murmur from the Priests No! No! We do not see. We cannot see.

Sensa Oh, send it away! Send it away. It frightens me!

Agmahd [*Triumphantly*] Our Queen is welcome.

Sensa No! No! Send it away. I shall die of fear! Send it away!

Agmahd Our Queen is welcome, and we do her all reverence.

[*Raising his arms with an Egyptian gesture of reverence. All the Priests do the same.*]

Will our Queen help her subjects? Will she remove the curse of blindness which has fallen upon the Lord Hesep-ti, and destroy his enemy? Will she show herself to the people? The fortune of the temple is at stake. Unless our Queen helps us, the Temple must fall.

[*Sensa has sat huddled with his hands over his eyes. He now moves and looks even more alarmed.*]

Sensa A voice! A voice! Oh, I hear a dreadful voice! A voice like ice! She is speaking.

[*General Stir.*]

Agmahd [*Strong and controlled*] She speaks? Repeat her words. We cannot hear them. What does she say?

Sensa What! Can you not hear her? Can you not hear her speak?

[*Looks fearfully at them.*]

Priests [*Murmuring low*] No, we cannot hear. We cannot see. All is dark and silent.

Sensa You cannot hear her? You cannot see her? It is only I -- I -- who hear her and see her?

[*In a trembling voice of great fear.*]

No! No! I cannot! I cannot! No! No! I will not go in alone with you!

Agmahd What does she say? You must obey her command.

Sensa She says that you shall have all you ask.

[*Murmurs of delight.*]

But that I must go in there alone with her. I cannot. I cannot.

[*Yet he rises with outstretched hand and moves toward the Sanctuary as if drawn by an invisible hand, resisting all the way.*]

Yet I must. She draws me with her hand. It burns. It holds. It draws me.

He enters the Sanctuary. The Priests follow his every movement and press forward. There is an intense pause of waiting and anticipation. Suddenly, a terrific cry is heard, and Sensa flings himself forth from the Sanctuary, dashing wildly to escape, and falls in the midst of the priests. "The Ten" gather round him.

Oh, horror of horrors! What have I seen! Shall I ever forget that awful face!

One of the Ten Ah, be not afraid. That face is but a mask, and through it you will see things most beautiful and desirable.

Sensa But that voice! That cold and cruel voice!

Another of the Ten [*Insinuatingly*] That voice can be most soft and sweet. You have but to yield to its commands.

Sensa But her hand. Her hand that burnt me -- it was like fire.

Another of the Ten In that hand are all the passion and all the fire of life and joy.

[*"The Ten" press closer with soothing words and gestures. Sensa has removed his hands from his face and looks at them with wonder.*]

Sensa Can that be so?

The Ten Yes, yes! Oh, yes!

Sensa That face of horror can ne'er be sweet -- that voice can ne'er be kind -- that hand be tender!

The Ten It can! It is! So sweet, so tender!

Sensa [*Bewildered*] Can it be so?

Agmahd It is so. Enter there.

[*Gesture towards the Sanctuary. Sensa turns. "The Ten" surround him, softly chanting.*]

The Ten Yes. Enter there! Enter there! Life is there. Joy is there. Love and wealth and power are here.

[*They are at the door.*]

Are here! Are here! She will give them to you. Come! Come! Have no fear. Life is here.

[*Sensa, being cajoled and soothed, disappears into the Sanctuary. Agmahd and Kamen-baka draw the Curtains across.*]

Agmahd [*Turning*] He is ours! On him I will raise the fortunes of the Temple!

CURTAIN

Scene ii - The Slave

The same Scene. The walls are hung with garlands of roses in great profusion. Incense vases stand against the five pillars. The couch stands, L. A pile of costly and beautiful fabrics is thrown on it. On the floor and an small stools are quantities of valuable articles -- jewelry, flasks of perfume, etc.

Sensa sits on his chair in the center of the stage, opposite the Sanctuary. He wears a white robe. He looks much older, and very weary and heavy. His head is sunk on his breast, and his arms hang over the arms of the chair. Agmahd stands Center, in a dress of cloth of gold, dominating the whole scene, triumphant, superb. "The Ten" stand by the pillars. The Four Priests still stand, two on either side of the steps. Neophytes light the incense in the vases. Priests and Neophytes move amongst the beautiful things, delightedly. Some twang softly on musical instruments. Kamen-baka's robe is rich and splendid, but not quite so gorgeous as Agmahd's.

Agmahd Does he sleep?

Kamen-baka He seems to sleep. He is exhausted. He suffers.

Agmahd He will recover. As I led him to this,

[*Wide gesture.*]

so I can lead him again. I have triumphed, and I shall go from one conquest to another.

[*Contemptuously.*]

Do you not remember how he feared to look upon the face of our Goddess? He has not been easy to break to my will. The common pleasures of ordinary men do not entice him. With those pleasures which reflect the life of the spirit -- with music, poetry, and great accomplishments, I led him. He played with the golden ball of success, and always won. To and fro he tossed it -- and the ball was always his. All is well. I have conquered.

Kamen-baka But the people clamor still to see the Goddess. They desire speech with her. "The Ten" are restive and rebellious. They complain that you drive them too far -- and our Seer seems near the end of his strength. There is no limit to your ambition.

Agmahd Nor to your desire. Even so. It is but right. The whole Temple is uplifted and made splendid. Hesep-ti is a royal giver -- he has sent us of his best.

[*To Priests.*]

Sing the song of triumph. Raise your voices in acclamation.

Certain Priests who seem frenzied with delight, cry out in unison, on a high note, an Egyptian word of triumph.

Agmahd *goes into the Sanctuary.*

Kamen-Baka *joins the Priests, L. center.*

Sensa *stirs. Also "The Ten" begin to move. They are beautiful, but sullen and depressed.*

Sensa What is that cry, as of triumph?

[*He raises himself, looks about.*]

Who can rejoice over such poor matter as this? Gold -- jewels? Is this all that the years have brought me?

Pause. The Stage is very silent, and for an instant, the playing of the fountain is faintly heard. The Priestesses by Door, Center, strike one chord on their harps. Sensa lifts his head painfully. "The Ten" and Kamen-baka are alert. Agmahd comes out of the Sanctuary.

Oh, I dimly recall a garden where flowers grew and lifted their sweet faces to the sun. But that was long ago, when I was young and full of hope.

The Lotus was in bloom that day. I heeded it not, and now I cannot reach it. But oh! there is a cry in my soul for a Far-away Peace; for a voice that is known to my heart alone -- and for a glimpse, but one glimpse -- of that Divine Lady. Why do I linger here in this spot, evermore?

[*Sensa rises and turns, and is confronted by Agmahd and Kamen-baka, one on either side of him. He falls back in his chair.*]

Oh, I shall stifle in this close place, all sickly with incense and perfume.

Kamen-baka [*Suavely*] You have been too much within doors. They shall not kill you with the ceremonies of the Temple, even though you are the only one who can receive the messages and obtain the spells.

[*Enter Neophyte.*]

Neophyte [*Excitedly*] My lord! The Lord Hesep-ti is entering!

Enter Hesep-ti, powerful, strong, full of lusty life, seeing, and gorgeously attired with jewels and panther-skin, and wearing a great, flashing jewel on his brow. He comes straight down, stands in front of Agmahd.

Hesep-ti [*Vigorously*] Life! Health! Strength!

Agmahd Peace.

[*Hesep-ti takes the jewel from his brow and hands it to Agmahd.*]

Hesep-ti This, my lord, is for you to place in your crown. You have more than fulfilled your pledge. Bring in that coffer -- bring in that casket. Are the bullocks driven into the yard of the Temple?

[*Assent from Attendants.*]

It is well. There is plenty, there is glory for you all. I have given from my thankful heart.

[*Sensa falls back in his chair, with a gasp.*]

Young Priests He is fainting, my lord -- he is fainting!

[*"The Ten" rush towards Sensa with restoratives.*]

The Ten Give him this! This. Give him this.

Sensa [*Turning away*] These things do not feed me.

Agmahd [*Waves "The Ten" aside*] He cares nothing for these.

Hesep-ti Is this a tortured slave? What has he done?

Agmahd He is our Seer. Through him we have worked the miracle which has restored your sight and destroyed your enemy.

Hesep-ti Then I pay him all homage.

[*Makes an obeisance, and goes out.*]

Sensa [*Half raises a drawn, white face*] Oh, Oh, I am dying.

The Ten No! No! You must not die!

They gather round him. One fans him, another soothes his hand. Another plays softly on a musical instrument. Another advances with a flask, kneels at his feet and pours out a fragrant liquid. A strong, pungent perfume fills the air. Sensa recoils in disgust.

Sensa [*Turning restlessly*] Peace -- Peace! I am too tired!

["*The Ten*" *linger. He pushes them away.*]

Leave me. Can you not see that I have a feeling like death? Surely it is Death, and I shall be released from this bondage.

The Ten [*In surprise*] Bondage?

Sensa Yes. Am I not a tool, a slave? To you -- and you and you -- all! I cannot move. I cannot breathe. Night after night, I am in the Sanctuary, while you run hither and thither in the world. You enjoy the air, the sunshine, the people, the sweets of the earth -- and what do you bring to me, who sit here alone, keeping alive the fire in the Sanctuary? Only empty husks of empty things! Oh, if I did not know that behind that closed door, is my divine garden! If it were not that in sleep, I wander free where you cannot follow! If it were not that in profound, sweet sleep I touch the Infinite Source of all Refreshment, -- I could not return to this prison where I am a stranger -- alone and unloved!

Agmahd [*Scornfully*] Love? What has love to do with raising the fortune of the Temple?

Kamen-baka Love! [*Scornfully*] Though all men love me, I love no man.

Agmahd To raise the fortunes of the Temple and to lift it above all others, I have renounced my humanity.

Sensa It is nothing to me that it should be raised above all other Temples.

Agmahd If it is not above all others, it will be crushed by others.

The Ten [*All murmur*] Yes! Yes! We cannot endure that!

Agmahd We are one within the walls of this Temple. All our fortunes are at stake. You must obey. We will compel you to obey for the sake of our Temple, to make it the greatest in all Egypt.

Sensa I cannot. Oh, I cannot. I am too tired.

Kamen-baka We are destroying our priceless possession. We are stupefying him. He must have rest -- nay, more. He must have pleasure.

Agmahd Then you, who are versed in the mystery and magic of number and music and rhythm, bid him enter into pleasure.

Kamen-baka I will send him into the realms of joy, and the Ritual of "The Ten" shall be danced for him.

The Ten [*joyously*] Yes! Yes! We will dance for him! Come, dance!

They begin the Ritual Dance of "The Ten," accompanied by rhythmic music or intoning, from the Priests -- up Center. They circle round and round Sensa in a rhythmic dance. A moment of darkness falls upon the Stage. When it is again light, the Scene is witnessed through gauze. Sensa can be seen wakening, and with a cry of joy he perceives a beautiful woman standing beside him. Her dress is of rosy red and pink shades. She has red roses round her head, and a great rope of roses round her shoulders, crossing her heart. "The Ten" continue a slow dance, over against the Curtains of the Sanctuary, now singly, now in unison. The dance is composed of strange Egyptian postures, and the effect against the curtains is that of a frieze. Their movements are slow and unobtrusive, but they continue through the scene.

Sensa Is it you?

Dream Woman Yes, it is I. Your love of the Ages, your Queen of joy.

[*She sways from him, down L.*]

Sensa [*Slowly rising*] My love of the Ages, my Queen of joy, my very Self. How I have longed for you. Now I can reach you, now I can touch you, now I can lose myself in you. Where have you been so long?

Dream Woman Revelling in the consciousness of joy, whilst you have been down in the place of fear. Come, dance with me. Am I not your joy self? Your pleasure self? Your very self? Come, be with me, be of me. Be mine!

[*He has approached as though drawn by an invisible thread. She clasps him to her.*]

Sensa [*After a protracted pause, draws back, looking down at his clothes*] Oh, but this Priest's dress! How I hate it!

Dream Woman Be no longer a Priest. Be mine.

[*She takes a glittering robe from the couch and casts it round him.*]

Sensa Now I am utterly yours, until I am recalled.

Lifting a part of the rope of roses from her own throat, she throws it about him, uniting them. Gently, with seeming carelessness, she leads him to and fro as she wills upon the stage. At last she is seated in his chair, and he is kneeling beside her.

Sensa [*Adoringly*] How beautiful you are -- how beautiful! How I have longed for beauty!

Dream Woman And you -- how tired you are. Rest here. I will give you back your youth.

[*She draws him to her.*]

Sensa Oh, for eons of pleasure. Ages and eons of pleasure!

Dream Woman They are yours! Come to me. I will give them to you.

[*She draws him into her arms. He sinks wearily into her lap.*]

Sensa You have come to your beauty and I have not known you. How my years have been wasted.

Dream Woman These shall be the years of your triumph. Do not leave me again. Stay with me, and my passion will make you strong, to fulfil your destiny.

Sensa [*Lies in her arms in a trance of delight*] These walls no longer hold me. Ah, what broad, what open spaces! We are surrounded by innumerable shapes of exquisite beauty -- Is it not so, dear love?

[*She laughs gleefully.*]

They are dancing. I see their gleaming feet, their flying hair. Their tresses fall across my face. I feel the soft petals, I smell their fragrance. Their hands touch me, they clasp and draw me. I, too, am dancing -- dancing, dancing -- through the years.

[*They laugh with delight. He buries his head in the roses at her breast.*]

Dream Woman Listen to the music! Do you hear it?

Sensa [*Raises his head*] That is no music of earth! it is not played on instruments. It is the music of the Spheres. We are amongst the stars, and it is the stars that dance round us! Is it for an hour? -- or is it for an age?

Dream Woman Think not of Time, dear one. These are the years of our life. Hark!

Sensa [*Listening rapturously*] Surely I hear all the birds of all the worlds, singing at once! What cries of joy! [*Rises*] O, what a glorious life is mine!

The Stage is again darkened for an instant. When it is light, the gauze has been lifted, and Sensa is seated in his chair as before -- the Dream Woman has vanished. Sensa has lost the worn, weary look, and is now alert, strong, upright.

The curtains are drawn back, revealing the low, dark doorway of the Sanctuary. A loud clamor of the voices of the People is heard without.

People We want the Goddess! Oh, Priests, let us enter! Let us behold the great Goddess!

Sensa Go to the people. Tell them I shall this night work a wonder. They shall not only see the Goddess: they shall speak with her.

[*Exeunt Neophytes.*]

[*Agmahd and Kamen-baka draw back the curtains from in front of the Sanctuary, with an air of triumph. Sensa enters the Sanctuary.*]

A Priest Open the doors! Admit the people!

[*Exeunt two Neophytes.*]

Another Priest Lower the lights! The great Goddess is about to show herself.

[*Exeunt two more Neophytes, and an instant later, the lights are lowered and the Stage is darkened.*]

Priests [*Chant*] Great Queen! Glorious Queen! We welcome you!

This continues, until suddenly, a ray of light streams down from above and impinges on a mirror which is placed at a point to reflect the light on to the center of the Stage, where it dimly reveals the veiled figure of the Dark Goddess. The People and the Priests take up an attitude of worship.

People The Goddess!

Priests The Goddess!

[*The Chanting ceases.*]

Goddess [*Stretching out her arms over the People*] My people, I see your hungry hearts. I recognize my servants. You are a worthy army. I trust you to obey, not from duty, but from Desire.

People Yes, yes, Lady!

Goddess [*Pointing to various people, touching some near her*] You desire gold. [*Hands are outstretched*] Oh, that is easy. [*Pours gold into their hands*] It is yours. Take it. [*To a woman and youth*] You desire pleasure. Have it. [*Gives a rope of roses to each. Then to a man, a rather rough type*] You desire love. [*Takes the hand of a woman*] Here is another hungry heart. Feed each other. [*Man draws the woman to him. Then to a Nobleman*]

I see your secret desire. It cannot be uttered. I will give it to you. It shall be your secret and mine. It shall never be known. [*To a Peasant Woman*] The jewels make your eyes sparkle? Here. [*Throws a jewelled collar round her throat. To an Old Man*] And you long for youth? Poor dotard. Only believe you have it, and it is yours.

[*He straightens him-self up. The People are getting excited, thronging forward. A woman grasps the robe of the Goddess and clings to it.*]

Peasant Woman Lady, I am childless. I long for a man child!

[*Big, rough peasants, pushing forward, grasp her robe from the other side.*]

1st Peasant Lady, I have never had a piece of gold in all my life!

2nd Peasant I have never seen a piece of gold!

Peasants Gold! Gold! Give us gold!

They all pull at her. The robe begins to tear. As the Goddess reaches for the gold and turns with her hands full, she staggers. The Crowd presses upon her, and she suddenly disappears. There is an uproar of baffled desire. The People are in a frenzy and tear at everything they can lay their hands on, and at each other. They run hither and thither.

People Where is she? Where is she? Here! No! Here! Here!

They now begin to rush out of the Temple, followed by all the Priests and Priestesses, except "The Ten." Some dash at the door of the Garden, Center, and tear it open. A great stream of light pours in, frightening them, and they rush shrieking away through the Exits. Sensa staggers from the Sanctuary and falls forward on the platform. The light streams on him.

The Lady of the Lotus appears at the Gate.

Lotus Lady [*With wrath*] Oh, Sensa, Beloved of the Gods was it for this that you were born?

[*Pause, Sensa stirs.*]

Was it for this that your eyes were opened, and your senses made clear to perceive?

[*Sensa half rises.*]

You know it was not. Have you fallen so low that you will be a slave for ever? [*Sensa rises.*]

Go, then. I will cleanse my Sanctuary. It shall no longer be the dwelling-place of selfish desire. It shall be silent, and none shall know that any gods exist. Go, and leave me to my silence. [*She turns.*]

Sensa turns and goes slowly with dragging footsteps towards Exit. He hesitates. A wild burst of song from the People can be heard.

Sensa That song! That song of degradation! It is Her song! The song of the Goddess! The song that is sung under all skies and in all ages. Ah, my Mighty Ones in passion -- Kings in lust, Monarchs in desire. We have lighted a fire that will bum through the ages! Are you satisfied at last? And I -- I -- what of me? [*Assumes an attitude of tense, introspective despair*] I die of hunger -- I am stupefied, and poor, and starved. I am beset on every side. Desire, Ambition, Greed, Passion crowd in on me, darken my life, and compel me to this slavery. I am alone -- alone, in the midst of this crowd.

[*Turns to the Lady of the Lotus, speaks with great passion.*]

What can I do? Queen of Wisdom -- Light of my soul, do not forsake me! Help me!

Lotus Lady [*Turns*] Sensa! You have called me!

Sensa Oh, Queen of Wisdom, save me!

[*He falls on his knees.*]

Lotus Lady [*Comes down, touches his head*] Sensa, you have called me.

Sensa [*Distractedly*] Lady, tell me -- what am I to do?

Lotus Lady Seek me. Daily, hourly, in holy meditation. Seek me in this garden, deep in the garden of your Soul. Look not out for help, but ever within the inner-most Sanctuary of your own Being -- within the Lotus bloom of your own Heart -- for there am I!

CURTAIN

ACT III

Scene i - The Solitary Soul

PLACE *The Temple Garden*

TIME *Before Dawn*

The *Scene is dim and shadowy, just enough faint light to show the outlines of the plants and trees and the fountain. The Lotus tank is Center, and from a rich tall growth of leaves, rises a glorious thousand-petalled Lotus.*

The Garden is full of tall, strong plants, covered with flowers -- myrtle, acacia, mimosa in great yellow, feathery masses, and a palm tree on each side. All round the sides, against the high wall of the garden is a trellis, on which roses are trained. Thousands of roses of all colors hang their heads from this trellis, necking a background of the most vivid coloring. By the side of the tank (or right in front of it), is Sensa seated deeply plunged in concentration and remaining in a correct Egyptian attitude of meditation. A faint movement stirs the leaves of the plants and there is a whispering amongst them. A delicate form emerges from the center of the trees and bushes. They step forward in charming attitudes and look at Sensa quite silently. Then, in perfect silence and unison, they dance in a circle round him, with gestures of blessing as they pass. At the climax of the dance, they all join hands above him, meeting in the center.

Magnolia The dawn is near!

Acacia I feel the ethereal glow upon me!

Magnolia With the first ray of light, our Queen, the Lady of the Lotus will be here.

Myrtle Dear leaves, arise and let the dew drop off!

[*The spirits of the Roses now appear, hiding their faces.*]

Roses [*In unison*] Alas! Today we die!

All the other Spirits Die? Die?

Magnolia [*In center of group*] No! Only change form and live again.

Roses We suffer! We suffer!

Magnolia Alas! For you are passionate.

[*All the Spirits try to soothe and cheer the Roses.*]

Acacia Rejoice! Rejoice! New life is all!

Mimosa Our flowers, too, are demanded by the High Priests for the festival.

Camelia But it is not death -- only entrance into new life.

Magnolia Raise your beautiful heads, dear Roses, ready to welcome our Queen! Let us think no more of ourselves, but give of our best to Sensa. Learn that Sacrifice is life. Let us waft our perfumes to him.

[*All the Spirits do so, except the Roses, who stand uncertain and questioning.*]

This poor little human soul has been terrified by the dreadful Ten; he has been the slave of the High Priests; he has been the mouth-piece of the Dark Goddess of Desire! Come, let us surround him with sweet airs.

[*They all sway round him.*]

Roses [*With more abandon than the others*] Soul of Love! We welcome you! We bless you. [*They shower rose-petals on him*] Take us! Take us! May our passion make you strong!

Magnolia Behold, the dawn approaches! [*To Sensa*] Sensa's vigil is ended -- and our long night of watching is past. Come! He has earned the right to stand in the presence of our Lady. This is his great day. Come! We will lose ourselves that he may live. Come!

They all cast petals upon him and then softly return to their places. A moment of once, and then a beam of light strikes directly upon Sensas forehead.

Sensa [*Rises*] I thank thee, dear flowers, for rousing me. [*He kisses the petals that lie on his hand.*]

My vigil is over.

[*He raises his arms in front of his head and stands with his hands lifted to heaven, turned towards the coming light.*]

"Hail! All hail! Thou who art Ra! When thou riseth, thou riseth! Thou shinest! Thou shinest! Thou who art crowned King of the Gods!"

[*The light grows stronger. The Lady of the Lotus appears.*]

Lotus Lady What would you hear and see, and what have you in mind to learn and know?

Sensa I long to learn the things that are, and comprehend their nature, and know God.

Lotus Lady Hold in your mind all you wish to know, and I will teach you.

Sensa Oh, Queen of Wisdom! I have passed through the blackness of desolation and have learned that no possession is permanent and that no thing endures. For many nights I have kept vigil, praying for speech with you when you should enter your garden.

Lotus Lady And yours! The garden of your soul, Sensa. You are at home here. Do you not feel new life within you?

Sensa Yes -- I am reborn. Tell me, Queen of Wisdom, what am I to do?

Lotus Lady Live according to the law of Love.

Sensa Oh, Lady -- what is Love?

Lotus Lady It is the losing of your self. It is the finding of your Self.

Sensa It is a thousand times harder than to live according to the law of Hate.

Lotus Lady Yes; but live according to the law of Love. Give all that you have. Teach the people. Rouse them! Awaken them! Tell them of the Three Truths great as life itself -- yet simple as the simplest heart of man. Feed the hungry with them.

Sensa Where can I find these truths?

Lotus Lady Within yourself. In every human heart, the Lotus blooms. For those who live in Love, there is no death -- for Love and Immortality are one!

Sensa To this great effort I now pledge myself. The divine satisfaction has fallen upon me. I am conscious that Love is infinite, though I can hold but one drop. I myself have nothing, and am nothing. Yet I am all, and have all.

[*Turns. In the perplexity of ecstasy.*]

I sleep and wake at the same time. Within me is the measureless content which is eternal Rest. My being is absorbed into the Absolute Peace.

Lotus Lady There is no rest, no peace, for him who has become a Brother of Love.

Sensa [Heroically] I am ready. I am ready for ceaseless activity. Thou hast armed me for perpetual warfare. I am Thine.

Lotus Lady [With great tenderness] My beloved. My child. There is no more any parting of the ways. All the different paths have become the One path which leads to immortal Life.

She steps back and vanishes. The Garden is now in the full blaze of the sunshine, radiant with beauty. Birds glance hither and thither. Sensa remains standing gazing upon the open Lotus flower.

Seboua enters, carrying a great basket, and a knife.

Seboua [To Sensa, with surprise] Have you been here all night?

Sensa [Still gazing] Yes.

Seboua But you must go. It is the day of the festival. So far as the eye can see, the people have gathered.

Sensa [Eagerly] There are people at the gate?

Seboua All Egypt is at the gate!

Sensa Then I must go to them.

[Turning to the Lotus.]

Divine Lady, Queen of Love and Wisdom, I go to do Thy bidding.

[Sensa goes out.]

Seboua Oh, Osiris, father of men, guard and keep him! *[Lifts his hands for a moment in prayer; then he commences to cut the roses and magnolias, and put them into his great basket.]*

CURTAIN

Scene ii - The Man

The Interior of the Temple, stripped and bare. All the Priests have a depressed, exhausted and poverty-stricken look, and are angry and morose.

Sensa's chair is in the middle of the stage, opposite the Sanctuary. He is sitting, leaning forward, his arms on his knees. "The Ten" are grouped about, some at their pillars and some near the chair. Two are sitting on the floor, their heads resting on the chair. They look pale, starved, lean and unhappy. Sensa looks pale, but clear-cut alert and determined, about 30 years of age. Agmahd stands Center. Kamen-baka by the Sanctuary. They are dressed as in Act One.

There is an uproar outside the Temple, as before.

Sensa Tell the people that I will speak to them at the Gate, as before.

[*The Neophytes hesitate. "The Ten" move uneasily.*]

Agmahd So you are determined to defy us.

Sensa Yes.

[*A murmur of protest from "The Ten." Sensa turns to them.*]

Come.

[*He moves L.*]

The Ten You are destroying us. You are destroying us!

Two of the Ten [*With their hands to their heads*] We are deaf.

Another I am blind.

Another I cannot see.

Another [*Touching a pillar*] The world has gone from me.

Another I cannot feel it.

Two Others You are starving us.

Others of the Ten No longer do you make sacrifices to our Gods!

Sensa Your Gods! The Gods of the Senses! No! Soon you will be blind forever. Soon you will be deaf forever! Soon the world will be utterly lost to you forever. Are we then to work for these little gods of the Senses who themselves must die?

[*The people are heard clamoring at the Gates. He stops and listens.*]

Come with me. We will serve the One and not the many -- Osiris -- who is the Eternal. Come!

[*Exeunt Sensa and "The Ten"*]

Kamen-baka Again he defies us! We cannot endure this!

Agmahd He is useless to us!

Kamen-baka He is worse -- he is dangerous. It is no longer safe. Bring him back. Do not let him speak again to the people! He incites them against us.

[*Agmahd turns to Neophytes.*]

Agmahd Go! Bring him back! Quickly!

[*Exeunt four of the Neophytes.*]

After a slight pause, the door of the Garden, L. opens, admitting a great stream of light, and Seboua enters, bearing a large quantity of red roses.

Seboua [*To the Priests by the door*] These are for the Seer's chair. I have but little time -- the garlands for the walls are being made.

[*Looks round.*]

Where is the Seer?

A Neophyte He is teaching the people at the Gate.

Seboua [*Lifts his hands*] Osiris, protect him. The night is at hand, and the darkness must fall. But the truth shall be taught by our Seer, and left in the hearts of the people!

Agmahd [*Coldly*] We are waiting for the garlands.

[*Exit Seboua.*]

The Four Priests, having distributed the roses, return to their places. Sensa enters, led by Neophytes. He is preceded by "The Ten."

Agmahd Your service is needed. The hour for the ceremonial is at hand. I demand your obedience.

Sensa [*In tense excitement, looking round*] I stand alone!

[*Pause. "The Ten" look ugly.*]

One among many -- a solitary soul in the midst of a united crowd. Among you all, I am the only one who knows, and will teach. I have taught the worshipers at the gate, because of the power which dwells within me. I am upheld by it! I am made strong by it!

Kamen-baka He is in an ecstasy.

[*"The Ten" advance closer.*]

Agmahd He is mad! He is dangerous!

The Ten Ah, this is Death! This is death! We shall all die!

Kamen-baka Yes, this is death! He is leading us to death!

The Four Priests [*Chanting*] Death is but a going home!

[*Sensa comes down to the chair, looks on the roses, with love.*]

Sensa The roses of my life! Cut and laid low! [*He sits*]

[*Voices of people heard without.*]

[*He springs up*] I hear the people! They are coming in. I will speak to them here!

[*A general murmur of protest.*]

The Ten [*Addressing him*] If you do, you will never again look on the light of the sun.

Sensa I have seen the Divine Light!

The Ten But what of the glory of the constellations? The majesty of the moon when it rises upon the darkness? Have you not loved the moon? Have you not gazed upon it through that high window, trembling as if in an ecstasy? All that pleasure will be lost to you. What of the beauty of the summer upon earth? Have you not looked at the palm trees, at the magnolia blooms, like one enrapt? Those roses that cover your chair. . . .

Sensa [*Interrupting*] Stay! I have seen their spirits. It is their spirits that I love.

The Ten What of the beautiful women of earth? It is not the beauty of their spirits you adore -- it is the beauty of their earthly shapes.

Sensa [*Triumphantly*] I have seen the Lady of the Lotus!

The Ten Listen, my lord. Are you willing to lose the songs of the birds? The melodies of the whispering trees? The voices of your friends?

Sensa I have no friends in this Temple.

The Ten What of the cries of life? The sounds of the city? Will you lose them forever? What of the voice of the beautiful woman whom you loved?

Sensa [*Flings them from him*] Ah! I care for none of these! Go! You are nothing to me! I have done with you! Leave me!

[*A gasp of horror from "The Ten."*]

Poor and paltry things that you are! When I think of the years I have wasted with you] Satisfying you, feeding you -- animating you --

[*Taking in Agmahd and Kamen-baka with his gesture. A pause, expressing unspeakable disgust.*]

Oh, I will go! No longer shall this Temple hold me!

[*"The Ten," with uplifted arms, utter a wild long drawn-out wail of despair.*]

The Ten Oh, we must die!

The People have rushed in from either side of the Temple and are crowding forward. Agmahd and Kamen-baka disappear into the Sanctuary. The Four Priests by the gate softly twang upon their musical instruments.

People Where is the young Priest? The young Priest who taught us?

Sensa [*Springing up, raises his voice*] People! My beloved people. [*Looks out over them*] Down-trodden, suffering, starving, untaught -- yet each with the divine spark within you. [*Holds out his arm*] Come near me, come round me, while I tell you of the three Truths which are absolute.

[*The People press closer.*]

People Yes! Yes!

Sensa "The soul of man is immortal, and its future is the future of a thing whose growth and splendor have no limit."

People [*Appreciatively*] Ah!

Priests No! No! He is a traitor! Untrue to the Temple!

[*They try to press the People back. They struggle.*]

Sensa [*Speaking above the tumult*] "The principle which gives life, the Divine principle, dwells in us and without us, is undying and eternally beneficent."

People [*Assent joyfully*] Yes! Oh, yes! Speak on!

Priests No! No! Silence him! Silence him!

[*Certain of them try to pull Sensa down -- people pull the Priests away.*]

Sensa [*Shouting, but with great effort*] "Each man is his own absolute law-giver, the dispenser of glory and gloom to himself, the decreer of his life, his reward, his punishment."

"The Ten" set upon him determinedly and drag him down. Others struggle with the People and drive them out through the Exit, L. All the Priests follow them, except "The Ten" and "The Four." The cries and shouts of the tumult gradually die away in the distance. All is quiet. "The Ten" are grouped round Sensa in attitudes of baffled despair. Sensa sits rigid in his chair in the Egyptian attitude of meditation. The Four Priests again play softly.

Sensa [*Introspectively*] "I go in like the Hawk, and I come forth like the Bennu bird, the morning star of Ra. May a path be made for me whereby I may enter in peace into the beautiful Amentit; and may I lie by the Lake of Horus, and may I lead the grey hounds of Horus; and may a path be made for me whereby I may enter in and adore Osiris, the lord of Life."

The Four Priests [*Softly chanting*] Death is but a going home! Enter across the hidden Lintel! Enter on light!

Sensa Oh, thou white crown of my Divine Form! Oh, thou resting-place of the Boat! I am the child! I am the child! I am the child!

["*The Ten*" *murmur low, and droop.*]

The Four Priests Yes. Enter across the hidden Lintel! Enter on light!

Sensa [*With strength*] The slaughter block is made ready, as thou knowest!

[*A long, low moan from "The Ten," as they fade into the Sanctuary.*]

My going forth is as the going forth of the Lord Ra!

The Four Priests, still chanting, open the door of the Garden, disappear into it. The opening of the garden door sends a great shaft of light upon Sensa. He rises and turns towards the Garden.

Hail, thou Lotus! I am the man who knoweth Thee! Grant that I may see the Gods who are the divine guides through the Underworld. Grant that I may come forth whithersoever I please.

[*Turning again to the front.*]

And let me not be driven away from the presence of the great company of the gods -- but receive me, Oh, all ye gods, into the presence of the Lord of Eternity.

Oh, Osiris, verily I have come! I behold thee! I see my divine father! I scatter the gloom! I see my divine father, Osiris! I will perform all the ceremonies! I will open every way in heaven and earth! I am the son who loveth his father Osiris! I have become a khou -- I have become a sahu -- I am furnished with what I need. Hail, every god! Hail, every khou! I have made a path for myself. I myself am Osiris!

CURTAIN

THE END

Made in the USA
Middletown, DE
10 May 2025